A Practical Guide to

Evaluation

Related books of interest

Research Methods for Social Workers:
A Practice-Based Approach, Second Edition
Samuel S. Faulkner and Cynthia A. Faulkner

Doing Research: The Hows and Whys of Applied Research,
Third Edition
Nel Verhoeven

Using Statistical Methods in Social Work Practice with a
Complete SPSS Guide, Second Edition
Soleman H. Abu-Bader

Clinical Assessment for Social Workers:
Quantitative and Qualitative Methods, Third Edition
Catheleen Jordan and Cynthia Franklin

Navigating Human Service Organizations,
Third Edition
Rich Furman and Margaret Gibelman

Social Service Workplace Bullying:
A Betrayal of Good Intentions
Kathryn Brohl

Policy, Politics, and Ethics: A Critical Approach
Thomas M. Meenaghan, Keith M. Kilty, Dennis D. Long, and
John G. McNutt

SECOND EDITION

A Practical Guide to
Evaluation

CARL F. BRUN
Wright State University

OXFORD
UNIVERSITY PRESS

OXFORD
UNIVERSITY PRESS

Oxford University Press is a department of the University of Oxford. It furthers the
University's objective of excellence in research, scholarship, and education by
publishing worldwide. Oxford is a registered trade mark of Oxford University Press
in the UK and certain other countries.

Published in the United States of America by Oxford University Press
198 Madison Avenue, New York, NY 10016, United States of America.

Library of Congress Cataloging-in-Publication Data

Brun, Carl F.
    A practical guide to evaluation / Carl F. Brun, Wright State University. — Second edition.
    pages cm
Includes bibliographical references and index.
ISBN 978-0-190615-46-8 (pbk. : alk. paper)
  1. Human services—Evaluation. 2. Evaluation research (Social action programs) I. Title.
HV40.B874   2014
361.3'2—dc23

                                                            2013030165

ISBN 978-0-190615-46-8

CONTENTS

FIGURES

CASE EXAMPLES

CHECKLISTS

PREFACE

Evaluation of social and educational services leads to better practice. That is the underlying premise of this text. Yet many beginning practitioners resist evaluation, citing the following justifications for not conducting evaluations: "Evaluations do not make a difference. Persons in authority have already decided what will happen in this program," or "It's too hard to evaluate the impact of multiple interventions," or "Not all aspects of practice or education can be measured." Many beginning social service workers and educators are not prepared to integrate evaluation into everyday practice.

The types of settings used as examples in this text include the following:

- Social and educational services delivered in public and private settings by social workers, educators, psychologists, and other social service workers
- Primary, elementary, and secondary education in which educational programs are measured by student performance and in which nonacademic programs are delivered to address nonacademic barriers (e.g., bullying, substance abuse, mental health concerns) to student performance
- Higher education in which every discipline is required to assess the impact of curriculum on desired student outcomes

In this book I combine my experience as a social work practitioner, administrator, educator, and evaluator to provide readers with an understanding of how agency politics, professional and personal values, diversity, theory, and research methods shape the evaluation decision-making process. Readers are encouraged to rely on the values, skills, and knowledge learned in practice and research courses of their discipline and to embrace the rewards of evaluation rather than resist the unavoidable reality that evaluation is here to stay.

The importance of evaluation has become the predominant focus of social services and education since the first edition of this book was printed in 2005. Yes, the need to focus on evaluation was present long before 2005; but look at the following professional changes that have occurred since 2005 that reinforce the need for social workers, educators, and social service workers to learn the skills of critical thinking and evaluating practice:

- The Council on Social Work Education's (CSWE) revision of the Educational Policy and Administrative Standards (EPAS) from an accreditation model that focused on curriculum content (2003) to an accreditation model that focuses on student practice behaviors (CSWE, 2012)
- Program cuts and new funding sources that reward outcomes in social services.
- Program cuts and new funding sources that punish negative outcomes in education
- Educational cuts and pressure for accountability in delivering student outcomes

SECOND EDITION

The second edition of this book retains the following tools from the first edition.

Interactive Model of Evaluation.

Evaluation is a fluid process that does not always have a clear beginning and ending. Many students, practitioners, and administrators want to begin an evaluation by discussing which surveys or other data-collection tools should be administered. Yet many other important planning decisions must be answered first to know that the right data-collection methods were used to answer the specific evaluation questions. The steps to the interactive model of evaluation are as follows:

1. Clarify the evaluation scope and purpose.
2. Negotiate with evaluation stakeholders.
3. Clarify the ethical values that guide the evaluation.
4. Clarify the program theory and evidence-based research that guide the evaluation.
5. Clarify the data-collection methods that best fit the scope, purpose, ethics, and program theory as agreed upon by the key stakeholders.
6. Document the decisions made at each of these steps.

The circular model emphasizes that decisions made in each step affect the other steps and that the decisions are not always linear and sequential. This book is divided up into the six parts of this Interactive Model of Evaluation.

Evaluation Decision-Making Model.

Evaluation, the systematic collection and analysis of information about one or more interventions, is a set of important and critical decisions. There are several decisions that must be made during each of the steps outlined in the interactive model of evaluation. Each chapter begins with evaluation decision-making questions for that step of the evaluation. Documenting evaluation decisions becomes the source of accountability for every evaluation and the justification for the decisions made. An outline of the evaluation decision-making questions from each chapter appears in the appendix.

SCREAM.

I once questioned whether the SCREAM acronym was functional until one student gave a campuswide presentation about a service-learning project she completed in the research course that used this text. Her accompanying poster contained an animated person with a megaphone with the letters S-C-R-E-A-M funneling into the sky. She then discussed how her project implemented the values captured by the acronym: strengths, culture, resources, ethics, agreement, and multiple-level outcomes. These values are discussed in chapter 3. At my own university, several of these values have become integrated into the institutional review board's petition for human subjects review, which is discussed in chapter 4.

Explore, Describe, or Explain.

The evaluation questions should drive the evaluation data-collection methods, not the other way around. The key stakeholders should be the persons agreeing on those evaluation questions. I argue that all evaluation and research questions are either exploratory (using qualitative methods only and having no independent or dependent variables), descriptive (using qualitative or quantitative methods to analyze the relationship among independent variables [the program, intervention, or policy] and dependent variables [client or student outcomes]), or explanatory (using quantitative methods only to test a predicted, causal relationship between independent and dependent variables). It is possible to use qualitative and quantitative data-collection methods to answer descriptive questions. Thus, the data-collection chapters (chapters 8–11) come later in the text after the discussion about the differences in the types of questions asked for any given evaluation.

Stakeholders.

Evaluation is political. Persons with power have a say in why, how, when, and what should be evaluated. For example, the outcomes and efficiency-test-based demands of the No Child Left Behind education policies have forever changed teaching in primary, elementary, and secondary schools. Every evaluation is influenced by persons who have a stake in the implications of the data collected during evaluations. Chapter 5 is devoted to negotiating with stakeholders. The A in SCREAM provides a way to document in writing the evaluation agreement made by stakeholders. Persons representing the participants in the evaluation (e.g., consumers, students, practitioners) should be on a committee that oversees the implementation of the evaluation.

Further Resources.

This text provides an overview of key concepts related to each step of evaluation. There are literally hundreds of books written about evaluation and hundreds more written about specific aspects of evaluation, such as data-collection methodology. There is a list of further resources, websites, and evaluation tools at the end of each chapter. These lists have been updated since the first edition.

AEA and NASW Guidelines for Evaluation and Research.

The American Evaluation Association (AEA) is the largest cross-disciplinary organization devoted solely to evaluation. A strength of this organization is that the theoretical and practical underpinnings of evaluation are merged within the membership of academics and evaluators in the trenches conducting evaluations for agencies or representing the large funding sources that require the evaluation. Members represent all disciplines, but especially education, psychology, health sciences, and social work. The AEA has published its *Guiding Principles for Evaluators* (2004) to establish minimal ethical standards for all evaluations. The National Association of Social Workers' *Code of Ethics* (NASW, 2008) guides all social work practice. Other international associations in education, psychology, social work, and evaluation also have ethical guidelines for evaluation. For the most part, this text focuses primarily on U.S. organizations, although there are references in some chapters to international evaluation organizations.

Case Examples.

Case examples are provided throughout the entire text, covering all aspects of the evaluation process. The examples include the evaluation of social service interventions and interventions in educational settings. The examples also include evaluations conducted by educators, social workers, researchers, and students.

The following sections discuss tools added to this edition of *A Practical Guide to Evaluation*.

Evaluation Decision-Making Table.

On the basis of using *A Practical Guide to Social Service Evaluation* to teach research and evaluation, I developed a table that helps students and practitioners know which data-collection procedures are appropriate given the type of evaluation questions that are being asked. This table appears in figure 10 in chapter 8.

Chapter Discussion Activities.

This text combines critical thinking (questioning why decisions are made) with a basic, practical approach (which decisions are made and how) to evaluation. At the beginning of each chapter, there are evaluation decision-making questions (called "procedural journal activities" in the first edition). At the end of each chapter are critical-thinking questions (called "reflective journal activities" in the first edition), which can spark important dialogue in class or with key evaluation stakeholders. These questions help persons clarify the purposes underlying the evaluation decisions.

Documentation Tasks.

Documenting the decisions made at each step of the evaluation is vital to accountability of the entire evaluation. In the first edition documentation was discussed primarily in the final chapter. In this second edition documentation is emphasized throughout the entire evaluation process. At the end of each chapter is a section called "Documentation Tasks."

Readers are asked to document the answers to the evaluation decision-making questions for that chapter as the questions pertain to the planning and implementing of an actual evaluation. These pages are perforated and can be torn out. Multiple copies of the pages can be made for multiple evaluations.

Data-Collection Chapters.

The section on research methods (chapter 6 in the first edition) has been expanded into four chapters. Chapter 8 discusses the range of the following procedures related to research methodology in all evaluations: research design, participant selection, data collection, data analysis, and data credibility. The following three chapters cover qualitative research methodology to answer exploratory evaluation questions in chapter 9, quantitative research methodology to answer explanatory evaluation questions in chapter 10, and mixed research methods to answer descriptive evaluation questions in chapter 11.

Workbook Format.

The evaluation decision-making checklists and documentation tasks are printed as perforated text to allow for tearing out the pages and handing them in as homework assignments for a class or to use as drafts of evaluation plans. These pages can be copied before using and applied to multiple evaluations.

Competency-Based Education and the 2008 EPAS.

Social service workers and agencies are accountable to evaluate the impact of their programs. A primary audience for this text is graduate and undergraduate students of social work. The 2012 Council on Social Work Education Policy and Accreditation Standards (EPAS) have specific core competencies expected of all BSW and MSW graduates:

> *Educational Policy 2.1—Core Competencies.* Competency-based education is an outcome performance approach to curriculum design. Competencies are measurable practice behaviors that are comprised of knowledge, values, and skills. The goal of the outcome approach is to demonstrate the integration and application of the competencies in practice with individuals, families, groups, organizations, and communities. (CSWE, 2012, p. 3)

Other disciplines also have competency-based education that fits the CSWE's definition here. I have used this text to help other academic departments in higher education develop an assessment plan. This text has been used by academic support services, such as the Office of Disability Services, to develop a logic model and ways to measure the program goals, objectives, and desired results. This text has been used by elementary and secondary education settings to measure the impact of educational and support services on student performance.

After understanding the concepts in this text, students should be able to master the following core competency of EPAS 2012:

> *Educational Policy 2.1.6—Engage in research-informed practice and practice-informed research.* Social workers use practice experience to inform research, employ evidence-based interventions, evaluate their own practice, and use research findings to improve practice, policy, and social service delivery. Social workers comprehend quantitative and qualitative research and understand scientific and ethical approaches to building knowledge. Social workers use practice experience to inform scientific inquiry and use research evidence to inform practice. (CSWE, 2012, p. 5)

The premise of this entire text is that research informs practice. All of the chapters help students learn skills to evaluate practice. Chapter 7 specifically addresses how students can conduct searches of prior research to inform their current practice.

Additional EPAS 2012 competencies and practice behaviors that can be enhanced by this text are the following:

> *Educational Policy 2.1.2—Apply social work ethical principles to guide professional practice.* Social workers have an obligation to conduct themselves ethically and to engage in ethical decision-making. Social workers are knowledgeable about the value base of the profession, its ethical standards, and relevant law. Social workers recognize and manage personal values in a way that allows professional values to guide practice; make ethical decisions by applying standards of the National Association of Social Workers' (2008) *Code of Ethics* and, as applicable, of the International Federation of Social Workers' *Statement of Ethical Principles* (2012) and the International Association of Schools of Social Work's *Ethics in Social Work Statement of Principles* (2004); tolerate

ambiguity in resolving ethical conflicts; and apply strategies of ethical reasoning to arrive at principled decisions. (CSWE, 2012, p. 4)

Ethics and values are discussed throughout the entire book. In chapter 4, there is a more detailed discussion of ethical guidelines for evaluation following the NASW's (2008) *Code of Ethics* and the AEA's (2004) *Guiding Principles for Evaluators*. Additional values emphasized are adherence to the strengths perspective, cultural competency, and assessment of multiple-systems-level impacts on desired results for clients:

Educational Policy 2.1.3—Apply critical thinking to inform and communicate professional judgments. Social workers are knowledgeable about the principles of logic, scientific inquiry, and reasoned discernment. They use critical thinking augmented by creativity and curiosity. Critical thinking also requires the synthesis and communication of relevant information. Social workers distinguish, appraise, and integrate multiple sources of knowledge, including research-based knowledge and practice wisdom; analyze models of assessment, prevention, intervention, and evaluation; and demonstrate effective oral and written communication in working with individuals, families, groups, organizations, communities, and colleagues. (CSWE, 2012, p. 4)

Readers are encouraged to constantly question how theory, values, and data-collection methods drive evaluation decisions that will ultimately help social service workers improve service delivery. Definition, purpose, and activities must be clarified for each new evaluation. No two evaluations are identical. Students at both the undergraduate and the graduate levels can apply the concepts in this book, especially as they apply the concepts to the field practicum setting. Social service workers with or without evaluation experience can also use this book:

Educational Policy 2.1.10(a)–(d)—Engage, assess, intervene, and evaluate with individuals, families, groups, organizations, and communities. Professional practice involves the dynamic and interactive processes of engagement, assessment, intervention, and evaluation at multiple levels. Social workers have the knowledge and skills to practice with individuals, families, groups, organizations, and communities. Practice knowledge includes identifying, analyzing, and implementing evidence-based interventions designed to achieve client goals; using research and technological advances; evaluating program outcomes and practice effectiveness; developing, analyzing, advocating, and providing leadership for policies and services; and promoting social and economic justice. (CSWE, 2012, pp. 6–7)

AUDIENCE

The change in the title of this revised book, *A Practical Guide to Evaluation*, conveys the intent of this book from the very beginning to be of value to all persons conducting an evaluation. The audience, then, includes social service personnel and also educators at all levels. All providers of service, whether it be education, counseling, health services, or social services, are accountable for the outcomes of that intervention. The examples throughout this book include all of those services. There are many examples of interventions provided in an elementary or high school setting whereby the outcomes measured were educational (e.g., grades, test scores, graduation, attendance rates) and supportive (e.g., decrease in office visits for behavioral issues, increase of positive behaviors, showing respect).

In general, the term *social service worker* or *educator* is used when describing the implementers of an intervention being evaluated. More specific references to a profession may be used within the context of specific case examples. For example, the evaluations set in a school setting may refer to teachers, principals, and counselors.

This text emphasizes the integration of practice and research skills. An undergraduate or graduate student in social work or related fields with a beginning understanding of the research process can use this text to apply theory, values, respect for diversity, and research methods in practice courses settings. For example:

- Readers can understand and be critical of the issues that underlie social service evaluation.
- They can plan an evaluation of an intervention discussed in a practice course when working with individuals, families, groups, or organizations.
- They can plan ways to evaluate the application in a practicum setting of a theory learned in a human behavior and social environment (HBSE) course.

- They can propose evaluations to test the impact of a state, federal, or local policy on worker and client behavior.
- Community organization courses can apply this text when discussing the role of a needs or strengths assessment in planning community-wide interventions.
- This book can be used for a capstone course that helps students use evaluation as a means to integrate all the content areas learned across the curriculum.
- Readers can use this text to design an evaluation at their agency practicum site.

Social service workers and educators embarking on evaluation can also use this book. For example:

- Readers can use it to develop a beginning evaluation plan as part of a request for proposals (RFP).
- Several workers from the same agency can use it to guide planning, practice, and evaluation decisions.
- Several workers from collaborating agencies can use it to arrive at agreement on the scope and activities of a specific evaluation.
- Agency administrators can use some of its suggestions to create an environment that encourages and supports staff evaluation activities.
- Readers can use the numerous lists contained in this book to concentrate on sections of the evaluation decision-making model that apply to a given evaluation. All sections of the book will not necessarily apply to all evaluations.
- The book can be used to develop evaluation contracts that specify the evaluation focus and the tasks of each person involved in the evaluation.

PLAN OF THE BOOK

Evaluation is both a process and a product. This book is about clarifying the components of an evaluation while also helping readers do an evaluation. Planning, implementing, and evaluating an intervention are interconnected steps. Social service workers and educators do not always have the time to separate these three activities. The discussions in this book show how to involve key people in the process of reaching agreement on evaluation decisions.

This book is organized in parts according to the following set of decisions (listed here) that all social service workers need to answer during an evaluation:

- What is the purpose and scope of the evaluation? (Part 1: chapters 1 and 2)
- What are the values and ethics that drive the evaluation? (Part 2: chapters 3 and 4)
- Who are the stakeholders that decide on the scope of the evaluation? (Part 3: chapter 5)
- What are the theories that drive the evaluation? (Part 4: chapters 6 and 7)
- What are the data-collection methods that drive the evaluation? (Part 5: chapters 8, 9, 10, and 11)
- What is documented throughout the evaluation and in the final report to show the connection between all the steps of the evaluation? (Part 6: chapter 12)

Although the evaluation process can begin at any of several points, the chapters in this book are organized in the order in which I prefer to conduct an evaluation. I believe that the scope of the evaluation as determined by key people invested in the evaluation should be the beginning point, but in reality, the scope may already have been determined before those key persons become involved. Similarly, in some situations, the expectation to follow certain values (e.g., focusing on client strengths) may be considered as an afterthought during the data-collection stage.

Clarifying the program theory or logic model of an intervention will lead naturally to the expected outcomes that can be measured in an evaluation, but some people may be expected to measure certain outcomes without having a clear logic model. The appropriate data-collection method can be selected more accurately after the previous components have been clarified, even though many evaluations start by stating a method that should be used (e.g., survey, focus group). The final report then becomes the written documentation that confirms the decisions made from the beginning to end of the evaluation.

Each chapter has the following structure:

- Evaluation decision-making questions, listed at the beginning of the chapter
- Case examples, to illustrate the main points
- Evaluation decision-making checklists, to help readers arrive at decisions on key issues in each chapter
- A "Further Resources" section, to provide readers with a list of other books and websites that give more detail about the key topics discussed
- Critical-thinking questions at the end of each chapter, to help readers become aware of subjective reactions to the material and to question the material that was presented
- Documentation tasks, at the end of each chapter, which focus on documenting the key evaluation decisions for the component of evaluation discussed in each chapter

Chapter 1, "Purpose of Evaluation," begins with the different ways that evaluation can enrich social service practice. The definitions of *research* and *evaluation* are given. Research is the implementation of reliable, valid, and credible methods to empirically explore, describe, or explain a theorized relationship between variables. Evaluation implements research methods to improve interventions or programs. How will the evaluation improve practice and program planning? How will the evaluation build knowledge? This chapter helps the reader clarify what important stakeholders expect from the evaluation and whether or not all evaluations are feasible.

Chapter 2, "Scope of Evaluation," builds on chapter 1 and places the evaluation in the context of the types of overall evaluation questions that are being asked. Evaluation questions can be exploratory, explanatory, or descriptive. Specifying the type of questions being asked will drive all other evaluation decisions. Needs assessment, a type of exploratory or descriptive evaluation question, is discussed in this chapter. Use of the evaluation process and results to improve practice is also discussed. The discussion of ethics, in part 2, has been moved up in this edition to emphasize its importance throughout the entire evaluation process.

Chapter 3, "SCREAM," begins by helping the reader understand the influence of personal, agency, community, and professional values on the evaluation process. Specific attention is given to ways in which the following SCREAM values can be respected during each evaluation: assessment of evaluation participants' strengths, respect for stakeholder and evaluation participants' culture, conducting evaluation feasibly within one's resources, ensuring ethical evaluation procedures, reaching a written agreement among stakeholders on the scope and activities of the evaluation, and measuring multiple-systems results.

Chapter 4, "Ethical Guidelines for Evaluations," discusses the minimal ethical guidelines expected of all evaluations, which are presented as ten "thou shalls" of ethical evaluation. An important documentation task for this chapter is to complete an institutional review board (IRB) petition that follows all federal and ethical guidelines for research with human subjects.

In part 3, "Negotiating with Stakeholders," chapter 5, "Politics of Evaluation," discusses the many different persons who have a stake in evaluation. These include funders, agency administrators, direct-care staff, clients, the general community, and the evaluators. The differences between internally and externally driven evaluations are discussed. Tips are given on how to develop an evaluation stakeholder plan that includes the following: the persons authorizing the evaluation, the persons advising the evaluation, the persons responsible for conducting the evaluation, the reports expected from the evaluation, and a timeline for meeting the expectations of the evaluation.

Part 4, "Theory-Driven Evaluation Decisions," covers "Developing a Logic Model" (chapter 6) and "Conducting Literature Reviews" (chapter 7). These two tools can help social service workers connect theory to planning, practice, and evaluation. Theory is a description or explanation of the relationship between a social service intervention or program and desired results for clients and consumers of the services. Theories help social service workers answer the question "Why do you plan to use, or why are you using, that intervention?" The logic model is a clarification of intervention goals, activities, and desired results and helps workers answer the above question by providing the answer "Because this is the best intervention to meet our goals and desired results." Theory learned through literature reviews and data-collection methods described in chapter 5 helps workers develop logic models. Theory and logic models become important tools for evaluating the planning and implementation of social services.

The literature review provides a partial answer to the question by helping the social service worker learn from written accounts of successful interventions and be able to provide the answer "Because this intervention has been shown in the literature to be effective." Chapter 7 also contains a discussion of systematic reviews, a tool to assess the empirical data from studies measuring the effectiveness of a specific intervention.

Part 5, "Data-Driven Evaluation Decisions," includes chapters 8–11. Chapter 8, "Research Methods," begins with a discussion of how evaluations transform information in an agency into data that are relevant to answering the evaluation questions. The purpose of this chapter is to familiarize the reader with the issues related to research methods. Differences in open-ended, qualitative and closed-ended, quantitative data-collection processes are compared across the evaluation process. Chapters 9–11 discuss the application of research methods to answering specific types of evaluation questions. Chapter 9, "Qualitative Research Designs: Exploratory Evaluation Questions," covers the use of qualitative research methods to answer exploratory evaluation questions. Chapter 10, "Quantitative Research Designs: Explanatory Questions," covers the use of quantitative research methods to answer explanatory evaluation questions. Chapter 11, "Mixed-Methods Research Designs: Descriptive Evaluations," covers the use of mixed methods to answer descriptive evaluation questions.

Part 6, "Documenting Evaluation Decisions: Coming Full Circle," aids the reader in writing the final report. The final report is the reader's justification for the decisions made and agreed on by key stakeholders during the give-and-take negotiation that all evaluations entail.

The appendix, "Evaluation Decision-Making Questions Outline," lists all of the evaluation decision-making questions for all twelve chapters. There is also a glossary of common terms used throughout the book.

AUTHOR'S BACKGROUND

Evaluation has been my tool for bridging academe and the practice setting in my role as a social work educator at Wright State University since 1993. I am a social worker. My baccalaureate, master's, and doctoral degrees are all in social work. I also have educational training in psychology, sociology, education, women's studies, cultural studies, and urban affairs. My social work practice has been in the fields of child welfare, mental health, and family violence prevention. I now make it my profession to influence future social workers through my teaching of micro and macro content in undergraduate and graduate social work courses. I also mentor students who are completing social work honors theses and graduate theses in applied behavioral sciences, psychology, and the humanities. Social work values, knowledge, and skills related to practice, planning, and evaluation are infused into every class I teach and every thesis committee on which I serve.

The case examples that I provide throughout the book range from evaluations initiated by social service workers or students in agencies with a small staff of five or fewer and a small operating budget of $100,000 or less to statewide evaluations of county-implemented programs with a large operating budget, often in the millions of dollars. The case examples cover different purposes (planning, implementation, and research), answer various types of questions (exploratory, descriptive, and explanatory), and were intended for different uses (continue, improve, create, or discontinue the evaluated interventions).

My involvement in all the case examples was connected to my university affiliation, which meant that all data-collection activities needed approval by an institutional review board, which is discussed in chapter 4. The case examples follow the SCREAM values that I describe in chapter 3 to different degrees. Some case examples show the utilization of a logic model to guide evaluation decisions. Some examples illustrate cases that required that the evaluated programs implement evidence-based practices. Qualitative and quantitative data-collection approaches are illustrated, sometimes in the same case example. Finally, actual products derived from case examples are provided and include journal articles, conference presentations, annotated bibliographies, and evaluation manuals.

My role as educator, facilitator, change agent, supporter, and mediator varied across the different evaluations. In some evaluations I was a member of an outside evaluation team that had little or no contact with the persons implementing the evaluated programs other than collecting data from them. In other evaluations I met with the direct-care staff or planners often to teach them about evaluation methods or to inform them of the theory most relevant to their service delivery.

I provide the case examples as a way to help the reader engage knowledgeably in the evaluation process. In all of the examples, I was an evaluator. The reader too can learn evaluation tasks. Minimally, readers should be knowledgeable about what to expect from those persons hired to evaluate their programs. The case examples, evaluation decision-making checklists, and further resources provide the applied tools that will help readers understand and successfully conduct evaluations of their practice interventions.

In each evaluation I applied the same social work processes as I did when I was a child welfare social worker. Just as I did with practice clients, I wanted evaluation clients to know the potential consequences of decisions that were being made mutually. The evaluation process, like the practice process, is itself a learning tool for all persons involved. Much of the knowledge gained from the evaluation examples in this book came from the process as much as from the outcomes measured.

I conclude this preface with these catchphrases that readers should remember as they use this book to ensure that evaluations are conducted *with* social service workers and clients rather than *on* them:

- *Clarify, clarify, clarify.* It is worth everyone's time to be clear about the purpose and expectations of an evaluation. The time spent to clarify in writing with key stakeholders the important components of the evaluation reduces the amount of time spent blaming persons for doing the evaluation the "wrong" way.
- *Practice, practice, practice.* Learn while doing. Try some of the ideas in this book on a small scale before applying them to an entire evaluation.
- *There is no perfect evaluation.* Some stakeholder will always be critical of evaluation decisions because there are always many different options in evaluations. Keep a journal during evaluations to document the decisions made, noting those persons who agreed to and those who opposed those decisions.
- *SCREAM as often as you can.* Measure client strengths. Respect the cultural backgrounds of all stakeholders. Work within the means of the available resources. Treat all participants ethically. Expect stakeholders to reach an agreement on how to conduct the evaluation

competently to the best of one's abilities. Measure results of multiple systems (i.e., individuals, families, agencies, and communities). These are values that most social services advocate in their daily interventions. The same should be true for evaluations.

- *Do not go out there alone.* Form an evaluation support group to help you get past writing blocks or stakeholder blocks or the logic model blues. Others can help you see the value of moving forward even when you seem to be spinning your wheels.

ACKNOWLEDGMENTS

I could not have completed this book without the support and patience of my wife, Karla, who understood when I spent hours, weeks, and years in the upstairs office—writing both editions of this book. She genuinely applies evidence-based interventions to deliver occupational therapy to children with special needs. My parents, siblings, and friends have given me much encouragement to finish this book at times when I got lost in the chapters. I thank all my colleagues in the Social Work Department who support my teaching and evaluation. Thank you Carolyn Staruch, Rebecca Holtkamp, Janae Corbett, Erin Ritter, and Kay Frazier, who helped edit the drafts of this edition. I thank all the social service workers and clients who taught me about evaluation through their questions and active participation in the evaluation process.

A theme of this book is that evaluation bridges practice and research. The following mentors and colleagues have helped me bridge all the different influences that created this book. Thank you, Drs. Patti Lather, Laurel Richardson, and Mary Katherine O'Connor, for your hands-on teaching and modeling of qualitative methods and constructivist, naturalistic approaches. Thank you, Dr. Elsie Pinkston, for teaching me the value of writing measurable behavioral outcomes and valid and reliable observation protocols. Thank you, Drs. Nolan Rindfleisch, Karen Harper, Beverly Toomey, Keith Kilty, and all my doctoral classmates, for building my confidence as a researcher and evaluator.

Thank you to the following evaluators with whom I have had the fortune to collaborate: Micko Smith, Betty Yung, Cheryl Myer, Katherine Cauley, Richard Rapp, Rhonda Reagh, Carla Clasen, Jane Dockery, Anya Senetra, Timothy Sweet-Holp, and William Mase.

Thank you David Follmer and the staff of Lyceum Books for guiding me through the long process of completing the second edition of this book.

Thank you to the following persons who gave helpful feedback and insight from multiple disciplines and worldviews by reviewing the draft of this edition: Jami Fraze, Lori Bakken, Gary Bess, Carol Lewis, and Karen Schwartz.

Thank you to all the people I reference in this book, for it is your writings that helped me conceptualize evaluation as an applied tool that belongs in the hands of social service workers and their allies.

A Practical Guide to

Evaluation

PURPOSE AND
SCOPE OF EVALUATION

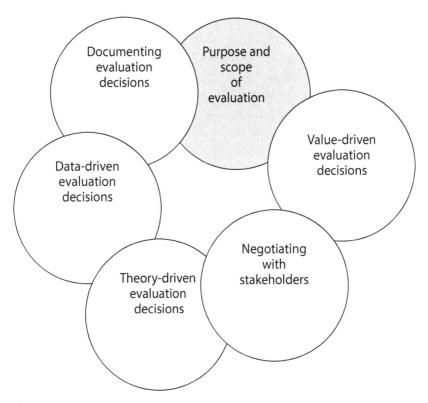

Figure 1.
Interactive model of evaluation: Purpose and scope of evaluation

Purpose of Evaluation

1

EVALUATION DECISION-MAKING QUESTIONS

Why evaluate?

Who wants the evaluation?

What are the goals of the evaluation?

What are the expected outputs of the evaluation?

Before my discussion of the importance of evaluation and the steps in the process, it is important to reiterate that the steps involved in evaluation do not occur in a set order and are each affected by the other. This text provides a model to help social service workers, educators, and students control the evaluation process. Evaluation is described in this text as a necessary process if practice and planning are to be enriched and if social service workers, educators, and students are to remain accountable to stakeholders. Each chapter summarizes separate but interconnected steps to evaluation, as seen in figure 1, "Interactive Model of Evaluation." As you read and conduct your own evaluations, remember that decisions you make in each step affect activities conducted in other steps of the evaluation.

This first chapter of this part begins with a discussion of the positive ways in which social service workers can benefit from evaluation. The second chapter emphasizes the importance of clarifying the scope of a current evaluation before proceeding with the other steps of the evaluation.

WHY EVALUATE?

Why are you reading this book? Look at checklist 1 and check off all of the reasons you are learning about evaluation. Even though your motivation to learn about evaluation may be external and not fully voluntary, the checklist includes the reasons that evaluation enriches practice.

Evaluation Is Practice.

Read case examples 1 and 2. Take note of the practice skills that were necessary to collect information during the evaluations. The purpose of the evaluations guided the actions of the social service practitioners, planners, and evaluators. Interviewing skills were needed to elicit accurate and credible information. The evaluators informed participants that their participation was confidential and voluntary. The results of the evaluation guided practice and planning decisions.

Case Example 1. Evaluation of Strengths-Based Case Management

The director of a strengths-based case management (SBCM) intervention contacted me to conduct open-ended, qualitative interviews with consumers to answer the following general descriptive question: "How do consumers experience SBCM?" The intervention was based on prior research that demonstrated the effectiveness of SBCM with persons discharged from an inpatient, substance-abuse rehabilitation program. Agreement on the data-collection process was reached with the three agency workers who were also interviewed to obtain their description of the intervention. The main source of information was ten consumers or evaluation participants with whom one-hour interviews were conducted at three different times over a six-month period. Initially, some of the staff was nervous about how the results might affect the program. The program director assured them that all information was confidential and would be used to improve the program rather than discontinue it. My summaries and interpretations of the interviews were shared with each participant. The written report was provided to the staff and shared with them during a staff meeting. The staff benefited from hearing about client experiences of which they had not pre-

Checklist 1. Why People Evaluate

Place a check mark next to each reason you are planning or conducting a current evaluation.

Program Improvement

___ It is required and/or recommended by an accrediting body.

___ It is required and/or recommended as part of an RFP.

___ It is required and/or recommended as part of receiving a grant.

___ It is required and/or recommended by the agency board of directors.

___ It is required and/or recommended by the agency director.

___ It is required and/or recommended by my supervisor.

___ It is required and/or recommended by a collaborating agency.

___ It was requested by an agency consumer.

___ I have to evaluate my staff's performance.

___ Other

Knowledge Building

It is required and/or recommended in one of these academic settings:

___ A class in a bachelor's program

___ A continuing education class

___ A class in a master's program

___ A class in a doctoral program

___ An honors, master's, or doctoral thesis

___ Other

viously been aware. For example, one man reported: "I did not trust the things the counselors were saying. The only time someone in the past said something nice to me, they were lying because they wanted something from me." The staff discussed ways to deliver SBCM that incorporated knowledge learned from the information I collected, analyzed, and reported to them. The costs of this project were covered as part of the operating budget for this program, which was funded by the National Institute on Drug Abuse. The primary expenses were compensation for the participants' time ($30 for each interview) and less than 10 percent reallocation of my and the staff's time from other responsibilities to complete the project. All data-collection procedures were approved by my university's institutional review board (IRB) to ensure that ethical guidelines were followed in data collection.

Case Example 2. Evaluation of Family Support Interventions

I, along with colleagues from my and seven other universities, submitted a response to a request for proposals to conduct a statewide evaluation of thirty-eight family support interventions (FSIs) over a two-year period. FSIs were community- and school-based programs that were locally planned and implemented. Goals of the programs were to increase collaboration among families, agencies, schools, and communities to improve child, family, agency, and community functioning. Intervention strategies included assessment, referral, after-school programs, tutoring, parent education, community organization, agency outreach, counseling, advocacy, health services, and mental health services.

This $250,000 evaluation was funded by three state agencies. Our evaluation plan included conducting open-ended, qualitative site interviews during the first year to answer the descriptive question, "How do different stakeholders (administrators, direct-care staff, community representatives, and consumers) perceive success of the programs?" The results of the site interviews would help the evaluators construct a list of common, desired results to measure across selected programs during the second year. At the same time, quantitative, closed-ended telephone surveys were conducted with consumers of the programs and a comparison group to test the following explanatory hypothesis: "Consumers of the FSIs will significantly improve family functioning."

There were varying levels of agreement about the evaluation among stakeholders. As the primary evaluator, I had at least quarterly meetings with the state funders and often much more frequent e-mail and telephone contact. There were legal mandates on school-based FSIs to measure the student performance outcomes of proficiency-test pass rates, attendance, retention, and graduation rates. Other FSIs had more flexibility to determine the best results to measure locally. Some FSIs targeted the larger community for change, whereas others targeted the family for change. This difference in program targets made it difficult to arrive at a feasible list of common results across FSIs to measure in the second year. On the basis of this information, the state funders and the evaluators agreed at the one-year point to continue the telephone survey of consumers and to conduct academic literature searches to determine the best standardized instruments to measure child health, family functioning, and parent involvement in children's education.

The following reports delivered at the end of the evaluation were made available to the state funders and local directors of the evaluated programs to assist them in future evaluations: (1) results of the statewide evaluation; (2) feedback about individual programs; (3) evaluation training material; and (4) critiques of standardized instruments that measure child well-being, family functioning, and parent involvement in children's education. During the first year, the funding for this project compensated my university for 100 percent of my time and 10 percent each of the time for ten faculty from other universities. For the second year, the funding covered 10 percent of my time and of about five other colleagues. The funding also covered the telephone survey expenses for both years. All data-collection procedures were approved by my university's IRB to ensure that ethical guidelines were followed in data collection.

Evaluation Improves Services.

In case example 1, the strengths-based case management (SBCM) intervention for men in recovery was adapted to take account of participants' skepticism of the approach. In case example 2, several reports emerged from the evaluation to help improve the implementation of the family support programs. Those evaluation reports were (1) a list of commonly desired results at the child, family, agency, and community levels that could be measured across all programs; (2) critiques of instruments to measure child health, family health, and parent involvement; and (3) a training model to help the participants conduct self-evaluations.

Evaluation Is Accountability.

Funding sources require practitioners to be accountable for producing desired results by conducting what are termed **summative evaluations**. Summative evaluations measure specific outcomes expected of the intervention. In case example 1, information from the client interviews supported positive outcomes previously reported from an evaluation of the same program. In case example 2, the desired outcome of improved family functioning across participants of community-based family support programs was not demonstrated partly because the instrument used to measure family functioning employed may not have been the best conceptual tool for this population. Yet the individuals, local agencies, and state administrators were still able to utilize the process and the results of the evaluation to improve practice and future evaluations.

Evaluation Is a Process.

In both examples, the evaluators negotiated with the key stakeholders to reach agreement on the evaluation activities, just as a social service worker or educator develops an intervention plan with clients or students and other systems to help targeted persons achieve change. In case example 1, the key stakeholders were the four staff, although the director had more influence on the evaluation decisions than did the three direct-care staff. The consumers' input was sought as part of the information-gathering process. There were many more stakeholders involved in the example presented in case example 2. The primary stakeholders were the state funders, although consultation on the evaluation plan was solicited from each director of the thirty-eight programs being evaluated.

Evaluation Is Applied Research.

In both case examples, the data-collection methods were finalized only *after* the following points were clarified with key stakeholders: (1) the purpose of the evaluation; (2) whether the evaluation questions were exploratory, descriptive, or explanatory; (3) important values to be guided by in the evaluation (e.g., to measure client strengths); (4) the logic model (listing the goals, interventions, and expected outcomes of the intervention, and listing how the outcomes will be measured) guiding the practice and evaluation; (5) preferred methods of data collection; and (6) the final products of the evaluation.

The two case examples illustrate that evaluation is a process of systematically collecting and analyzing information to improve practice. In the first example, the evaluators employed qualitative, open-ended interviews with participants in a structured manner. The interview format was based on descriptive questions pertaining to the evaluated intervention. In the second example, a longitudinal, comparison-group survey design was implemented to test an explanatory hypothesis related to the programs. Open-ended site interviews with key stakeholders were conducted to answer descriptive evaluation questions.

In both examples, the knowledge of specific evaluation designs (e.g., qualitative, single subject, experimental) and data-collection methods (e.g., surveys, observation, secondary data analysis) was then implemented on the basis of the negotiation of the factors listed. No evaluator can master all possible data-collection methods. The benefit of conducting the evaluation as a team, as in case example 2, is the ability to utilize the skills of the different evaluators and social service staff.

In both examples, stakeholders and participants in the evaluation stated that they learned methods of self-evaluation that they could employ in the future. Clients changed destructive behavior (using substances) and increased healthy behavior (positive interaction with their children) on the basis of insight gained from the open-ended interviews. Evaluators sought out studies conducted on interventions similar to their own, located the best instruments to measure their desired outcomes, and designed self-evaluations. Administrators arranged time for practitioners to design and conduct evaluations. They also arranged training on a specific, empirically based intervention.

This text provides a model to help social service workers and educators control the evaluation process. Evaluation is described in this book as a process, a necessary process, if practice and planning are to be enriched and if social service workers are to remain accountable to stakeholders. This is not a technical, research methods book. Those texts already exist. This is a book to help students, practitioners, and planners become active participants in evaluation by understanding and clarifying the terms and expectations of a given evaluation.

The discussions throughout this text do require the reader to understand the interrelated roles of research and evaluation. Research in the social sciences is the rigorous implementation of data-collection methods and designs to answer questions that will contribute to the knowledge base about human behavior. All students of social work are expected upon graduation to "comprehend quantitative and qualitative research and understand scientific and ethical approaches to building knowledge" (Council on Social Work Education, 2012, p. 5). As is discussed in chapter 8, there are different views of what constitutes "scientific inquiry." Some researchers advocate only for quantitative, experimental designs, which are not feasible in most agencies.

For the purposes of this text, I define **research** as the implementation of reliable, valid, or credible methods to empirically explore, describe, or explain a theorized relationship between variables. This definition allows for the rigorous implementation of quantitative and qualitative methods. **Evaluation** is the systematic collection and analysis of information about one or more social service interventions and targeted clients to improve practice, planning, and accountability and to contribute to knowledge building. So, the primary purpose of evaluation is to use data to assist agencies and schools in making data-driven decisions. A secondary goal is to contribute to the knowledge base and help other persons who are evaluating similar interventions. As the next section covers, different stakeholders may have demands on the evaluation that affect the data-collection process.

EVALUATION STAKEHOLDERS

Put yourself into case examples 1 and 2. Imagine yourself in different roles: clients, direct-care workers, supervisors, agency directors, funding-source representative, and evaluators. On the basis of these different roles, what would be your goals and expected outcomes of the evaluations?

Stakeholders are those persons affected by the intervention or program and the process, results, and reports of the evaluation. Stakeholders can include funders; service providers; consumers of services; community members; and those individuals involved in the planning, implementation, and utilization of the evaluation. An evaluation can have an impact on many people. Within a three-year period, one small multiservice program that began with only one funding source obtained four additional funding sources after the project director demonstrated the success of the program through evaluation.

There is a difference between a stakeholder and an evaluation participant. Stakeholders are most often involved in advising the evaluation process. They give feedback about the purpose and manner in which information will eventually be gathered. **Participants**, called research subjects in studies, are those persons from whom data are gathered through interviews, surveys, observations, and documents to answer evaluation questions.

Stakeholder and participant roles may overlap during an evaluation. In one evaluation, a prominent businessperson was surveyed about her understanding of violence prevention in the workplace. On the basis of her participation in the evaluation, she eventually joined the team planning future violence-prevention programs and evaluations. In another evaluation, interviews with all members of the evaluation planning team were included in the final evaluation report. Thus, stakeholders (the planning team) were also participants, providing information for the evaluation.

Funders are those individuals who represent the source that is financing the intervention and who have input about the evaluation activities. Funders usually communicate in writing their expectations of the evaluation in the request for proposal (RFP) and grant contract. Some funders require that an evaluation plan be developed but not necessarily carried out. Others require that a specific type of evaluation (e.g., outcomes evaluation) be implemented. Optimally, workers from the funded agency have ongoing face-to-face contact with the funder to clarify and gain approval of all evaluation decisions. Sometimes, the funding source may have a team of several staff members overseeing the evaluation.

Service providers are those persons responsible for implementing the intervention. Service providers should be clear about the goals of the intervention, details of the strategies for reaching the goals, and the expected short- and long-term results of the intervention. For example, the goal of a school-based family support program was to improve the school readiness of all children in grades 1–4. The strategies included annual physical examinations and referrals, tutoring, after-school reading assistance, and assessment and referral for emotional concerns. The desired short-term results were that a specified percentage of the children be physically and emotionally healthy; have passing grades; reach grade level in spelling, reading, and comprehension; and have minimal absences from school. The desired long-term result was that a specified percentage of all children pass the fourth-grade proficiency exam.

Consumers are those persons who receive the intervention. Some agencies use the term *clients* rather than *consumers*. In school settings, student outcomes are the primary focus. Many funding sources seek consumer input about the intervention and how to evaluate it. For example, consumers of the school-based family support intervention (FSI) described earlier included students, parents, and caregivers. Parents' consent is required for services delivered to children. Guardian consent must also be given for those persons who are determined unable to make the decision to participate on their own, such as those with a severe mental illness. Consumers can be those persons with an identified concern, such as low academic performance, or persons considered at risk, such as children living in poverty. Consumers of a prevention program could all be residents of the targeted community.

Evans and Fisher (1999) described five levels of consumers' or service users' involvement in evaluation decision making. From least to most involvement of service users in the evaluation, the levels are the following: "(1) Service users receive information about the evaluation. (2) Service users are consultants to the evaluation. (3) Service users participate in evaluation decisions. (4) Service users have power to veto evaluation decisions. (5) Service users control all aspects of the evaluation" (p. 108). The authors then provided an example of a user-controlled evaluation of a private cash-assistance program for disabled persons. A research group that included service users controlled the evaluation budget and design, served as interviewers during the data-collection process, and analyzed the interview results.

Community members are persons who belong to a constituency (e.g., neighborhood, city, school district) that is affected by the intervention and evaluation. For example, family violence prevention in a school setting may include students in a class on healthy dating relationships that is part of the health education curriculum for all sophomores. In this example, community members may also include the entire school, other family members, neighbors, and other service providers.

Evaluators are stakeholders, too. **Evaluators** are those persons who design and carry out the systematic collection and analysis of information to improve program practice, planning, and accountability. In addition, most evaluators—especially those connected with a university or a professional evaluation organization—want to utilize evaluations to promote knowledge building. Thus, they can produce written reports that are used by agency workers, conference presentations, and journal articles that can be used by other social service workers not associated with the evaluated agency. An evaluator may have multiple reasons for conducting an evaluation. Discuss those reasons honestly with the evaluator and at the beginning of the evaluation. Do not assume that the evaluator has the same purpose as you or anyone else involved in the evaluation.

Evaluators, like social service workers and educators, take on multiple roles in addition to that of evaluator. For example, evaluators may take on the roles of educator, consultant, negotiator, practitioner, change agent, coach, or consoler (Fetterman & Wandersman, 2005; Patton, 2012). For any given evaluation, what is expected of the evaluator?

- Do stakeholders expect the evaluator alone to determine the merit or worth of the programs evaluated?
- Do stakeholders expect the evaluator to reinforce social service workers' self-evaluation of the program?
- Do stakeholders expect total objectivity from the evaluator, or do they acknowledge the evaluator's influence on the evaluation setting?

There are many evaluation models, each taking a different view of the role of the evaluator. References for some of the more common evaluation models are listed in the "Further Resources" section of this chapter.

Just as social service workers can function "simultaneously as change agents and evaluators of their interventions" (McClintock, 2003, p. 95), social service evaluators can also function as change agents. With this dual role, however, come potential ethical issues. Consider, for example, the hypothetical scenario presented by Morris (2003) of an evaluator suggesting that questions about youth sexual behavior be part of a needs assessment about pregnancy prevention strategies. The evaluator faced objections raised on moral grounds by stakeholders taking the position that the evaluator should function only as an evaluator. The stakeholders felt that sexual behavior questions suggested by the evaluator imposed the evaluator's values on the needs assessment. The stakeholders wanted the needs assessment to contain only abstinence as a pregnancy prevention strategy. What should the evaluator do?

When it comes to resolving such role conflicts, the quick answer is that there is no quick answer. As Leviton (2003) made clear in responding to Morris's (2003) "ethical challenge," evaluators need to be competent, honest, and responsible. This means that they will sometimes find themselves taking positions that are in conflict with those of some evaluation stakeholders—and that the resulting role conflict must be clarified through discussion. Clarifying role conflicts begins with clarifying who the client actually is, in much the same way that social service workers begin an intervention by identifying the client system.

See case example 3 for a description of evaluators also serving the roles as educator and facilitator.

Case Example 3. Negotiating Evaluator Roles

All the evaluation case examples in this book were conducted to guide program planning, practice, and evaluation decisions. In all the case examples, I provided findings and results based on the purpose and evaluation questions deemed important by the stakeholders. In some cases, stakeholders wanted the final report to include recommendations as well. Two additional roles requested by evaluation stakeholders are described below.

Educator

In a statewide evaluation of thirty-eight family support interventions (FSIs), the state funders requested that the evaluators provide education and technical assistance so that the program staff could eventually conduct self-evaluations. The education component was implemented through workshops given throughout the evaluation. An evaluation manual and instrument critiques were among the final products that the evaluator provided so that the workers could conduct future evaluations on their own.

In the evaluation of a countywide family violence prevention planning grant, the stakeholders asked me to provide one-hour presentations on practices that were effective in preventing child abuse and neglect and family violence, two areas in which I had research and practice experience.

In the statewide evaluations of the Children's Health Insurance Program (CHIP), the evaluation team presented the successful outreach efforts to the state funders, who then disbursed the information to the participating county workers.

Facilitator

As the primary evaluator for the statewide evaluation of FSIs, I was a facilitator of negotiations among three stakeholder groups: (1) an advisory group, consisting of at least one representative from each of the three state funders; (2) a group representing directors of the local FSIs; and (3) the evaluation team, which over the two-year evaluation period included faculty from more than seven different universities and up to thirty-five different staff persons who were responsible for collecting survey and site-visit information. A great deal of time was devoted to facilitating discussion and negotiation among these different groups.

I was a member of the evaluation team described that administered a survey to stakeholders statewide to assess agreement on the competencies that all direct-care mental health workers should possess. One member of the evaluation team served on the evaluation advisory board as a co-facilitator. Also serving on the advisory board were direct-care workers, supervisors, trainers, union representatives, client advocates, and vendors that contracted for services. The final survey had to meet the approval of this advisory board.

There were times during the family violence prevention project that I co-facilitated advisory board meetings, although this was not my primary role. I also facilitated discussions about the scope of the grant with the funders, the directors of four other programs funded by the same grant, the evaluators hired by the funder, and the local directors. The local directors sought my advice as well in developing the final plan, which was based on the information collected both from the research literature and from needs assessments conducted over a one-year period.

Negotiating with stakeholders is the focus of chapter 5. For now, be able to identify the key stakeholders of an evaluation and to determine their goals and expectations of the evaluation.

GOALS OF EVALUATION

Goals are general statements of a desired state. Looking back at checklist 1, of possible reasons people conduct evaluations, those reasons fall into two general goals: (1) to improve programs that help people and (2) to build knowledge. Evaluation is initiated for program improvement purposes when decisions to continue, change, or discontinue interventions or programs are grounded in knowledge gained from the information collected. Program improvement can occur by evaluating existing programs and by collecting data about current needs that are not currently being met. The latter type of evaluation, often called a needs assessment, helps workers plan for future interventions on the basis of data. Evaluation is initiated for knowledge-building purposes when decisions are grounded in and contribute to knowledge gained from research conducted on similar interventions or programs reported in the literature. A theme of this book is that university-agency partnerships promote evaluations that achieve both purposes at the same time.

Program Improvement.

Many authors define *evaluation* as the collection of data or information for the purpose of helping persons make program-management decisions (e.g., Grinnell, Gabor, & Unrau, 2012; Patton, 2012; Posavac, 2011; Royse, Thyer, & Padgett, 2010). A goal for this text is that persons at all levels in an agency, including direct-line practitioners, agency planners, administrators, and even consumers of services, participate in evaluation decision making.

Agency workers are likely to view evaluation for administrative purposes as jumping through bureaucratic hoops. It may seem that the motivation for the evaluation comes from an outside source such as a funder or program administrator. That is, the evaluation is simply a program requirement. In such cases, workers are unlikely to participate in the evaluation if participation is not required. The objective of evaluation in such situations can be rationalized as helping make program decisions. Evaluations can involve the collection of data to determine whether there is a need for services. In this case, evaluation is used for planning purposes. Evaluation can involve collecting data about an intervention or program that already exists. In this case, the evaluation is used for practice purposes.

Social service planning involves the selection of the interventions that will be delivered to a group of persons to achieve desired results. Planning may involve assessing the needs and assets of those affected by the program to establish goals and consulting the literature and key websites to learn about other programs that address similar concerns in other communities. In the planning stage, information is gathered to justify implementing a new program or modifying an already-existing program. The term **formative evaluation** is used to describe those evaluations in which data are collected to develop or improve programs and interventions. During program planning, information about potential clients is also collected. Planning or formative evaluations are sometimes called

needs assessments because data are collected to determine whether there is an issue or problem shared by large groups of people that requires intervention.

Descriptions of formative evaluations for planning purposes can be found in case example 4. In each of the examples, the evaluator stayed with the purposes established for the evaluation in question. For example, in the United Way example, the need to identify the targeted populations and interventions described in the reports analyzed was the basis of the evaluators' findings and recommendations—hence the need for the advisory group of agency directors *not* to consider other targeted populations and interventions when planning their five-year vision.

Case Example 4. Formative Evaluations for Planning Purposes

A United Way that funded services in a two-county region contacted my university to conduct a content analysis of four separate research studies conducted in the region over the previous several years. The purpose of the evaluation was to answer the question, "What are the targeted populations and interventions described in the four analyzed studies?" The results guided the selection of priority areas for funding by United Way over the following five years. I was a member of the evaluation team that provided the results of our content analysis to an advisory team of approximately fifteen agency directors and community leaders.

A local agency director contacted me to collect information to help a collaboration of agencies and community residents develop a pregnancy prevention proposal to be submitted for state funding. Information was collected by means of focus groups and surveys with teenage parents, teenagers who were not parents, parents of teenagers, teachers, religious leaders in the community, and directors of social service agencies providing services to youth.

A local agency director contacted me to collect information to help a collaboration of agencies and community residents develop a family violence prevention proposal to be submitted to a private foundation for funding. The members of the collaboration asked that I educate them about family violence prevention since I had a great deal of practical experience in the field of child welfare and domestic violence. They also wanted help constructing instruments and surveys to send to social service providers and were active in conducting literature searches. My role was as much educator, facilitator, and planner as it was evaluator.

I was a member of an evaluation team that conducted a quantitative, closed-ended survey of state mental health workers and an open-ended, qualitative focus group with key stakeholders of nine mental health facilities to answer the question, "What are the competencies expected of all direct-care mental health workers?" The results of the project were shared with stakeholders to determine priorities for developing a training program for mental health workers (Clasen, Meyer, Brun, Mase, & Cauley, 2003).

Social service practice is the actual delivery of services to a group of persons to achieve desired results. Evaluation activities include collecting information that describes or explains the relation between the intervention and desired results. In the practice stage, information can be gathered to justify continuing, changing, or eliminating the program.

Case examples 1 and 2 were both evaluations of the delivery of social service programs. For descriptions of other practice evaluations, see case example 5. The evaluators in each of these examples reported their findings within the limitations of the evaluation questions asked.

Case Example 5. Social Service Practice Evaluations

A facilitator of a local support group and summer camp for children experiencing the loss of a close relative contacted me to collect information that described the activities of the interventions. The information was collected through participatory observations and interviews in which I was a co-facilitator of a group and recorded observations of the other volunteers and family participants. The information was utilized primarily to train volunteers facilitating the support groups.

A staff person directing the diversity committee of a county public child welfare agency contacted me to describe possible reasons for the disproportionate number of African American children placed in out-of-home care compared to white children. I helped the diversity team analyze national research on the same topic and develop a plan to review case records for factors hypothesized to be related to this phenomenon.

I was a member of an evaluation team that conducted qualitative, open-ended site visits in ten separate counties to answer the question, "What are the successful outreach strategies for enrolling eligible children in the Children's Health Insurance Program (CHIP)?" (Meyer, Brun, Yung, Clasen, Cauley, & Mase, 2004). The information was shared with the state and local funders to guide CHIP outreach efforts across the state.

The Government Performance and Results Act (GPRA) of 1993 mandated that both public and private agencies improve their efforts in conducting summative evaluations by measuring results, outcomes, and other program-performance indicators. As a way to enforce the GPRA of 1993, most federally funded grants have minimum GPRA outcomes that must be measured as part of the evaluation. For example, in a 2005 Safe Schools Healthy Student grant with the U.S. Department of Education, the required GPRA outcomes that were expected of the funded programs were (1) to improve school attendance rates of middle and high school students by 5 percent per year; (2) to reduce the percentage of violence-related school suspensions by 10 percent each year of the grant; (3) to reduce use of alcohol and other drugs of middle and high school students by 20 percent; and (4) to increase referrals to outside agencies for specialized health, mental health, and family needs by 30 percent annually. The evaluators worked with the federal grant contact person to agree on the methods for measuring the GPRAs.

A second example of measuring GPRAs was an Integrating Schools with Mental Health Services (ISMHS) grant funded by the U.S. Department of Education and the Substance Abuse and Mental Health Services Administration (SAMHSA). The purpose of this grant was to facilitate proper referrals among the schools, mental health agencies, and juvenile court. The two required GPRA performance measures were (1) the percentage of schools served by the grant that have comprehensive, detailed, linkage protocols in place and (2) the percentage of school personnel served by the grant who are trained to make appropriate referrals to mental health services. The participating agencies could choose how to measure these two outcomes and could add other outcomes to their collaboration.

A premise of this text is that, in order for social service workers to meet external demands to evaluate their interventions, they must have available to them internal motives and supportive resources, such as those listed earlier. Further, evaluation takes many shapes in addition to performance- or results-oriented models. Other types of evaluations discussed in this book include exploratory, empowerment, needs-assessment, assets-assessment, theory-driven, and evidence-based evaluations. It is important to be aware of any disconnect between the social service staff's purposes for the evaluation and the funder's purposes for the evaluation. For example, the staff may produce information for the purpose of demonstrating performance and supplying evidence as to why a grant should be renewed when those are not the funder's goals. Rather, the funder may want the evaluation to produce data supportive of policy agendas, a purpose that might not even occur to the program staff.

The evaluation stakeholder agreement tool discussed in chapter 5 is one way of ensuring in writing the expectations from all stakeholders at the beginning of the evaluation process.

Knowledge Building.

People also conduct evaluation for academic reasons, to learn and promote knowledge building, most often under the name "research." Students may be required to evaluate agencies as part of a class assignment, practicum requirement, or mandatory research project. Similarly, agency workers often contact university faculty to obtain assistance with evaluations required by funders. If the evaluation for academic purposes is not conducted in such a way that the agency decision-making process benefits, then the staff may view the evaluation negatively, as merely an academic exercise that achieves nothing more than the completion of a class assignment.

An evaluation for academic purposes may sometimes seem to focus more on methodology and less on how the knowledge gained will directly benefit a social service worker's daily decision-making process. As a student, think of evaluation as an opportunity to benefit the agency. As an agency worker, think of students as a potential resource to assist with the planning and implementation of evaluation activities. See case example 6 for several descriptions of student research projects that social service agencies have used to improve service delivery.

Case Example 6. Student Research Projects Benefiting Social Service Agencies

A master's student conducted a single-system design evaluation of a behavioral modification intervention that resulted in the parents implementing reinforcement and time-out procedures that decreased hitting and fighting behaviors between their two sons. The mother of the two children gave a formal presentation to the agency staff of the changes for her family, including displaying baseline and post-intervention charts of the frequency of the boys' fighting.

Two master's students conducted a multiple single-systems design evaluation of a youth outreach intervention. The students used the Goal Attainment Scale (GAS) to measure whether the youth attained their goals. The GAS was selected because it was an unobtrusive measure that fit with the informal interactions between the youth and the staff. The results identified for staff common goals among the users of the drop-in center.

A doctoral student conducted a naturalistic, exploratory study of parents identified as at risk to neglect their child. The findings from qualitative, open-ended interviews conducted with six mothers were reported as six individual case narratives with questions such as, "How do parents who are predicted to be at risk for child abuse and neglect successfully raise their children?" The common strengths among the parents were conceptualized as the Interactive Model of Parent Strengths, which has been used to train Head Start family service workers to focus on positive parent assets.

An undergraduate student consulted the literature and adapted a survey to measure experiences of dating violence. She administered the survey to undergraduate social work majors. The results that many participants scored high on being victims of dating violence were reported to the faculty, who incorporated more discussion of violence prevention throughout the social work curriculum.

A director of a local mental health care agency contacted the instructor of a research course to assist with a needs assessment. The students in the class were trained on how to conduct face-to-face interviews with residents in a rural area with no health-care facility. The residents were asked how often and where they used health services and whether they would use a health center if it were located in their community.

An undergraduate student conducted a content analysis of procedural manuals written by a school district's nurse to determine how school staff should respond if children arrive at school with lice. The standard policy was for teachers to dismiss such children. The student researcher was concerned, however, because some children were missing many days of school, and often no one followed up on cases to assist the parents in removing the lice and to institute measures to prevent future infestation. The student reported to a collaborative team of nurses, social workers, and teachers that nothing in the procedural manuals indicated that children should be sent home. On the basis of the student's analysis, procedures were established for a nurse and a social worker to follow up on any reports of children having lice to reduce the number of days those children were absent from school.

Some authors distinguish between evaluation and research by stating that evaluation is conducted to help make program decisions, whereas research is conducted to promote knowledge. This distinction between evaluation and research *can* dichotomize practitioners and academics, both in the literature and in the practice setting. It is difficult, if not impossible, to conduct an evaluation without appearing academic. Still, it is desirable not to appear academic. Research and knowledge building are necessary tools for evaluation. So are the tools of relationship building and negotiation, which ensure that the needs of the program staff and clients are met. The social work value of going where the client is guides evaluation as much as it does practice. Good social work practice is good evaluation practice.

Throughout this book the term *evaluation* is employed instead of the term *research*, except in chapters 8–11, because the latter often implies methods of data collection rather than the entire evaluation process. Standards in many research texts focus on obtaining researcher objectivity through the use of comparison-group design and standardized instruments and the application of inferential statistical analyses. Standards in qualitative research texts focus on ensuring data credibility and trustworthiness (e.g., peer review, member check, data triangulation, journaling, decision audits). Mixed-methods designs employ both quantitative and qualitative methods that are feasible and rigorous for the specific evaluation conditions. Discussion of data-collection methodologies is the focus of chapters 8–11.

Checklist 2 provides a list of items for students to consider when conducting evaluation as part of an academic research project.

EVALUATION OUTPUTS

Evaluations include activities that are inputs and outputs. Inputs include the expectations of the key stakeholders concerning the purpose and scope of the evaluation and the data-collection methods. Outputs are the tangible, concrete products expected from the evaluation. See checklist 3 for possible outputs of an evaluation.

The writing of each of the outputs is discussed in more detail in chapters 12 and 13. The important point here is to clearly document which written and oral communications are expected from the evaluation. Who is responsible for the communication? Have all key stakeholders approve the outputs prior to beginning the evaluation? Be clear about what information each output should contain.

Have approval from all stakeholders to produce the outputs. For example, students and faculty may want to submit manuscripts for publication related to the evaluation or to present the findings at a professional conference. Include these outputs in the initial contract between evaluator and funder. Also, students and faculty will be required to receive approval from an institutional review board (IRB) before collecting any data. Again, include this requirement in the initial contract between evaluator and funder.

MAJOR POINTS

Evaluation is the systematic collection and analysis of information about one or more interventions and clients to improve social work practice, planning, and accountability. A premise of this text is that there may be disagreement among key stakeholders on the purpose of the current evaluation. Funders may require an agency to collect information for an evaluation without being clear about how that information will be used to guide future program decisions. Disagreement can arise as to what kind of information is to be collected. Service providers may argue that reporting high client satisfaction is evidence of program effectiveness, but funders may argue that only measuring positive change in client behavior is evidence of effectiveness.

This chapter discussed decisions to clarify the purpose of an evaluation, including (1) agreeing on the definition of *evaluation* for the current situation, (2) clarifying who wants the evaluation and why, (3) clarifying the goals of the evaluation, (4) clarifying how formative evaluations will guide program planning and practice decisions, (5) clarifying the specific outcomes that will be measured by summative evaluations, (6) clarifying how evaluation will contribute to knowledge building, and (7) clarifying which outputs or products will be expected from the evaluation.

Checklist 2. Items for Students to Consider When Conducting Research in the Agency

For a current agency research project, place a check mark next to each item that is needed.

Verification of the requirement from the academic institution:

___ Syllabus
___ Form from professor
___ Website explanation

Verification that ethical guidelines will be followed:

___ IRB approval form (all theses and dissertations are required to have IRB approval, but class assignments may be exempt)
___ Consent forms
___ Form stating how the evaluation will be used

Verification of approval from the agency:

___ Agency evaluation advisory board
___ Other committee approves such activities

Verification of how the results will be reported:

___ To the teacher only
___ To a thesis committee
___ Published as a thesis or dissertation
___ Published as an article
___ Presented as a paper

Verification of how authorship will be shared:

___ Agreement of whether or not the agency will be mentioned
___ Agreement of whose names will appear as authors
___ Other

Checklist 3. Evaluation Outputs

The following outputs are expected from the evaluation. Check all that apply to a current evaluation.

___ Written evaluation proposal or plan
___ Written evaluation logic model
___ Written amendments to the evaluation plan (approved and signed by key stakeholders)
___ Written evaluation progress reports submitted every _____ months
___ Written final evaluation report containing the following components:
___ Executive summary
___ Key stakeholders overseeing the evaluation
___ Purpose and scope of evaluation
___ Evaluation questions
___ Evaluation methodology
___ Copy of all data-collection tools used
___ Evaluation findings: summary
___ Evaluation findings: all statistical tables
___ Evaluation findings: all narrative responses
___ Discussion of findings
___ Recommendations
___ Bibliography
___ Literature review
___ Written educational material on how to conduct evaluations
___ Presentations on _____ given to the following stake-
     holders: _____
___ Manuscripts written by _____ to be submitted to
     _____
___ Call for papers written by _____ to be submitted to
     _____

CRITICAL-THINKING QUESTIONS

Universities and colleges prepare students to be critical thinkers. As mentioned in the preface, standard 2.13 of the Council on Social Work Education's (2012) Education Policy and Accreditation Standards requires all students to be critical thinkers by "distinguishing, appraising, and integrating multiple sources of knowledge, including research-based knowledge, and practice wisdom" (p. 4). Evaluation requires students and practitioners to be critical thinkers, to question what is being evaluated, and to ask why.

"Critical thinking is the art of analyzing and evaluating thinking with a view to improving it. A well cultivated, critical thinker: raises vital questions and problems, formulating them clearly and precisely; gathers and assesses relevant information, using abstract ideas to interpret it effectively; comes to well-reasoned conclusions and solutions, testing them against relevant criteria and standards; thinks open-mindedly within alternative systems of thought, recognizing and assessing, as need be, their assumptions, implications, and practical consequences; and communicates effectively with others in figuring out solutions to complex problems" (Paul & Elder, 2006, p. 4).

At the end of all chapters, there are critical-thinking questions to help readers question the content presented and to form their own synthesis of the material.

The critical-thinking questions for this chapter are the following:

1. Do you agree that evaluation enhances practice? Why or why not?
2. The author argues that evaluation is necessary for good practice. Do you agree and why?
3. What are the differences between research and evaluation? Do you value one over the other and why?
4. Do you agree that evaluators can also serve as educators to the other stakeholders? As facilitators? Why?
5. Do you take the position that evaluators should be objective data collectors without influencing the stakeholders? Why?

6. What are the possible conflicts of goals and desired outcomes among the stakeholders described in case examples 1, 2, and 3?

7. At the beginning of planning for an evaluation, ask key stakeholders to define evaluation. How did persons define the term *evaluation*? In what ways did their definitions differ? What were persons' expectations of the evaluation? How did their expectations differ? How were those differences resolved?

8. Thinking of a specific evaluation, ask key stakeholders about their perceptions of the evaluation. Did persons view the evaluation as jumping through administrative hoops? If so, why? Did staff persons view the evaluation as merely an academic exercise? If so, why?

9. How can evaluation improve program practice at the agency?

10. How can evaluation improve program planning at the agency?

11. Turn to checklist 1 and check off those purposes that apply to a current evaluation. If you checked more than one box, how do any of the purposes conflict with each other?

12. What are similar skills used by practitioners and evaluators?

13. What are similar skills used by planners and evaluators?

14. What are your strong practice skills? How can you apply those skills to evaluation?

15. What are your strong planning skills? How can you apply those skills to evaluation?

16. Look at checklist 3 of evaluation outputs. Can you think of any item with which a key stakeholder would disagree? Why?

17. Who are the stakeholders who may want the final evaluation report to contain recommendations? Which stakeholders may object to a section on recommendations? Why?

18. Which items in checklist 3 pose potential concerns about protecting the participants' confidentiality? How would you assure participants of confidentiality if you were required to include those items?

19. What can social service or educational settings do to make their programs ready for evaluation?

20. What are your reactions to the material presented in chapter 1? How is the material different from that presented in other books you have read on evaluation or research?

21. Cite at least two works from the "Further Resources" section at the end of this chapter that support your answers to any of the foregoing questions.

DOCUMENTATION TASK INSTRUCTIONS

Documentation of the decisions made at each step of the evaluation will help the reader in writing an accurate and detailed final report. Documentation also provides evidence of why the decisions were made. Remember, evaluation involves many overlapping decisions made by many stakeholders. Evaluation is a series of negotiations and documentation captures how those decisions were reached.

At the end of each chapter, the evaluation decision-making questions posed at the beginning of the chapter are repeated. A brief outline is provided of the material in the chapter that addressed each question. The documentation tasks for each chapter can become assignments that lead up to a student's final evaluation proposal. The documentation tasks can also be used to help stakeholders arrive at agreements related to evaluation decisions.

When completing these tasks, be expansive, honest, and reflective. Cover all of the ideas in your mind related to the questions. Be critical of the questions. Do not rely solely on the possibilities discussed in the chapter. Consider "other" to be an additional response to the list after each question. Explain your answers. Convince yourself and others of your answers.

The documentation tasks become your reflective and procedural account of the evaluation decisions you make. Reflect on the conflicting emotions and thoughts that are created by negotiating the evaluation process. At the same time, document the final decisions made. The reflections will not become part of the final report, but your reactions to the process will shape your decisions. Your reflections can become a source of discussion with persons supervising the evaluation to help uncover all influences on the evaluation.

Answer the following questions in relation to a current evaluation. Answer each of the boldface questions by considering the options that follow each question.

FURTHER RESOURCES

Web Resources

American Evaluation Association—http://www.eval.org
Canadian Association for Social Work Education—http://www.caswe-acfts.ca

Canadian Evaluation Society—http://www.evaluationcanada.ca
European Evaluation Society—http://www.europeanevaluation.org
Foundation for Critical Thinking—http://www.criticalthinking.org
National Center for Education Evaluation and Regional Assistance—
    http://ies.ed.gov/ncee
Social Work Research Network—http://www.bu.edu/swrnet
W. K. Kellogg Foundation—http://www.wkkf.org
Western Michigan University Evaluation Center Checklist Project—
    http://www.wmich.edu/evalctr/checklists/evaluation-checklists/

Other Resources

Alkin, M. (2011). *Evaluation essentials from A to Z*. New York, NY: Guilford
    Press.
Alkin, M. (Ed.). (2013). *Evaluation roots: A wider perspective of theorists' views
    and influences* (2nd ed.). Thousand Oaks, CA: Sage.
Dudley, J. (2013). *Social work evaluation: Enhancing what we do* (2nd ed.).
    Chicago, IL: Lyceum Books.
Fortune, A., McCallion, P., & Briar-Lawson, K. (Eds.). (2010). *Social work prac-
    tice research for the twenty-first century*. New York, NY: Columbia University
    Press.
Ginsberg, L. (2001). *Social work evaluation: Principles and methods*. Boston, MA:
    Allyn & Bacon.
Mertens, D., & Wilson, A. (2012). *Program evaluation theory and practice: A
    comprehensive guide*. New York, NY: Guilford Press.
Preskill, H. (2005). *Building evaluation capacity: 72 activities for teaching and
    training*. Thousand Oaks, CA: Sage.
Smith, N., & Brandon, P. (Eds.). (2008). *Fundamental issues in evaluation*. New
    York, NY: Guilford Press.
Stufflebeam, D., Madaus, G., & Kellaghan, T. (Eds.). (2000). *Evaluation models:
    Viewpoints on educational and human services evaluation* (2nd ed.). Boston,
    MA: Kluwer.

DOCUMENTATION TASKS

Why evaluate?

Evaluation is good practice.

Evaluation improves services.

Evaluation is accountability—summative evaluation.

The evaluation process is beneficial—formative evaluation.

Evaluation is applied research that builds knowledge.

Other reasons: _____

_____

Who wants the evaluation?

Write the specific names of persons who fit each category below for the current evaluation:

    Recipients, consumers, and/or clients of the services

    Funders

    Service providers

    Community members

    Evaluators

    Other persons: _____

_____

What are the goals of the evaluation?

To improve existing programs by measuring program outcomes—
summative evaluation

To conduct a needs assessment and plan for needed programs—
formative evaluation

To build knowledge

Other goals: _____

_____

What are the expected outputs of the evaluation and due dates?

___ Written evaluation proposal or plan due ___

___ Written evaluation logic model due ___

___ Written amendments to an existing evaluation plan due ___

___ Written evaluation progress reports due ___

___ Written final evaluation report due ___

___ Executive summary due ___

___ Recommendations due ___

___ Bibliography due ___

___ Literature review due ___

___ Presentation on the evaluation findings due ___

___ Peer-reviewed manuscript on the evaluation due ___

___ Call-for-papers submission due ___

___ Response to request for proposal (RFP) submission due ___

___ Other:

Scope of Evaluation

2

EVALUATION DECISION-MAKING QUESTIONS

Which current interventions will be evaluated?
What exploratory evaluation questions are being asked?
What explanatory evaluation questions are being asked?
What descriptive evaluation questions are being asked?

The discussion in chapter 1 provided the rationale that evaluation is good practice. Evaluation is a skill and knowledge base that is just as important as learning clinical or teaching skills and knowledge. Evaluation is a team effort among many stakeholders. The foundation for evaluation is that a program has a clear set of goals and desired outcomes connected to the intervention so that the achievement of those goals and outcomes can then be measured. The values and premises of evaluation discussed in chapter 1 underlie all of the other chapters in this text. The six questions at the beginning of this chapter cover the scope and purpose of the evaluation. Clarifying the scope and purpose of the evaluation first is key to choosing the most appropriate data-collection methods later.

PRACTICE AND PROGRAM EVALUATIONS

Following a systems perspective, social services or educational services can be delivered to individuals, families, groups, organizations, and communities. The word *intervention* is sometimes used interchangeably with *service, practice, program, lesson, agency,* or *school.* **Interventions** are those services delivered to an identified client or client system with intended theoretical goals and desired results. One intervention provided to one client and implemented by one person can be evaluated. One intervention provided to multiple clients by the same worker can also be evaluated. An example is the use of cognitive behavioral therapy (CBT) by one therapist with clients who abuse substances. Another example is the use of pairing motor skills with reading skills in one classroom by one teacher. The scope of the evaluation is the intervention as applied by one person. Evaluating one's own practice or intervention is called **practice evaluation**. The research designs for such evaluations are called single-systems design and are discussed in chapter 10.

The same intervention provided to multiple students or clients by multiple persons can also be evaluated. The scope of the evaluation then becomes the intervention—sometimes called the program—as administered by the group of workers or agency. Examples are evaluating multiple therapists' implementation of CBT or multiple teachers implementing the motor skills and reading intervention. This type of evaluation is most commonly called **program evaluation**. The scope of the evaluation is the agency or the school's implementation of the intervention. All of the data-collection methods described in chapters 8–11 can be applied in program evaluations. The specific methods used are determined by the specific evaluation questions posed, which are discussed later in this chapter.

A **social service program** is one or more interventions delivered to achieve specified goals and desired results for identified needs of clients. A program can be delivered by one worker, by several workers in the same agency, or by several collaborating workers from different agencies or schools.

Social service workers, educators, and students are expected to know both how to evaluate their own practice and how to evaluate larger systems' implementation of interventions. As stated in the Education Policy and Accreditation Standards of the Council on Social Work Education

(CSWE, 2012), "Social workers use practice experience to inform research, employ evidence-based interventions, evaluate their own practice, and use research findings to improve practice, policy, and social service delivery" (p. 5). The methods discussed in this book can be used to help students and practitioners evaluate a single intervention and to help students and practitioners design, and in some cases implement, evaluations of programs, agencies, or schools. In demonstrating mastery of the competency to "evaluate one's own practice," many students choose to implement a single-systems design of an intervention they implemented in their field practicum. Other students have met the same competency by helping agencies utilize data to evaluate the agency's implementation of a specific intervention or program using some of the group designs discussed in chapter 10.

So, the first step is to be clear about which interventions are the foci of this evaluation. Often times, the funding source is interested in evaluating only their funded programs. For example, I have been involved in more than one grant-funded evaluation in which the same intervention was funded by more than one source, but only one source required the evaluation. In one case, the intervention was an evidence-based program called Families and Schools Together (FAST; http://www.familiesand schools.org). FAST is an eight-week, evening program in which parents and children meet with volunteers and workers to discuss specific child and family issues. The evening begins with all family members sharing a meal. Then, parents meet separately to discuss parenting concerns and the children meet in developmentally appropriate groups. The evening ends with all members coming back together. FAST was already being provided in three schools before the school district received a Safe Schools Healthy Student (SSHS) federal grant. Under the SSHS grant, three more schools received funding to implement FAST. The implementation of FAST in the three new schools was the scope of the SSHS grant. As a member of the evaluation team, we encouraged the FAST facilitators to evaluate the original three programs and taught those facilitators how to implement the same evaluation plan used for the three new schools.

Another complication to identifying the programs to be evaluated is that many funded grants are actually administered collaboratively across several agencies. In the SSHS grant mentioned, the school district received the funding and contracted with more than ten other agencies to deliver seventeen different programs. The collective goals of the grant were to reduce violence or aggressive acts of students and to reduce substance use by students. The underlying premise was that the seventeen programs together would reach the goal and achieve the expected student outcomes. Separately, each intervention had different short-term goals that were related to the overall long-term goals of the grant. For example, the goal of FAST was to build family cohesion among those families in which students were struggling in school. Family cohesion would help reduce student aggression and substance use. Another intervention was the evidence-based program Positive Behavior Intervention Systems (PBIS; http://www.pbis.org). The goal of PBIS was to reward positive behavior of students and to track disciplinary data (e.g., office visits, detention, suspension, expulsion) as evidence that PBIS was reducing the number of disciplinary actions. Although PBIS focused on all student disciplinary action, the grant was able to focus on those actions taken in response to acts of aggression such as fighting and bullying.

Besides identifying the intervention to be evaluated, there needs to be an explanation connecting the intervention to the goals and outcomes of the intervention. A tool called a **logic model** is used to help identify the goals, interventions or strategies, short-term results, and long-term results of programs being evaluated. Constructing a logic model is discussed in chapter 6. Remember from chapter 1 that an intervention should have clear, theoretical grounding of why it is expected to create desired results.

All interventions should be evaluated. Remember, "research informs practice and practice informs research" (CSWE, 2012, p. 5). Yet resources, feasibility, and pressure from external sources are usually the main motivators behind interventions getting evaluated. Be clear about what the focus is of your current evaluation. Also, be aware that people will react to being part of an evaluation. All participation in evaluations must be voluntary and confidential, issues that are discussed in chapter 4. Participants in evaluations sometimes feel that they personally are being evaluated. Remember, the intervention is being evaluated because the intervention is assumed to create the changes in clients and students. The evaluation may demonstrate that the intervention is not being delivered in the manner it was intended. Agencies can then improve the intervention and evaluate the improved implementation.

In some evaluations, the focus of information is the activities, behaviors, and views of individuals. The following are some examples:

- The clients' narrative descriptions of strengths-based case management (SBCM) were the primary information reported in the findings of an evaluation, although there also were interviews with intervention staff. The decision was made to foreground the clients' views.
- In an evaluation of persons receiving family support interventions (FSIs), a telephone survey was conducted with clients. The site interviews were expanded to include clients, workers, and people from the community who participated in the program. Findings from the site visits were, thus, reported by comparing information collected from individuals representing different groups.

In other evaluations, the focus of information is the activities, behaviors, and views of groups and organizations. Ways in which information can be collected about groups include the following:

- In the SBCM evaluation, the evaluator reviewed all of the forms that the group of workers used with clients: assessments, intervention plans, referral plans, and discharge plans.
- In the FSI evaluation, the site interviewers asked focus-group participants to share written documentation that offered evidence of program success. Documents provided to the site interviewers included annual reports, evaluation reports, media coverage of the program, and client stories.
- In a United Way planning evaluation, the information analyzed was needs assessments and studies conducted and written by sources other than the evaluators. These sources provided information about organizational activities in the community.
- In a family violence prevention planning evaluation, one source of information was police reports of domestic violence offenses to which the county sheriff's office responded in a one-year period.

In other evaluations, the focus of information is the policies that shape the behaviors of individuals, groups, and organizations. Evaluation has a way of bringing home the point to the evaluation participants that service delivery is greatly shaped by public policy:

- In the FSI evaluation, participants of the school-based interventions were mandated (by state law at the time and by federal law now) to report specific student performance outcomes.
- In the family violence prevention planning evaluation, child welfare reporting laws, elder abuse reporting laws, and criminal court procedures for responding to domestic violence all needed to be reviewed.
- In an evaluation to determine common competencies for mental health workers, many different stakeholders had a vital interest in the findings. Those stakeholders included union representatives who influenced training policies and client advocates who demanded competent services.
- The evaluation of outreach efforts to enroll eligible children in the Children's Health Insurance Program (CHIP) revealed much information about how the eligibility requirements for CHIP were often an obstacle to enrollment. Successful enrollment interventions were conducted by agencies that found ways to overcome these obstacles, for example, by bringing portable copiers on home visits to process applications on the spot.

Evaluations of policies are relevant for planning and practice purposes. This discussion is connected to the concepts of formative and summative evaluations mentioned in chapter 1. At the planning or formative stage, persons can ask, "How will we show evidence that the policy or grant requirements will be followed?" At the practice or summative stage, persons often need to justify the answer to the question, "How did we follow the policy or grant requirements?" Most people feel more secure having answered the former question before being asked the latter one.

One last example demonstrates the interrelation between policy and practice in the planning, delivery, and evaluation of interventions. An evaluation advisory team was formed to evaluate the out-of-home placement patterns for African American children. The members of the evaluation team agreed to analyze how individual family case plans, steps taken by the agency's diversity committee to educate the entire staff about out-of-home placement patterns, and the state law to reduce the number of children in long-term care were all related to placement patterns for African American children.

TYPES OF EVALUATION QUESTIONS

Asking the right type of evaluation questions is the next component pertaining to the scope of an evaluation that needs to be clarified. Many students and practitioners find data collection to be the fun part of evaluation. Practitioners and students usually like to learn and solve problems. Data collection and analysis are tools for accomplishing these tasks. But different tools are required to answer different evaluation questions.

I organize evaluation questions into three categories: exploratory, descriptive, and explanatory. In part 5 there is more discussion of how the type of question posed dictates which data-collection methodologies will be implemented. For this section on the scope of the evaluation, the discussion focuses on how the evaluation question influences the general approaches to data collection, qualitative or quantitative, and how the evaluation question builds and tests theory. Figure 2 outlines the evaluation question continuum discussed in this chapter.

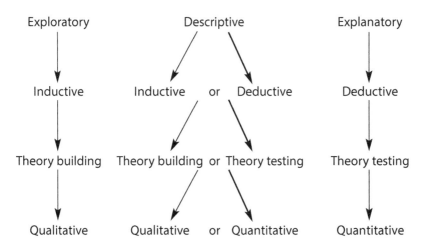

Figure 2.
Evaluation question continuum

Exploratory evaluation questions are open-ended, meaning that there are not predetermined answers. Truly exploratory questions use *only* qualitative research methods to seek and find themes that emerge from the evaluation participants. An example of an exploratory question is to ask clients or students, "What is it like to be a client here? What is it like to be a student in this program?" The evaluators make all attempts methodologically to genuinely capture the experiences of the participants. Exploratory questions are often asked during formative evaluations to learn about the process of the intervention or to identify needs for a new program.

Explanatory evaluation questions are on the other end of the methodological continuum and use closed-ended instruments to measure hypothesized relationships between interventions and client or student change. Evaluations answering explanatory questions use *only* experimental research designs, random assignment to a control or comparison group, and quantitative statistical analysis to objectively analyze whether the intervention was responsible for the expected client or student outcomes. For example, an explanatory evaluation would test the hypothesis "Clients with substance abuse problems will decrease their substance use after receiving cognitive behavior therapy (CBT) compared to persons with substance abuse problems who do not receive CBT." Explanatory questions are asked during summative evaluations to measure the intended outcomes of an intervention or program.

Descriptive evaluation questions fall in the middle of the methodological continuum and pose a relationship between interventions and client outcomes. Descriptive questions can use qualitative or quantitative methods. An example of a descriptive evaluation question is, "What is it like to be a client of strengths-based case management (SBCM)?" The participants were asked specific questions related to specific components of the SBCM, such as the strengths assessment, establishment of goals, setting a strengths-based treatment plan, identifying resources in the community, and establishing outcomes. This question is not exploratory because the evaluators have limited their data collection and analysis to specific, *predetermined* components of the intervention. The question is not explanatory because the evaluators do not want to create an evaluation methodology that would test a hypothesis. Rather, the evaluators chose to ask open-ended and closed-ended questions to learn the client's experiences with SBCM in comparison to presumed outcomes of the

SBCM based on prior research. Descriptive evaluation questions are asked in formative and summative evaluations.

The explore-describe-explain continuum guides evaluators to apply the appropriate data-collection method on the basis of the questions being asked. In simple terms, exploratory questions are open to all possible answers and thus have no predetermined relationships between an intervention and outcomes. Qualitative designs, which are discussed in chapter 9, are the appropriate methodology for answering exploratory questions. Explanatory questions test a causal relationship between an intervention or program and intended outcomes. Quantitative, experimental designs, which are discussed in chapter 10, are the appropriate methodology for answering explanatory questions. Both purely qualitative and purely experimental designs are not always feasible for agency or school evaluations. Thus, most social service and education evaluations employ rigorous implementation of qualitative and quantitative methods to answer descriptive evaluation questions.

There is not consistency in the evidence-based literature of the use of the explore-describe-explain continuum. It is not uncommon to see researchers refer to some quantitative studies as exploratory, which confuses my discussion here. There also are times when it is not clear whether the study is testing a hypothesized, causal relationship between intervention and client outcomes or whether the study is describing a relationship between the intervention and outcomes, but a true causal relationship cannot be proved. Matching methodology to the type of question makes it easier to determine the type of question actually posed in a study reported in the literature.

The discussion in this section refers to the overall evaluation question and not to specific questions asked in data-collection instruments. Also, some evaluation questions may actually appear as statements rather than questions. For example, explanatory evaluations test hypotheses, which are statements of predicted causal relationships between intervention and outcomes. Also, some descriptive evaluations also state the relationship of intervention and outcomes.

For a summary of the exploratory, descriptive, and explanatory evaluation questions that social workers most commonly ask, see checklist 4. Data-collection methods employed to address each type of question are discussed in chapters 8–11. Each type of evaluation question is now discussed in more detail.

EXPLORATORY EVALUATION QUESTIONS

Exploratory evaluation questions ask clients, workers, or community members about their experiences or circumstances, the answers to which will lead to program improvement and knowledge building. Examples of exploratory questions are the following:

- What is it like to be a graduate student in this program?
- What is it like to receive services from this agency?
- What is it like for you to be a parent?
- What is it like to be a worker at this agency or school?

The understanding of the contexts shaping participants' perceptions and experiences to be gleaned from their responses to exploratory questions is important information that can guide social service planning and implementing. Here is an example from a recent Integrating Schools and Mental Health Systems (ISMHS) evaluation funded by the U.S. Department of Education and the Substance Abuse and Mental Health Services Administration (SAMHSA). At the beginning of the two-year evaluation, project directors visited the thirty-seven schools across one county. The directors approached the school secretary and simply asked, "Can we speak to the person who administers the mental health referrals of youth in this school?" The project directors then asked the appropriate person (usually a counselor or principal), "How do you refer youth to mental health services?" This open-ended, exploratory approach allowed the project directors to learn how the mental health process varied a great deal across schools, even though the mental health staff had a prescribed protocol that each school had been instructed to follow.

Persons collecting information to answer exploratory questions must be critical of any preexisting ideas that they might carry into the evaluation or research setting. In the ISMHS example, the mental health program staff were discouraged that the prescribed mental health protocol was not being implemented. The exploratory approach, though, allowed them to learn this fact. In addition, the mental health staff discovered legal and procedural barriers in school districts, which resulted in school districts adapting their own mental health referral process. For example, some school administrators were concerned that the school district would have

Checklist 4. Clarifying the Evaluation Question: Explore, Describe, or Explain

Listed below are common evaluation questions grouped as exploratory, descriptive, or explanatory. Check all that apply to an evaluation you are currently conducting.

This evaluation is being conducted to answer exploratory questions such as:

___ What is it like to be a client?
___ What is it like to be a worker?
___ What is it like to be a resident?

This evaluation is being conducted to answer descriptive questions such as:

___ What is the relationship between ___ and ___?
___ What are the needs of ___?
___ What are the strengths of ___?
___ What are the program outcomes?
___ Who are the persons who utilize the program?
___ How many persons use the program?
___ Are persons satisfied with the program?
___ Which agencies in the community provide what services?
___ Are the requirements of a grant funder met?
___ Are the requirements of an accrediting body met?

This evaluation is being conducted to answer explanatory statements such as:

___ This program resulted in the following outcomes: ___.
___ This program achieved the following results: ___.
___ This program had the following impacts: ___.

to pay for mental health services if school personnel initiated the referral. Thus, rather than expecting a common mental health referral process for each of the thirty-seven schools, the mental health staff used the exploratory information to develop unique referral plans to meet different circumstances.

Exploratory questions require qualitative research methodology, which is discussed in chapter 9. As the ISMHS example illustrates, exploratory questions yield important information. Here are some practical items to consider when asking exploratory evaluation questions:

- Qualitative designs are time consuming. Asking open-ended questions, transcribing the interviews, and coding the transcriptions takes about ten hours for every hour of interview.
- Qualitative designs often have fewer participants than quantitative designs, and some stakeholders prefer larger sample sizes.
- Most evaluations are of interventions that are based on a predetermined, theoretical relationship between the intervention and outcomes. Thus, being open to other data is considered less efficient and not relevant.
- Even in needs assessments, there is the pressure to narrow the focus to already-determined categories rather than allowing the participants to describe their needs. There may just be too much variation to be able to capture, especially with large participant sizes.

What does happen more often is the use of qualitative methods to help answer descriptive questions, which is discussed later in this chapter.

EXPLANATORY EVALUATION QUESTIONS

Explanatory evaluation questions test whether an intervention produced the desired results for clients, workers, or members of the larger community. Answering explanatory evaluation questions leads to program improvement and knowledge building. The selection of desired results should be based on evidence-based practice. My definition of **evidence-based practice** is an intervention or program shown through empirical evaluation methods to have the desired impact on client or student outcomes. This definition allows for the "evidence" to be collected through qualitative, quantitative, or mixed research methods. Evidence-based practice is discussed in more detail in chapter 7. In this section, I am referring specifically to evidence collected through quantitative methods.

Explanatory questions are often posed as hypotheses or statements of expected intervention outcomes. For example, "Consumers of family support interventions will significantly improve family functioning." This hypothesis was tested by administering a standardized assessment of general family functioning to intervention clients and a comparison group at three different times over an eighteen-month period. The evaluation to test this hypothesis received sufficient funding to conduct the telephone survey to persons throughout the state to a relatively large participant group. The evaluators also contacted persons with similar demographic backgrounds who were not recipients of the intervention. The surveys were conducted at three different times. Much time was used to analyze the statistical data. Most agencies do not have the resources to administer experimental designs or to have a comparison group. Also, the study more accurately used a quasi-experimental design because persons were not randomly selected to the intervention or comparison group. It is also difficult to isolate a causal relationship in order to implement an experimental design.

Two findings pertinent to the intervention evaluations were that there was not a significant difference in family functioning between time 1 and time 3 and that there was not a significant difference in family functioning between the clients and the comparison group. One reason such findings were obtained was that both the clients and the comparison group had high scores on family functioning during the first survey. Thus, there was not much room for improvement. Another, and probably more important, reason was the assumption that family functioning would improve immediately in all interventions. However, open-ended narrative data collected through site focus groups showed that some interventions targeted change in the entire community rather than change in specific families. Also, the school-based family support interventions targeted individual children, not entire families.

An expectation for students and practitioners is to implement only evidence-based practice that has been proved through rigorous research methods to be effective. More discussion of conducting literature searches of evidence-based practices occurs in chapter 7. Many researchers posit that the most valid evidence that an intervention is effective is evidence collected through the experimental design, with participants assigned randomly to the intervention or control group. One research site that contains systematic reviews of evidence-based practice is the Campbell Collaboration (http://www.campbellcollaboration.org). Systematic reviews of interventions are available at this website. In most systematic reviews, the number of random-controlled-trial studies cited are much lower than the actual number of studies on the same intervention that appear in peer-reviewed sources. Thus, on the one hand, there is the expectation that interventions need to be proved effective through explanatory research designs, and on the other hand, the reality is that such studies make up a minority of studies conducted on social service interventions.

DESCRIPTIVE EVALUATION QUESTIONS

Descriptive evaluation questions are questions about the demographics, attitudes, behaviors, and knowledge of clients, workers, and community members, as well as information about interventions. The answers to descriptive evaluation questions will lead to program improvement and knowledge building. Examples of descriptive evaluation questions are the following:

- Do consumers experience strengths-based case management (SBCM) in the same way that case managers perceive the implementation of SBCM?
- How do different, direct-practice caseworkers, program administrators, community advisory board members, and clients perceive success of the programs?
- How do mental health workers, mental health clients, and mental health advocates define the competencies that every mental health worker should implement?

See case example 7 for examples of evaluations posing descriptive, formative evaluation questions. The questions are descriptive because the stakeholders had categories by which they grouped the needs rather than totally open-ended, exploratory questions. The questions are not explanatory because the stakeholders did not have an intervention in mind. The stakeholders were more interested in identifying the issues and past best practices from this literature. The evaluation was formative because after identifying the needs and potential interventions to meet the needs, the stakeholders could then conduct summative evaluations of outcomes after implementing the new interventions.

Case Example 7. Research Methods Used to Answer Descriptive, Formative Evaluations

---

Evaluation Question: What should be the priority area for funding for United Way in the following five years?

Data-Collection Methods: As agreed upon by the stakeholders, the four reports in the United Way strategic planning evaluation were analyzed according to the categories outlined in the white paper "Community Impact: A New Paradigm Emerging" (United Way of America, 1998). The most reported target populations and interventions became the top five priority areas.

Evaluation Question: What is the most effective pregnancy prevention program for this county?

Data-Collection Methods: A literature review was conducted to identify the pregnancy prevention programs that were shown through credible research methods to be the most effective in preventing teenage pregnancy. Those interventions were discussed in the open-ended focus groups with stakeholders. Some stakeholders valued abstinence-only interventions even though interventions that educated about both abstinence and birth control were shown to be more effective. The focus-group data shaped final decisions about interventions as much as the literature review.

Evaluation Question: What is the best family violence prevention plan for this region?

Data-Collection Methods: The stakeholders divided family violence into three categories: Domestic violence or partner abuse, child abuse and neglect, and elder abuse and neglect. A literature review showed the participants of the family violence prevention plan that successful plans require the collaboration of multiple agencies, including social services, police, courts, and the government, if intolerance of abusive and violent behavior is to be reinforced. Focus groups with representatives of the same agencies were conducted. Data were collected from public sources of the incidences of each type of family violence. A "state of family violence" report was presented to the community at the end of the data-collection stage that included the incidence data, focus-group data, and literature review of evidence-based practice. This report became the data that drove the decision for interventions in the second year of the grant.

Evaluation Question: What are the competencies expected of all direct-care mental health workers in the state?

Data-Collection Methods: More than one hundred competencies for direct-care mental health workers described in the literature were narrowed down to twenty-six by eliminating categories that covered the same content. These top twenty-six competencies were then narrowed down to five on the basis of the results of the stakeholders completing the survey and through focus groups with all stakeholders. The top five competencies then became the basis for training of all new direct-care, mental health workers in the state.

As the examples demonstrate, the selection of categories for descriptive questions is assisted by a review of research related to the interventions in question. The point here is that social service workers often assume certain relationships between interventions and client change. The accuracy of such assumptions is often challenged when those assumptions are compared to the results of other social service evaluations and research.

The other point about descriptive questions is that data are collected from multiple sources. The data are not collected just from one source, such as the clients. The data are not controlled only by the evaluator. Having multiple sources of data helps bring credibility to the results if there are similar findings and helps question the results if there are conflicting findings.

MAJOR POINTS

This chapter focused on the following areas that constitute the scope of an evaluation. First is identifying the specific interventions or programs being evaluated. Evaluating one's own intervention is called practice evaluation. Evaluating an entire system's implementation of multiple interventions is called program evaluation. Second is clarifying whether the evaluation will answer exploratory, descriptive, or explanatory questions.

Exploratory questions are open-ended, meaning that there are not prede-termined answers. Truly exploratory questions use *only* qualitative research methods to seek and find themes that emerge from the evaluation participants. Explanatory questions are on the other end of the method-ological continuum and use closed-ended, quantitative instruments to measure hypothesized relationships between interventions and client or student change. Descriptive evaluation questions fall in the middle of the methodological continuum and pose a relationship between interventions and client outcomes. Descriptive questions can use qualitative or quanti-tative methods.

CRITICAL-THINKING QUESTIONS

1. Think of exploratory questions related to persons in an agency set-ting. Write the general evaluation question in a way that does not imply a possible theory or explanation. What preexisting theories or values must you abandon to be truly open to people's descriptions of their experiences?

2. Everyone in the class, write a one-page answer to this question, "What is it like to be in a class about evaluation?" In a class discus-sion, everyone reads their answer verbatim—no ad-libbing. Discuss how persons may have described the same reactions using different words. Each word has a different meaning. What did you learn about the other classmates from their one-page answer?

3. Can you think of any circumstance when an explanatory evaluation design could be implemented at your agency or school setting?

4. How would you design an explanatory study to test the hypothesis, "Social work and education majors are more liberal than engineering majors"?

5. What are the ethical concerns about implementing an explanatory evaluation in a social service agency or school setting?

6. All of the examples in case example 7 are from needs assessments, which help persons plan new programs. Write a descriptive evalua-tion question of an intervention at your agency. Do you agree that the question is descriptive and not exploratory or explanatory? Why?

7. Why are most social service evaluations descriptive rather than exploratory or explanatory?
8. Should agencies strive to conduct explanatory evaluations, or is it sufficient to have the majority of evaluations to be descriptive? Why or why not?
9. Read a peer-reviewed journal article of an evaluation and answer the following questions:
   a. What are the exploratory questions, if any, being asked? Why are they exploratory? Did the author also identify the question as being exploratory? If not, why?
   b. What are the descriptive questions, if any, being asked? Why are they descriptive? Did the author also identify the question as being descriptive? If not, why?
   c. What are the explanatory questions, if any, being asked? Why are they explanatory? Did the author also identify the question as being explanatory? If not, why?
10. Refer to one of the general texts on evaluation listed under "Further Resources." How does the text help clarify some of the points discussed in this chapter?

FURTHER RESOURCES

Campbell Collaboration—http://www.campbellcollaboration.org
Families and Schools Together—http://www.familiesandschools.org
Positive Behavior Intervention Systems—http://www.pbis.org

DOCUMENTATION TASKS

Answer the questions below in relation to a current evaluation. Answer each of the questions below by considering the options that follow each question.

What current interventions or programs will be evaluated?

What exploratory evaluation questions are being asked?

What explanatory evaluation questions are being asked?

What descriptive evaluation questions are being asked?

VALUE-DRIVEN
EVALUATION DECISIONS

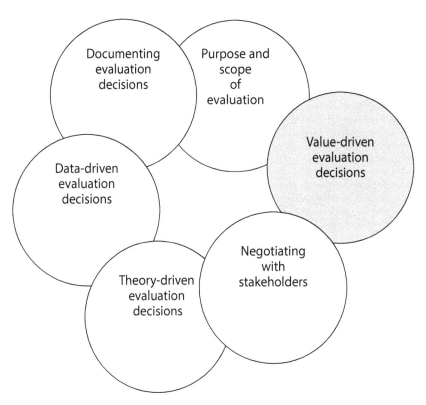

Figure 3.
Interactive model of evaluation: Value-driven evaluation decisions

SCREAM

3

EVALUATION DECISION-MAKING QUESTIONS

What are the values underlying the evaluation?

How will the evaluation measure strengths?

How will the evaluation be culturally competent?

What are the resources available for the evaluation?

What multiple systems-level results will the evaluation measure?

The discussion in this chapter will help social service workers prioritize the values that should drive evaluation decisions. The values discussed in this chapter follow the guidelines of the National Association of Social Workers' Code of Ethics (NASW, 2008) and emphasize the different client systems, focusing on their strengths. The prioritization of values guiding evaluation decisions will lead to key evaluation activities. The values to consider in this chapter fit under the acronym SCREAM—strengths, culture, resources, ethics, agreement, and multiple systems. The SCREAM values should be applied when answering exploratory, descriptive, and explanatory evaluation questions. Chapter 4 covers in more detail the ethical guidelines for conducting evalua-tions. Readers should follow the ethical guidelines of their profession and national organizations.

Before we turn to the SCREAM values themselves, we must first discuss the distinction between personal values, group values, and professional ethics.

VALUE-DRIVEN EVALUATION

Values are preferences, beliefs, cherished ideas, worldviews, assumptions, traditions, and morals that consciously and unconsciously shape and influence decisions of individuals and groups. Values are observed in actions, behaviors, customs, language, and attitudes. Each stakeholder involved in a social service evaluation has a unique set of values concerning evaluation, beginning with whether he or she considers evaluations to be important. Values supported in any given evaluation reflect the values held by the individual stakeholders involved and the agencies, communities, and professions that they represent.

Personal Evaluation Values.

Individual stakeholders have different values when it comes to the purpose of evaluation, the preferred methods for collecting information, and the role of theory in evaluations. Even in the evaluation and research literature one can find different preferred foci for evaluations. To illustrate this point, complete checklist 5. Compare your responses to how other students, colleagues, professors, social service workers, and clients respond to the value statements listed in checklist 5. Discuss why you value the statements you marked. Can you negotiate or adjust those values? It helps to understand how value preferences can influence evaluation decisions.

Agency Evaluation Values.

Value-based policies influence evaluation decisions. An assumption of evaluation is that agency program implementation and planning decisions are made on the basis of the information collected in the evaluation. Evaluation is not the only process that guides agency practice. Values inherent in policy may influence agency decisions more than information gained during an evaluation. Policies may be internally driven—by an agency's mission, goals, and procedures set by a local board of directors or administrators. Or they may be externally driven—by state law mandating the mission, goals, and procedures of publicly funded agencies. In some external-

Checklist 5. Understanding Stakeholders' Personal Values Related to
Evaluation

Values are preferences, in this case, about the general activity of evaluation. Persons' values are shaped by experience, socialization, and learning.
They tend to be applied to general situations with little regard to specific
circumstances, in this case, the specific scope of the evaluation at hand.
Consider having all stakeholders at the beginning of an evaluation check
whether they agree with the following value statements:

___ I do not see the value of evaluations.

___ Social service workers must be accountable for the services they
deliver.

___ All program changes should be based only on results from rigorous
evaluations.

___ All program decisions should be based only on evidence-based
research.

___ All evaluations should follow quantitative data collection.

___ All evaluations should follow qualitative data collection.

___ Evaluations should always use both quantitative and qualitative
data collection.

___ All programs should follow a logic model that guides evaluation.

___ All programs should have clear, measurable outcomes.

___ All evaluations should have the input from the following stake-
holders: _____.

___ All evaluations should be conducted by an evaluator not connected
to the agency.

___ These additional values should be present in all evaluations: _____.

evaluation case examples given in this book, programs were discontinued regardless of the evaluation results because of cuts in state funding.

When an evaluation involves more than one program, differences in values among staff from the different programs become apparent. In the evaluation of family support interventions (FSI), all FSIs evaluated had as their state-mandated goal the improvement of family functioning. No FSI employed the same methods to achieve that goal. Some employed methods that had not yet been proved to be effective.

Here we see the important role that values can play in an intervention. Consider how each of the following value statements of different FSIs could lead to different interventions and outcomes:

- We prefer to start with helping children because healthy children lead to healthy families.
- We prefer to start with helping families because healthy parents lead to healthy families.
- We prefer to start with changing the agency environment because accessible services lead to healthy families.
- We prefer to start with changing the community environment because healthy communities lead to healthy families.

The statewide evaluation helped the state-level planners and the local agency staff clarify not just their preferred interventions but also the values and program theories guiding those preferences. Program theory and logic models guiding program decisions are discussed in chapter 6.

Community and Societal Evaluation Values.

The political climate of the United States and many other countries is one that values producing outcomes, implementing programs that have proved to be effective, and above all, accountability. No publicly funded agency can escape accountability. These values may influence some stakeholders, especially those from external funding sources, to prefer specific evaluation activities assumed to "prove" the effectiveness of social service programs. These activities include the following:

- Measurement of client outcomes
- Use of standardized instruments

- Implementation of only evidence-based interventions
- Hiring of external evaluators to assess the effectiveness of the program objectively

For an example of the influence of current public policy on service delivery, consider the national and state policies that school systems be held accountable for the educational outcomes of all students. One of the goals of the school-based FSIs was "All children will be ready to perform academically." All FSIs were required to demonstrate that they had attained that goal by measuring attendance, graduation, and the percentage of students passing the proficiency tests during and after the fourth grade.

The debate about values among participants in this evaluation mirrored the national debate about values. Among concerns raised were the following:

- Are proficiency scores a fair way to measure educational performance?
- Who is accountable for student performance: students, parents, or teachers?
- What noneducational support, if any, should schools be providing students in order to improve their performance?

Professional Ethics.

Ethics are embodied in an organization's written statement, or **code of ethics**, of the values, principles, and behaviors expected of all members of that organization. Professional standards are embodied in a professional organization's written statements of the principles and behaviors expected of all members of that organization. The professional standards most often applied to evaluation are the *Guiding Principles for Evaluators* of the American Evaluation Association (AEA, 2004). For a range of evaluation competencies that adhere to these standards, see King, Stevahn, Ghere, and Minnema (2001). Social service workers must also abide by the standards enforced by their agency, standards that are most often influenced by larger accrediting organizations, such as the Child Welfare League of America or the National Head Start Association, and public overseeing organizations, such as the U.S. Department of Health and Human Services.

Evaluation Values.

Evaluation values, then, are found at the intersection of personal, agency, and community values; professional ethics; and professional standards that influence the decisions made during an evaluation. The term *evaluation values* is more inclusive than the term *evaluation ethics* for three reasons.

First, framing the discussion in terms of evaluation values instead of evaluation ethics allows room for the consideration of values beyond those of one's profession or organization. For example, an ethical guideline is that all evaluation data are collected in a competent manner. Some persons involved in the evaluation may prefer that the data be collected quantitatively. In another evaluation, some persons may prefer that the data be collected qualitatively. Thus, the ethical value of competence is met in both evaluations even though the value or preference of research methodology differed.

Second, the term *ethics* usually implies coercion. That is, discussions framed in terms of ethics tend to focus on the negative consequences of not adhering to professional codes, whereas discussions framed in terms of values tend to focus on the positive rewards of acting in accord with personal value systems.

Third, a focus on ethical behavior tends to obscure the underlying values motivating that behavior. For example, social service workers conducting evaluations may focus on the amount of time it takes to develop procedures to protect participants' confidentiality and lose sight of the underlying value motivating the development of such procedures, the protection of human dignity and privacy. Values are applied throughout the evaluation process.

Decisions as to what is right and what is wrong involve practitioners, agency management, and community representatives, including funders or public administrators. Social service workers follow personal values and standards. They also work for agencies and belong to organizations that establish standards. Every evaluation brings together individuals with different personal values and professional standards, all of which must somehow be made to work together. When values and standards clash, it is important to remember that there is no one, right evaluation code.

Value decisions are all about preferences and making choices. What compromises, if any, are made when stakeholders disagree on a list of preferred behaviors or values? Social service workers can approach value preferences optimistically, as a set of positive choices that they themselves can make, or pessimistically as a set of negative requirements that someone else forces on them. Be clear about the values and behaviors that you prefer in an evaluation and communicate those preferences to other stakeholders.

Clarifying Evaluation Values.

Sometimes stakeholders simply list expected values without clearly stating the reason for their inclusion. But the reason makes a difference and must, therefore, be made explicit. Consider the expected value "involve stakeholders from different cultures." Cultural inclusion could be a purely methodological consideration (ensuring that the distribution of cultures among those involved in the evaluation matches the distribution of cultures in the general population) or simply a matter of fairness (ensuring that all cultures have a say in the evaluation process regardless of the distribution of cultures in the general population). It is also important that enforcement mechanisms, or the consequences of not operationalizing an expected value, be made explicit. For example, continued funding could be made contingent on the involvement of different cultures in the evaluation. Finally, what it is that constitutes evidence of compliance must be established as well. For a schematization of the clarification process, see checklist 6.

Standard ethical procedures as dictated by a university institutional review board (IRB) were the ethical values guiding most of the evaluation examples in this book. The reinforcement for meeting IRB standards was the authority to conduct the evaluations. The consequences for not following these procedures would have been reprimands, resulting in possible discontinuation of academic studies and employment and loss of funding for current and future projects.

Clarify with stakeholders which values and behaviors are legally binding and which stakeholders are legally bound to follow them. Any evaluator working for a university will be required to have the information-gathering procedures approved by an IRB to ensure ethical conduct.

Checklist 7 offers a form that will help the reader identify the general values expected of any evaluation.

Checklist 6. Clarifying Evaluation Values

Apply these three steps to an evaluation in your agency or practicum setting. Use the example as a model. Check off each step as you complete the step.

Steps	*Example*
___ 1. Identify the preferred and acceptable values underlying the evaluation.	Ensure that evaluation planning and participation involves key community stakeholders.
___ 2. Define the behaviors that exemplify acceptable values.	Invite key community stake-holders to participate in the evaluation advisory board.
___ 3. State how values and behaviors will be reinforced or the consequences, if any, if the values are not held.	Funding will not be extended if stakeholder participation is not demonstrated.

Checklist 7. Identifying Stakeholder Evaluation Values

Complete this form as it applies to an evaluation in your agency or practicum setting.

The following preferred or valued activities are expected by stakeholders to be present in the evaluation:

State Value 1: _____.
Is it requested or required by the following stakeholder? _____.
What is the reinforcement for meeting the value? _____.
What is the consequence for not meeting the value? _____.

State Value 2: _____.
Is it requested or required by the following stakeholder? _____.
What is the reinforcement for meeting the value? _____.
What is the consequence for not meeting the value? _____.

State Value 3: _____.
Is it requested or required by the following stakeholder? _____.
What is the reinforcement for meeting the value? _____.
What is the consequence for not meeting the value? _____.

The remainder of this chapter is devoted to the common evaluation values that should underlie every evaluation. These values are summarized by the acronym SCREAM:

- Measure strengths.
- Respect culture.
- Conduct evaluations within the capacity of your resources.
- Follow professional codes of ethics.
- Reach a written agreement about evaluation decisions with evaluation stakeholders.
- Measure changes across multiple systems.

Reaching stakeholder agreement is covered in chapter 5. Following ethical guidelines is covered in chapter 4. Discussion of the remaining SCREAM values follows.

STRENGTHS

Acknowledging the strengths of individuals, agencies, and communities participating in program planning, practice, and evaluation is a common expectation of many agency grants. Yet the desired results more often identified by stakeholders are a decrease in deficits or negative behavior (e.g., clients will no longer rely on public assistance) or the prevention of a negative behavior (e.g., there will be a decrease in family violence). Individuals such as youth and older adults can be viewed as gifts to a community rather than as delinquent, poor, or dependent.

Strengths are behaviors and beliefs that help individuals, families, and communities reach their optimal level of social functioning. There is a wide social work and social service literature base dealing with the integration of strengths into practice and evaluation. Several of these resources are listed in the "Further Resources" section at the end of this chapter. The strengths perspective arises from the profession of social work's commitment to social justice and the dignity of every human being.

Strengths can be measured for all systems levels: healthy individuals, healthy families, healthy communities, healthy societies. Strengths lead to emotional and physical health. Strength behaviors of agencies are evident when systems function well or function beyond minimally expected levels. Systems rely on strengths to cope with normal challenges and stressful situations. Strengths are behaviors and beliefs that systems want to increase and promote. Strengths are measurable and can be incorporated into all evaluations. For descriptions of how strengths have been measured as part of an evaluation, see case example 8. For a checklist of measurements of strengths, see checklist 8. To locate strengths-based instruments, see the "Further Resources" section at the end of the chapter.

Case Example 8. Valuing a Strengths Perspective in Evaluations

The following are examples of measuring strengths as part of an evaluation:

- A strengths-based case management approach with persons discharged from a substance abuse rehabilitation program was evaluated.
- A desired result across all of the thirty-eight evaluated family support interventions was increased family functioning. Several of the evaluated programs implemented a strengths-based intervention with children, families, and community groups.
- A family violence prevention planning group worked collaboratively with a similar community grant activity that measured youth assets rather than youth deficits. The evaluation process in this same example utilized evaluation advisory board members' motivation and knowledge to carry out some of the information-gathering activities.
- Evaluation advisory boards described in several case examples in this book began with the assumption that they would rely on community members' assets in planning and implementing the evaluation.
- The qualitative focus-group approach to collecting information in several of the case examples allowed participants to focus on their own strengths and the strengths of others.
- The consumer of a behavioral parenting intervention reported to the agency staff the increase in the amount of time that her two boys were able to interact positively.
- The exploratory, naturalistic dissertation study of parents built on the academic literature that demonstrated the strengths that African American families utilize to raise their children.

Checklist 8. Measuring Strengths

Check all items that you have included in the evaluation:

___ Measured strengths as part of the agency assessment form

___ When conducting a needs assessment, also described resources, assets, and strengths

___ Built strengths into the program logic model that describes the agency goals, activities, and results

___ Measured strengths of individuals, families, groups, and communities

___ Utilized the assets of stakeholders by valuing their feedback

___ Utilized consumers' motivation to assist with evaluation planning

- The Safe Schools Healthy Students federal grant in one city school district evaluated several strengths-based programs, including Families and Schools Together (FAST) and Positive Behavioral Interventions and Supports (PBIS).
- The federally funded Integrating Schools and Mental Health Systems grant evaluated several strengths-based interventions, including the evidenced-based Good Behavior Game (http://www.paxis.org).

CULTURE

Culture is the values, beliefs, customs, language, and behaviors passed on among individuals, families, communities, and societies. Cultural groups are composed of persons who are connected by a similar heritage, purpose, or identity that includes a set of values, beliefs, customs, and behaviors and a common language. Cultural groups can be based on race, ethnicity, age, gender, sexual orientation, physical abilities, religious belief, income, geographic location, political belief, and other group membership. Each person is unique because behaviors and values are shaped by the interaction of the individual with the group culture. Social service workers need to question generalizations that are made about an entire cultural group.

Culture, and how it affects program planning, implementation, and evaluation, needs to be clarified in every evaluation. Stakeholders may expect culture to be treated as a component of an evaluation—even though that expectation may remain unstated. One reason culture is often ignored is that persons tend to equate culture with race. In communities where there is minimal racial diversity, some stakeholders may claim that culture was not measured because there was no racial diversity among clients. Stakeholders can expand their definition of culture to include other expressions, such as income, status, and personal values.

Stakeholders should make a point of identifying diversity within targeted cultural groups. In the evaluation of the family violence prevention planning grant, one advisory board member questioned the need to target the faith-based community for educational workshops on violence prevention. The assumption was that the workshops would literally be preaching to the choir, that churchgoers were less likely to be violent toward family members than were non-churchgoers. A minister on the advisory board quickly gave national and local statistics demonstrating that family violence occurs among persons who attend church at rates higher than the public perception.

For more discussion of ways to reduce the cultural biases that are ingrained in evaluation, see this chapter's "Further Resources" section.

Culturally Competent Evaluation.

Culturally competent evaluation is a process of social service workers becoming aware of their own cultural values and beliefs. It also requires the workers to reflect on how those beliefs differ from those of the participants and stakeholders of an evaluation. The workers also need to become knowledgeable of the research and evaluation reported in the literature related to cultural groups represented in the evaluation. Culturally competent evaluation is a multiple-systems approach that acknowledges that macro-level racism and oppression affects social service implementation and evaluation (Fong & Furuto, 2001).

Social service workers can apply the following principles of culturally competent evaluation:

- Become aware of your own cultural limitations in understanding the culture of stakeholders.
- Become aware of the cultural values, knowledge, and skills of stakeholders.
- Identify the best interventions and evaluations available within the mainstream and clients' cultural groups, that is, those that support clients' growth, values, knowledge, and skills.
- Construct an evaluation advisory team that has representatives from different cultural groups to review all aspects of the evaluation, including the interpretation of findings.
- Try to locate instruments that display sensitivity to the cultural groups participating in the evaluation; norm instruments with the cultural group in a current evaluation.
- Reexamine your own definitions and perceptions of cultural groups that will negatively influence the evaluation process.

Selected examples of culturally competent evaluation taken from Fong and Furuto (2001) are contained in case example 9. These examples emphasize a commitment among stakeholders to value culturally competent evaluation by accepting the range of choices available in evaluations. This means choosing both qualitative and quantitative measures and individual, group, and community measures, as well as measuring both strengths and weaknesses.

Case Example 9. Conducting Culturally Competent Evaluations

All examples are taken from Fong, R., & Furuto, S. (Eds.). (2001). *Culturally competent practice: Skills, interventions, and evaluations.* Boston, MA: Allyn & Bacon.

Villa developed a two-factor model called *la fe de la gente* that addressed "issues of culture, traditions, values, religion, and spirituality among Mexican Americans." The first factor, the vertical dimension of spirituality, contained eleven variables, including belief in God and "feelings of faith, hope, and love as critical aspects of coping" (2001, p. 374). The second factor, the horizontal dimension of spirituality, focused on the importance of caring for others and the impact of social conditions, such as poverty, on one's spirituality.

Gilbert and Franklin described a seven-step evaluation process that emphasizes the trusting, working relationship between the social worker and the Native American client during intervention and evaluation. The authors provided a case example that utilized a single-system and qualitative design with an eighteen-year-old Native American woman. Qualitative, open-ended interviews and journaling were used to identify in the client's own words her target behavior and goals. The charting of behaviors following the AB single-system design showed a decrease in flashbacks about a car accident that took her boyfriend's life and an increase in completed assignments at school.

Lewis discussed the importance of Patton's utilization-focused evaluation and provided clear, practical guidelines to follow when conducting evaluations with Native American groups including the following: (1) knowing the specific evaluation protocol, (2) actively involving Native American leaders in the process, (3) determining outcome indicators, and (4) writing final reports. She advised persons to measure outcomes among those who participated in the intervention rather than using community-wide outcome measures. She advised analyzing the relevance of a standardized instrument for Native Americans, searching the literature for evidence of use with Native Americans, and utilizing statistical factor analysis to determine whether the concepts apply to the current population. Lewis discussed writing two reports: one addressing the community's questions, needs, and cultural values and a second, technical one focusing more on specific questions asked by a source outside the community, usually the funder.

Matsuoka emphasized the implementation of qualitative data collection through participatory-action research methods and the use of quantitative indicators of different systems levels, including a person's spirituality and the role of the family, community, and social influences. He provided a case example of using Geographic Information System (GIS) mapping to display visually statistical information. His example displayed residential, farming, and fishing communities as areas on a specific Hawaiian island that should remain protected from land development. Matsuoka provided a case example of using a logic model to assist a Hawaiian community's evaluation of its economic plan.

Mertens (2003) recommended ways in which all evaluations could be made inclusive of multiple cultures. "An inclusive approach has implications for every step of the evaluation process: the design of the study, definition of the problem, selection of indicators of success, sampling and data-collection decisions, development of intervention strategies, addressing power differentials in the study, and setting standards for good evaluation" (p. 96). She concluded by providing a list of questions that, when added to an evaluation, can ensure cultural inclusiveness. The list is reprinted in checklist 9.

RESOURCES

Resources are the time, materials, and training needed to complete evaluation tasks. Some agencies set aside absolutely no time or budget for evaluation. Some grants may require evaluations but provide a very minimal budget for them, often as little as less than 10 percent of the entire program budget. Evaluations should be conducted within the budgeted resources. Listed below are the Joint Committee on Standards for Educational Evaluation's standards (Yarbrough, Shulha, Hopson, & Caruthers, 2011) of feasibility that are intended to ensure that an evaluation will be realistic, prudent, diplomatic, and frugal:

Checklist 9. Mertens's Questions for Conducting Culturally Inclusive
Evaluations

Mertens (2003) stated that all stakeholders of all evaluations should
answer the following questions to ensure culturally inclusive activities
(pp. 104–105). Check all questions that you have addressed for a specific
evaluation:

___ What are the influences of personal characteristics or circumstances, such as social class, gender, race and ethnicity, language,
disability, or sexual orientation, in shaping interpersonal interactions, including interactions among evaluators, clients, program
providers, consumers, and other stakeholders?

___ What evidence is there that the evaluation was conceptualized as a
catalyst for change (e.g., shift the power relationships among cultural groups or subgroups)?

___ Were the time and budget allocated to the evaluation sufficient to
allow a culturally sensitive perspective to emerge?

___ Did the evaluator demonstrate cultural sophistication on the cognitive, affective, and skill dimensions?

___ Was the evaluator able to have positive interpersonal connections,
conceptualize and facilitate culturally congruent change, and make
appropriate cultural assumptions in the design and implementation
of the evaluation?

Feasibility Standard 1 (F1)—Practical Procedures. The evaluation procedures should be practical, to keep disruption to a minimum while needed information is obtained.

Feasibility Standard 2 (F2)—Political Viability. The evaluation should be planned and conducted with anticipation of the different positions of various interest groups, so that their cooperation may be obtained and so that possible attempts by any of these groups to curtail evaluation operations or to bias or misapply the results can be averted or counteracted.

Feasibility Standard 3 (F3)—Cost Effectiveness. The evaluation should be efficient and produce information of sufficient value, so that the resources expended can be justified.

These feasibility standards and the other educational evaluation standards are available at the Joint Committee's website (http://www.jcsee.org).

Time is the most valuable resource for conducting a thorough and accurate evaluation. Time is related to all three feasibility standards listed here. It is needed to plan an evaluation well before information is collected from participants. It is needed to ensure that the ethical guidelines discussed in the next section of this chapter are followed, thus ensuring minimal disruption to services provided to clients (F1). It is needed to explore possible political implications and conflicts of interest and to obtain input from all key stakeholders (F2). It is needed to clarify the purpose of the evaluation, the appropriate data-collection methods, and how the evaluation will be utilized. Producing processes, results, and products that were not intended by the key stakeholders wastes valuable time (F3).

Time costs money. Some of the many time-consuming tasks involved in evaluation are the following:

- Conducting a thorough literature search for research and evaluations similar to the task at hand
- Negotiating the evaluation purposes as agreed on by the funders, evaluators, service providers, and clients
- Convening an evaluation advisory committee
- Developing the evaluation plan
- Writing an evaluation progress report every three to six months
- Having conference telephone or face-to-face sessions with the evaluation team

- Completing the human subjects review material to be approved before data collection begins;
- Implementing these data-collection procedures:

    Securing copyright permissions and purchasing standardized instruments

    Developing the questions for individual or focus-group interviews

    Writing the instructions for informed consent

    Selecting and inviting the persons to participate

    Collecting and entering quantitative data into statistical software programs; Taking notes during interviews and transcribing interviews (set aside up to ten hours to transcribe verbatim a one-hour interview, longer if there is more than one respondent)

    Running the appropriate statistical analysis

    Conducting the theme analysis of the narrative data (set aside three hours to develop themes from a transcript of a verbatim, one-hour interview, which is usually at least fifteen pages long)

    Analyzing all the data together and writing the final report that chronicles the connection between each step of the evaluation

    Conducting a formal presentation for stakeholders of the results and implications of the evaluation

- Journal article writing

Some people's time is much more expensive than others. Assess how the tasks listed here can be completed in the most efficient way (e.g., perhaps some of the staff, rather than an outside consultant, can conduct some of the literature review). Have a written contract that specifies whether persons will be compensated on the basis of the final product or the time spent on the evaluation. Most consultants charge by the hour rather than by the product. Be clear about the total budget for an evaluator's time, and ask him or her for a reasonable prediction of the amount of time that it will take to complete the tasks listed here.

When contracting with a consultant from a university, be aware of indirect costs (e.g., phone use, office equipment, minimal administrative support) that may be assessed automatically. Usually, these administrative costs are calculated as a percentage established by the university research office that is based on typical government-funded grant rates. For some federal grants, the indirect costs for 2013 could be 45 percent and higher of the total cost. Ask an evaluator to provide a beginning budget at no cost before agreeing to enlist his or her services. All contracts should be reviewed at regular intervals, usually every three to six months.

Many stakeholders will be participating in the evaluation voluntarily, especially during the planning and negotiation stages. Count this time as leveraging when writing evaluation reports. **Leveraging** is the allocation of funds and other resources by organizations other than the primary funder. Many funders expect that the percentage of leveraged funds will increase each year until the point at which the funder is no longer supporting the activities financially. Many agencies allow social service workers to use agency time to participate in evaluation planning. Turn that time into a financial figure based on the person's hourly wage.

The best conservation of time and money is to clarify what you need from the evaluation. Consider all the options that are generated as you read this book. In one evaluation, the logic model might already be established, saving you much time in terms of meetings with stakeholders. In another evaluation, implementing a standardized instrument may be the best methodological option, saving you much time in terms of transcribing and analyzing open-ended interviews. This entire book is about making evaluation choices. Get in the habit of putting a price tag on each choice. Also get in the habit of establishing a time limit for each task. Think efficiently, and conducting evaluations may become easier.

Just as social service workers involve clients in the assignment of tasks while compiling an intervention plan, social service workers can also clarify who will complete each activity of the evaluation plan within the allotted timeline. If a team is completing the evaluation activities, one person should be the director of the overall project, making sure that all tasks are completed and coordinated. If practitioners contract with a university evaluation team, the director of the project is often called the primary investigator. This person is the main liaison between the evaluation team and other stakeholders.

MULTIPLE SYSTEMS

Multiple-level systems are the individuals, families, groups, organizations, and communities that are the targets for change and the sources for creating change. Sometimes systems levels are divided into micro, mezzo, and macro systems. *Micro* refers to desired changes in the individual. *Mezzo* refers to changes in informal systems, such as the family or other intimate groups and small formal systems, such as organizations to which a person may belong. *Macro* refers to large, societal organizations and groups and communities.

Social service workers often implement a systems approach, meaning that a change in one system will affect all other systems. For example, Kretzmann and McKnight's (1993) community asset mapping can be used to identify individuals and community resources that can be tapped to influence positive community change. A premise of community asset mapping is that local organizations (e.g., churches, neighborhood groups, cultural organizations) and institutions (e.g., parks, libraries, schools, colleges, police, hospitals) can make communities economically stronger. Economic assets can be measured through investment by local companies in the local economy, community development credit unions, and improved physical assets (e.g., acquiring and utilizing abandoned buildings, conserving energy sources, improving parks).

A systems approach applies to evaluations, also. In the evaluation of thirty-eight different family support interventions (FSIs) statewide, one of the evaluation questions for the first year was "What are the common desired results across all of these multiple service programs?" Figure 4 contains a diagram of the findings based on open-ended interviews with consumers, direct-care staff, administrative staff, principals, and other community service providers at each of the thirty-eight sites. Case example 10 provides a written description of each of the desired multiple-systems results.

Case Example 10. Description of Desired Results across Multiple Systems

Below are the most often mentioned multiple-systems levels measurements in the evaluation of the family support interventions listed in figure 4:

Measurements of *positive community change* were as follows:

1. *Increased service coordination*: (a) increased number of referrals between agencies; (b) updated information and referral database available to members of the community; (c) implementation of cross-agency, client consent-for-information form; (d) increased number of agencies participating in a specific program.
2. *Increased community involvement*: (a) increased sense of community (based on narrative interviews); (b) increased community assets; (c) increased number of volunteers; (d) increased economic investment by local businesses; (e) increased funding from local services.

Figure 4.
Desired results based on data collected from FSI stakeholders

Measurements of *positive agency change* were as follows:

1. *Increased parent involvement*: (a) increased number of parents attending a program; (b) increased number of times an individual parent attended an activity; (c) increased number of parents who volunteer or work at the agency.
2. *Expanded service capacity*: (a) increased number of services provided; (b) increased number of persons participating in program activities.
3. *Agency quality, positive rapport with consumers*: positive responses on satisfaction surveys.
4. *Agency quality, increase in supportive services*: providing transportation, child care, financial assistance, free services, and so on.
5. *Increased child involvement*: (a) increased number of children attending a program; (b) increased number of times an individual child attends a program; (c) increased child satisfaction with the program.

Measurements of *positive family change* were as follows:

1. *Reduction of child abuse and neglect*: (a) decreased child abuse and neglect reports; (b) decreased out-of-home placements.
2. *Prevention of child abuse and neglect*: (a) participating in prevention programs; (b) desired emotional and behavioral changes in family; (c) achievement of service goals for family.
3. *Family status, physical needs are met*: (a) parent(s) acquired employment; (b) parent(s) acquired further education; (c) family received food, clothing, financial assistance, or housing.
4. *Family status, increased knowledge and behavior related to appropriate parenting*: measured on pre- and post- standardized instruments.
5. *Family status, health*: (a) improved health among members; (b) health concerns treated; (c) children received immunizations; (d) family members were referred to health care.

Measurements of *positive changes In an individual* child were as follows:

1. *Increased learning*: (a) increased attendance at school; (b) passed the proficiency test; (c) improved grades; (d) progressed along normal developmental milestones.
2. *Positive social interaction*: (a) positive peer interaction; (b) positive child-adult interactions; (c) not being suspended for conduct.
3. *Positive emotional development*: (a) self-reported or observed positive self-esteem; (b) referred for emotional health services; (c) desired emotional changes in the child; (d) progress toward child service goals.
4. *Other problem-specific changes in child*: (a) not becoming pregnant; (b) not using substances or alcohol.

Before using multiple systems levels of measurement, a participating agency needs to take the following four steps:

1. Agree on the logical connection between changes at each level. In the evaluation of FSIs, some programs targeted community change first, theorizing that positive changes in the community and agencies were related to positive changes in families and children, whereas some stakeholders assumed programs would target child and family change first.
2. Clarify the following terms: *results*, *process*, and *outcomes*. Results are changes to participants that can be attributed to the intervention.

Results can be outcomes (e.g., an increase in referrals) or processes (e.g., interagency collaboration). Some stakeholders may have different definitions of these terms. Some stakeholders may define agency results (e.g., the provision of day care) as processes only, whereas others may conceptualize agency changes as outcomes.

3. Agree on the methods for measuring the agreed-on results, for example, through observation, surveys, or secondary documents (e.g., agency records or county abuse and neglect reports). Methods for collecting information are discussed in chapters 8–11.

4. Remember that this chapter is all about *values*. Stakeholders may prefer targeting different systems from those the funding source wants to target. Persons need to be able to justify those preferences.

MAJOR POINTS

Evaluation values reflect personal, agency, and community values. Evaluation stakeholders follow professional ethics such as the NASW's (2008) *Code of Ethics* and professional standards such as the American Evaluation Association's (2004) *Guiding Principles for Evaluators*. Actual activities and stakeholder behaviors can be clarified to demonstrate that agreed-on values are followed in an evaluation. Examples and tips were given for adhering to the SCREAM values described in this chapter: measure strengths, respect culture, conduct evaluations within the capacity of your resources, and measure changes across multiple systems.

CRITICAL-THINKING QUESTIONS

1. Complete checklist 4 and then complete steps a–d below.
   a. Compare your responses to how other students, colleagues, professors, social service workers, and clients respond to the value statements listed in checklist 4.
   b. Discuss why you value the statements you marked.
   c. Under what circumstances would you negotiate or adjust those values?
   d. Which values would you not negotiate for any reason? Would you choose not to participate in the evaluation if these values were not part of the evaluation?

2. The author has identified the five SCREAM values that should be part of every evaluation.
   a. Are there any SCREAM values you think are not vital to every evaluation?
   b. Are there any additional values you think should be in every evaluation?
3. Locate an agency assessment form or a referral form.
   a. Highlight any question that identifies a person's strengths. Do you agree that identifying those strengths is important to helping that person? Do you agree that a measurement of those strengths should be included in an evaluation? Why?
   b. If there is no mention of strengths on the form, develop three new questions that will identify strengths.
4. Why do you think evaluations tend to measure a reduction of deficits rather than an increase in strengths?
5. What are your strengths that you rely on to plan an evaluation?
6. Is it easy for you to identify your strengths? Can you see why some persons may not accurately identify their strengths as part of an evaluation?
7. Read a peer-reviewed journal article of an evaluation and answer the following questions.
   a. When describing the participants, which cultural demographics were identified?
   b. What other important cultural demographics of the participants were not identified? Why do you think those demographics are relevant to the evaluation?
   c. What other research methods did the authors use to ensure cultural competency?
8. How many hours have you spent so far working on an evaluation or working on a class that uses this book? Document every hour you spend on this class or on this evaluation project. At the end of the class or project, multiply the total number of hours by the hourly rate you make in a current job and that is your total budget for your time.
9. If you work in a social service or educational setting, how many hours per week within your normal workday are you able to devote toward evaluation? Is this sufficient? Why?

10. If you work in a social service or educational setting, how many noncompensated hours do you devote toward evaluation? Is this acceptable? Why?

11. It is sometimes difficult for students or practitioners to see how a micro intervention has larger societal impacts. In an evaluation of a school district's implementation of Positive Behavior Intervention Systems (PBIS), micro-level outcomes measured for every student were number of visits to the office, number of detentions, number of suspensions, and number of expulsions.

    a. List some potential mezzo-level outcomes for this same evaluation. How can those outcomes be measured?

    b. List some macro-level outcomes for this evaluation. How can those outcomes be measured?

12. Do you agree that every evaluation should include micro, mezzo, and macro outcomes? Why?

13. What other measurements would you include for each of the four systems-level measures outlined in case example 10?

14. What other values not covered in this chapter do you think should be part of every evaluation? Why?

FURTHER RESOURCES

Strengths-Based Evaluation

Web Resources

Asset-Based Community Development Institute (ABCD), Institute for Policy Research, Northwestern University—http://www.abcdinstitute.org

Orlena Hawkins Puckett Institute—http://www.puckett.org

Paxis Institute—http://www.paxis.org

Search Institute (SI), Minneapolis—http://www.search-institute.org

Other Resources

Glicken, M. (2004). *Using the strengths perspective in social work practice.* Boston, MA: Allyn & Bacon.

Green, G., & Goetting, A. (Eds.). (2010). *Mobilizing communities: Asset building as a community development strategy.* Philadelphia, PA: Temple University Press.

Green, G., & Haines, A. (2012). *Asset building and community development.* Thousand Oaks, CA: Sage

Helton, L., & Smith, M. (2004). *Mental health practice with children and youth: A strengths and well-being model.* New York, NY: Haworth Social Work Practice Press.

Saleebey, D. (Ed.). (2013). *The strengths perspective in social work practice* (6th ed.). Boston, MA: Pearson.

Culturally Competent Evaluations

Web Resources

Affilia Journal of Women and Social Work—http://aff.sagepub.com

Other Resources

American Evaluation Association. (2011). *Cultural competency statement.* Retrieved from http://www.eval.org/ccstatement.asp.

Guzman, B. (2003). Examining the role of cultural competency in program evaluation: Visions for new millennium evaluators. In S. Donaldson & M. Scriven (Eds.), *Evaluating social programs and problems: Visions for the new millennium* (pp. 167–181). Mahwah, NJ: Erlbaum.

Hesse-Biber, S. (Ed.). (2012). *Handbook of feminist research: Theory and praxis* (2nd ed.). Thousand Oaks, CA: Sage.

Hood, S. (1999). Assessment in the context of culture and pedagogy: A collaborative effort, a meaningful goal: Introduction and overview. *Journal of Negro Education, 67*(3), 184–186.

Hood, S. (2004). A journey to understand the role of culture in program evaluation: Snapshots and personal reflections of one African American evaluator. *New Directions for Evaluation, 102,* 21–38.

Hopson, R. (2005). Reinventing evaluation. *Anthropology and Education Quarterly, 36,* 289–295.

Lum, D. (Ed.). (2011). *Culturally-competent practice: A framework for understanding diverse groups and justice issues* (4th ed.). Belmont, CA: Brooks/Cole.

Mertens, D. (2009). *Transformative research and evaluation.* New York, NY: Guilford Press.

Mertens, D., & McLaughlin, J. (Eds.). (2004). *Research and evaluation in special education.* Thousand Oaks, CA: Corwin Press.

Nagata, D., Kohn-Wood, L., & Suzuki, L. (Eds.) (2012). *Qualitative strategies for ethnocultural research.* Washington, DC: American Psychological Association.

Seigart, D., & Brisdara, S. (Eds.). (2002). Feminist evaluation: Explorations and experiences [Special issue]. *New Directions for Evaluation, 96.*

DOCUMENTATION TASKS

Clarify the values driving the evaluation.

What strengths will be measured in the evaluation?
    Participants' strengths _____
    Agency strengths ___
    Community strengths ___
    Other strengths ___

What culturally competent steps will be taken in the evaluation?
    Appropriate language ___
    Respectful interactions ___
    Participant involvement in planning and implementing the
       evaluation ___
    Other ___

What are the resources available for the evaluation?
    Available funds ___
    In-kind resources ___
    Hourly amount of time needed ___
    Other ___

What multiple systems-level results will be measured in the evaluation?
    Individual results ___
    Family or group results ___
    Agency results ___
    Community results ___

Stokes, H., Chaplin, S., Dessouky, S., Aklilu, L., & Hopson, R. (2011). Addressing social injustices, displacement, and minority rights through cases of culturally responsive education. *Diaspora, Indigenous, and Minority Education,* 5(3), 167–177.

Thompson-Robinson, M., Hopson, R., & Sen Gupta, S. (Eds.). (2004). In search of cultural competence: Toward principles and practices [Special issue]. *New Directions for Evaluation, 102.*

Tripodi, T., & Potocky-Tripodi, M. (2003). Research on advancement and empowerment of women. *Journal of Social Work Research and Evaluation,* 4(1), 3.

Resources and Feasible Evaluations

Bamberger, M., Rugh, J., Church, M., & Fort, L. (2004). Shoestring evaluation: Designing impact evaluations under budget, time and data constraints. *American Journal of Evaluation,* 25(1), 5–37.

Robson, C. (2000). *Small-scale evaluation.* London, UK: Sage.

Multiple-Systems Measurements

Web Resources

Annie E. Casey Foundation—http://www.aecf.org
Center for Community Change—http://www.communitychange.org
Neighborhood Reinvestment Corp (Neighbor Works America)—
http://www.nw.org/network/home.asp

Other Resources

Anderson-Butcher, D., Lawson, H., Bean, J., Flaspohler, P., Boone, B., & Kwiatkowski, A. (2008). Community collaboration to improve schools: Introducing a new model from Ohio. *Children & Schools,* 30(3), 161–172.

Anderson-Butcher, D., Lawson, H., Iachini, A., Flaspohler, P., Bean, J., & Wade-Mdvanian, R. (2010). Emergent evidence in support of a community collaboration model for school improvement. *Children & Schools,* 32(3), 160–171.

Borrup, T. (2006). *The creative community builder's handbook: How to transform communities using local assets, art, and culture.* St. Paul, MN: Fieldstone Alliance.

Concepts Systems. *Publications in concept mapping methodology.* Retrieved from http://www.conceptsystems.com/content/view/publications.html.

Ethical Guidelines for Evaluations

4

EVALUATION DECISION-MAKING QUESTIONS

What is the ethical review process before any data can be collected in the evaluation?

Is there potential harm to participants?

Is there an informed consent form?

Are participants' confidentiality protected?

Are participants openly aware of all aspects of participating in the evaluation?

Are the evaluation procedures respectful of the cultures of all participants?

What are the procedures for evaluating the evaluation?

Have the evaluators openly discussed potential conflicts of interests or values?

What are the benefits of conducting the evaluation?

EVALUATION ETHICS

Professional ethics are the values, principles, and behaviors expected of all members of an organization. Ethics protect consumers from unprofessional behavior of those providing the service. In evaluations, ethical guidelines must be followed to protect the evaluation participants from unprofessional and harmful practice. In a survey and interview study with thirty-one evaluators, "there was nearly unanimous agreement" that ethical conduct was a competency expected from all evaluators (King,

Stevahn, Ghere, & Minnema, 2001, p. 239). Know your agency's ethical standards for evaluation. Apply the agency's practice standards to evaluation if there is not a separate policy for evaluation.

The key to ethical evaluations is to prevent the violation of a participant's or stakeholder's rights, whether intentional or unintentional. Checklist 10 contains a positively focused list of ten "thou shalls" of evaluation ethics. The first ethical value, "Thou shall evaluate . . ." is a theme of this entire book and is supported by the National Association of Social Workers' (NASW, 2008) *Code of Ethics* and the American Evaluation Association's (2004) *Guiding Principles for Evaluators*. Discussion of the remaining ethical points in checklist 10 follows.

INSTITUTIONAL REVIEW BOARD

Thou Shall Establish an Ethical Review Process.

There is a discussion in chapter 5 about the role of an agency evaluation committee in coordinating evaluation activities that overlap existing goals, such as strategic planning or maintaining a management information system. Once an evaluation project is planned, assurances need to be given that the evaluation procedures will follow ethical guidelines, procedures, or protocols regulating human interaction. Settings that receive federal funding are required to have a formal structure to approve the evaluation protocol. This structure is often called the human subjects review (HSR) or the **institutional review board** (IRB).

The primary purpose of an IRB is to ensure that people participating in evaluations are not harmed, physically or emotionally. The need for such safeguards arose from the well-publicized Tuskegee syphilis studies, which cost the lives of many African American men. In this study during the 1930s, an experimental study design was implemented in which some infected men were given treatment for syphilis and others were given a placebo that contained no effective treatment for syphilis. The study was funded by the American government and was implemented under the premise that the benefits, finding a cure for syphilis, would outweigh the costs. The costs were the lives of twenty-eight men in the study and hundreds of others who became infected from the men who were not treated. See the U.S. Department of Health and Human Services (2011) study and the reparations that have been implemented to require informed consent for all government-funded studies.

The discovery of the injustices committed in the Tuskegee study were not publicly revealed until the 1970s, whereas the war crimes trials at Nuremberg revealed biological experiments conducted on prisoners of war and victims of concentration camps during World War II. These unethical violations led to the U.S. Department of Health and Human Services' (1979) *Belmont Report*, which guides federal funding today. The ethical principles guiding the *Belmont Report* are (1) respect for persons; (2) beneficence; and (3) justice. The tools to carry out these principles are informed consent, assessment of risk and benefits, and the humane and voluntary selection of research and evaluation participants, respectively.

There are potential psychological harms to being a participant in research and evaluations. Potential psychological harms include emotional stress from recalling adverse events, having the perception of placing someone else in stress, being deceived, or reliving a painful event. Evaluators must take all precautions to not cause psychological harm during the evaluation. Evaluators must provide participants with information about how to receive counseling or other services if they experience psychological stress during the evaluation. For example, in a needs assessment about family violence prevention, persons answering questions about being the victim of family violence were given the names and phone numbers of community agencies providing prevention and services to victims of family violence.

There are also harms of injustice, intentional or unintentional. Evaluations can continue views of cultural inequality by only including persons of one race, gender, age, sexual orientation, or other areas of cultural diversity. Most IRBs now require researchers and evaluators to demonstrate that the participant selection process will include an equal representation of gender and culture of the population from which the participants are selected.

The role of an IRB is primarily to answer the question, "Are the procedures ethical?" To make sure that this question is answered positively, accurate and competent evaluation methods must be implemented and humane interaction between evaluators and participants must be ensured.

Checklist 10. Ten "Thou Shalls" of Ethical Evaluation

Check each item below that has been followed for an evaluation in your agency or practicum setting:

___ Evaluate social service interventions.
___ Establish an ethical review process.
___ Do no harm.
___ Do not coerce.
___ Do not use a participant's name in vain.
___ Be honest.
___ Be respectful of participants' culture.
___ Evaluate the evaluation.
___ Explore one's own values and conflicts.
___ Leave the setting better than when entered.

The **petition for approval of research involving human subjects** at my educational institution, "Wright State University Research and Sponsored Programs Human Subjects Review" (Wright State University Institutional Review Board, 2013) minimally requires the researcher and/or evaluator to demonstrate the following:

- No physical harm will befall participants.
- Participation is voluntary.
- Participants will be informed of the purpose of the evaluation, the type of information being gathered, the activities expected of them, and that they will have access to the results.
- Participants will give written informed consent before participating.
- Participants' names and identifying information will remain confidential.

Since 2005, the petition has been reorganized to emphasize the above key items and to more deliberately highlight that these additional safeguards are in place:

- There is no financial conflict of interest between the evaluators, participants, or other key stakeholders.
- There are sufficient resources to adequately manage the protection of human subjects.
- The subject population is representative of the population base from which subjects could be selected with respect to gender representation.
- The subject population is representative of the population base from which subjects could be selected with respect to minority representation (Wright State University Institutional Review Board, 2013).

These ethical principles are supported by federal policies and do match the SCREAM values presented in the previous chapter related to the evaluation being culturally competent and utilizing sufficient resources.

Be patient when undergoing the peer-review process, and allow sufficient time to collect the information required by the IRB. Also, be aware that most proposals submitted to IRBs are not approved the first time but must be resubmitted after incorporating or otherwise addressing suggested amendments. If you are conducting an evaluation with agencies or schools that do not have an IRB, Dudley (2013) has guidelines for creating one's own IRB. No evaluation data should be collected until a process of ensuring ethical implementation is completed.

POTENTIAL HARM

Thou Shall Do No Harm.

The infliction of physical harm during the course of a social service evaluation is never warranted, even if the benefits seem to outweigh physical discomfort or pain. Among evaluation situations that may result in physical harm to participants are the following:

- Withholding an intervention
- Implementing an intervention that is not warranted and/or monitored by a social service agency
- Forcing people to participate in an intervention that has been refused
- Participating in an evaluation that exposes participants to the danger of retaliation by, for example, an abusive partner
- Participating in an evaluation that you know will result in participants losing political power, status, or financial security.

Social service workers have a responsibility to be sensitive to the emotional nature of evaluation. Some evaluations collect very sensitive information. Some sensitive evaluation questions I have conducted included whether consumers of services were victims of child abuse, whether they have ever been victims of partner abuse, their beliefs about the role of sex education in the prevention of teen pregnancy, whether they have a history of mental illness, whether they have a criminal record, and whether they have a history of substance abuse.

Train all persons collecting information to interact empathetically. In one evaluation involving a telephone survey, stakeholders were appropriately concerned about questions dealing with partner abuse asked of all women participants. A videotape presentation explaining the dynamics of power and control used by abusive partners was produced and shown to the interviewers to help them recognize indications that participants were victims of partner abuse. The interviewers were instructed not to intervene should they recognize such indication but instead to make it a point of explaining at the end of all interviews how to get more information about the services available to victims of domestic violence.

Provide evaluation participants with a list of support services. Have agency staff help compile a resource packet to give participants after the information is collected. Leave contact information in case participants become distressed during or after the evaluation. Debrief participants on the purpose and results of the evaluation at the time the evaluation report is made public.

Also debrief those who helped collect the information. The data collectors, often students, hear many heart-wrenching stories. In one evaluation, three telephone interviews were conducted with parents at six-month intervals. At the two follow-up times, the student telephone interviewers asked the parents whether a specific child was still residing in the home. And it turned out that, in two cases, the child had died in the preceding six months. The student interviewers were, naturally, shaken and not sure how to respond. Project supervisors provided emotional support for the interviewers and counseled that, in such situation, the best response was to listen attentively and direct the participants to agencies that provide assistance in the grieving process.

VOLUNTARY PARTICIPATION

Thou Shall Not Coerce.

The fact that evaluators must think about evaluation every day means that clients must think about evaluation every day also. The easiest way to reinforce that evaluation may be part of receiving services is to include a statement about evaluation on the agency release of information or **consent form**. Agencies have consent forms because providing services entails consulting with persons who have information that is needed to complete the current assessment and service plan. The same is true for evaluation. Evaluating practice is just as important as the assessment and service plan.

Some social service practitioners express a concern that evaluations burden clients by taking up their valuable time. But this is not necessarily the case. Clients often enjoy being involved in an evaluation, especially when information is gathered through open-ended interviews, in which they can express their views in their own words. Contrary to concerns that they will give only positive feedback about evaluated programs, clients can be very open in providing negative feedback about services.

Include on the normal agency consent form a statement that any information collected can be used and follow-up calls made for evaluation purposes. This statement ensures that a potentially useful data source is not lost. If permission to release names and locating information to an evaluator has not previously been secured, agency workers must first contact all clients requesting permission and only then, after permission has been obtained, send a letter describing the evaluation along with a consent form. By the time the process has been completed, many participants are no longer available.

Most clients participating in program evaluations have limited resources. Therefore, many agencies offer the incentive of compensation in return for participation. Compensation can take many forms: cash, grocery store coupons, gas station vouchers, baskets of household supplies, and so on. A common argument against compensation is that it renders participation involuntary, making clients an offer they can't refuse. A counterargument is that compensating clients for their time is only fair. Besides, the practice is commonplace in marketing evaluation in which the targeted population is usually the middle and upper classes.

When compiling consent forms for client participants, it is necessary to include a statement that the agency will continue providing services whether or not the client chooses to participate in evaluation. An outside evaluator needs assurances from the agency that it will comply with this stipulation. The same openness and trust could be extended to social service worker participants. That is, funders could agree that information provided by the agency workers would not result in discontinuing funding for the service. This expectation is not always feasible, however, because one of the reasons for conducting the evaluation is often to make decisions about continuing, changing, or stopping the evaluated program.

Participants should be told how they can obtain the results of an evaluation. If feasible, establish a toll-free number. Alternatively, develop a website. Minimally, leave participants with a telephone number, an e-mail address, and/or a mailing address to contact. Be prepared to be asked for the results, especially by agency representatives.

See case examples 11 and 12 for samples of an informed consent. In case example 11, the consent forms are distributed in person before conducting the survey. In case example 12, the survey is conducted online with information about the survey provided. Thus, there is not a signed form, but rather consent is assumed by the participants' completion of the survey after being informed about the conditions of participation.

Case Example 11. Informed Consent to Participate in Evaluation Form:
Face-to-Face Survey

FAMILY AND SCHOOLS TOGETHER
Monday Groups
Day 8 Survey
March 17, 2008

Thank you for taking a few minutes to fill out this family survey. This survey will help you and the FAST group leaders better understand how FAST can help you.

This FAST group is partially funded by a grant awarded to the _____ Public Schools called Safe Schools Healthy Students. This survey is part of an evaluation required by the grant. Your participation in this survey is voluntary, meaning that you can choose not to answer any or all of the questions. Your participation or choice not to participate will not impact your involvement in FAST or any other service with the Family Service Agency.

Your participation is also confidential. Your name will not be disclosed on any of the results of the evaluation. The answers below will only be matched to the survey number at the top of this page. Please do remember your number, because you will be given another survey at the end of the FAST group.

Are there any questions? If not, please sign this form and take the time to answer the questions on the other side of this paper. Please let _____ know if you have any questions about this evaluation.

I agree that I have been told about the details of taking this survey.

_____   _____
Name   Date

Case Example 12. Informed Consent to Participate in Evaluation Form: Online Survey

Teacher Perception Survey
Announcement to be made by each school principal (can be made by e-mail, written memo, or in person)

_____ is conducting a survey of teacher and staff perceptions of making a referral for students to receive mental health services. I am asking for your participation in this survey. You can complete the survey by going to the following web link: www._____. You should be able to complete the survey in 5 minutes. We also ask you to complete the demographic information sheet available at www._____.

Your participation is voluntary. Choosing to answer or not answer any questions will not impact your employment with _____ schools.

Your participation is confidential. Only evaluators working with _____ will have access to individuals' responses. Your specific answers to any question will not be disclosed to me or any other person. The survey is being collected and analyzed by the Center for Urban and Public Affairs at Wright State University. The overall results will be analyzed and reported as a group.

If you have any questions about this survey please contact _____ at ___-____.

Please go online and complete the survey by November 1, 2010.

Thank you for participating in this important survey.

Sincerely,

_____, Principal
School Name and Address

Checklist 11 lists items that are required parts of consent forms for evaluations that are being conducted for research purposes. This means that the evaluation process and results will be disseminated as a peer-reviewed publication, including student theses, or as a conference presentation, or distributed as research through a website.

Checklist 11. Requirements for Consent of Participation in Research

Check all that apply to a consent form you have prepared for an evaluation:

___ A statement that the study involves research.

___ An explanation of the purposes of the research.

___ The expected duration of the participant's participation.

___ A description of the procedures to be followed.

___ Whom to contact for answers to pertinent questions about the research.

___ An explanation of whom to contact for answers to pertinent questions about the research participants' rights.

___ An explanation of whom to contact in the event of a research-related injury to the participant.

___ A statement that participation is voluntary.

___ A statement that refusal to participate will involve no penalty or loss of benefits to which the participant is otherwise entitled.

___ A statement describing the extent to which confidentiality of records identifying the participant will be maintained.

___ A statement that the participant may discontinue participation at any time without penalty or loss of benefits to which the participant is otherwise entitled.

Taken with permission from the Wright State University Institutional Review Board (2013).

If the evaluation is being conducted in collaboration with a university, one will be required to submit a petition for approval by the institutional review board (IRB). Even if the evaluation is being conducted in an agency or school setting that does not require IRB approval, all of the items on checklist 11 should be contained in the informed consent. If desired, the word *research* can be changed to *evaluation*. Most social service agencies, some educational settings, and all health agencies must comply with Health Insurance Portability and Accountability Act (HIPAA) of 1996 privacy protection (U.S. Department of Health and Human Services, 2013). For more information, see the U.S. Department of Health and Human Services website (http://www.hhs.gov/ocr/privacy/). Following the requirements of consent listed in checklist 11 should meet HIPAA requirements for protecting the privacy of evaluation participants.

CONFIDENTIALITY

Thou Shall Not Use a Participant's Name in Vain.

The necessity of protecting the confidentiality of individuals (e.g., clients, workers, community representatives) participating in an evaluation is often understood, but it is not always clear whether it is necessary to protect the confidentiality of agencies as well. In the evaluation of family support interventions (FSIs), the evaluators reported the interview data collected from clients, direct-care staff, and administrators collectively for the entire state. Some stakeholders asked that findings be reported separately by county. The IRB decided that only the confidentiality of individuals, not that of agencies, was protected. Also, state "sunshine" laws permitted stakeholders to access the data summaries since they were public documents. Ultimately, agency-specific reports were provided to each county and the state funders. The lesson learned was to discuss at the *beginning* of an evaluation the confidentiality of all systems, not just of individuals.

Participant confidentiality must be protected by having the participants sign a form stating that the evaluators will protect their confidentiality. This form is often called a consent form. Consent forms were discussed under "Voluntary Participation" and are discussed more under "Informed Consent."

INFORMED CONSENT

Thou Shall Be Honest.

The lead-in sentence of section C of the American Evaluation Association's (2004) *Guiding Principles for Evaluators* states: "Evaluators ensure the honesty and integrity of the entire evaluating process." The "entire evaluating process" begins with the first discussion of the evaluation with stakeholders and continues through the evaluator's final contracted task and any further uses of the evaluation results long after the evaluation itself has ended.

The application of the AEA guideline for integrity and honesty is discussed in chapter 5. Also discussed in chapter 5 is the evaluation contract that should be signed by all key stakeholders before any data are collected. It is key that all persons openly discuss expectations for the evaluation and agree in writing about the scope, purpose, ethical guidelines, methodologies, and outputs of the evaluation.

Honesty must be extended to the participants also. The consent form becomes a contract between evaluator and participant, much in the same way that a syllabus becomes a contract between a teacher and student. Begin with why participation in the evaluation is important. Most evaluators give general statements of purpose, such as "Your participation in the evaluation is valued and will help the agency better improve services." Many evaluators remain general because they do not want to lead the participants in their responses to the data-collection instruments. An example of a leading purpose statement is "Your participation is valued because the responses to this evaluation will determine whether or not to keep this program." Some participants may give all favorable or all negative responses on the basis of such a purpose statement. Participants need to know that it is permissible to give their honest views, but the responses should be driven by their own experiences and not by the influences of the evaluators.

All participants have the right to see the overall results of the evaluation. Evaluators can make the results available at a website or through a report delivered to key stakeholders. There usually is a long lag between the actual collection of data and the final report because of the amount of time it takes to analyze the findings.

Evaluators must be honest in their reporting of the evaluation findings. Evaluations are best implemented by an evaluation team, so that there are multiple people reviewing the findings and reporting of the results. Some honest mistakes can occur by oversight or miscalculations. These mistakes should be noted in the final report. Evaluators are sometimes accused of reporting only positive results, fearing that negative results may lead to the termination of an intervention. Evaluators need to report all results, positive and negative findings. Program improvements occur from learning from successes and challenges.

CULTURALLY COMPETENT EVALUATIONS

Thou Shall Be Respectful of a Participant's Culture.

The value of cultural respect was discussed in chapter 3. State very clearly at the beginning of an evaluation the expectations for including persons from different cultural backgrounds as evaluation stakeholders and participants. Consider the following points when clarifying culturally competent evaluation activities:

Define culture for the evaluation. Is it defined by race, ethnicity, gender, sexual preference, age, income, religion, political views, or some other characteristic? Should there be representation by some stakeholder constituency (e.g., consumer, direct-care worker, administrator, community resident)? What other cultural groups do stakeholders want represented in the evaluation? For example, in the family violence prevention planning evaluation, stakeholders agreed that age was an important cultural difference. Including high school youth on the advisory board led to the identification of dating violence as a subset of domestic violence.

Define cultural group inclusion. Once the cultural groups involved are identified, how should representatives from the different groups be included in the evaluation process? Should each group have one representative on the evaluation advisory board? Consumers of services should be one of the cultural groups represented on the evaluation advisory board. The consumer representative should not also be in the role of service provider. For example, in one evaluation, a service provider was also a parent. Some stakeholders wanted this person to represent service providers and parents on the advisory board. It was decided that she would represent the service providers and another person from the community represented parents.

Define culturally sensitive methods of collecting information. How will the values, attitudes, and beliefs of different cultural groups be respected during the information-gathering process? Is the wording of consent forms changed as necessary to ensure that it is understood by the targeted cultural group? Are evaluation materials translated into the primary languages of all cultural groups involved in the evaluation? Should information be collected by persons of the same cultural group as the participants? Are standardized instruments normed to different cultural groups? During one evaluation of the Families and Schools Together (FAST) program, one parent participant was not completing the written survey. The evaluators asked one of the FAST volunteers to read the survey to the parent and record the parent's answers. This was done in a way to avoid embarrassment to the parent. In the evaluation of FSIs, one community group stated that participants would not come to the agency for focus groups. Instead, as suggested by the agency workers, the evaluators attended a neighborhood summer barbecue and conducted focus groups there. This process increased the number of participants and led to more information in the participant's own words.

Define culturally sensitive methods of reporting results. How will the final reports reflect the cultural representation of the evaluation? Will the art used on the report cover reflect the cultural diversity involved? Are discussions of persons from different cultural groups conducted in a respectful manner, one that does not reinforce negative stereotypes? How will the confidentiality of cultural groups with only a small representation be protected? An evaluation of a behavioral parent-training intervention used a single-systems design to measure a mother and her children's positive change in behaviors as a result of the new parenting techniques. The mother observed and documented her two sons' fighting behavior and appropriate play daily, weekly, and monthly. She graphed the incidences of these behaviors and was visually able to see the positive changes made as she used positive reinforcement and time-out rather than yelling and hitting. The mother was invited to present her findings to the clinical team. She attended the meeting wearing a dress (which shows the importance she gave to making her presentation in front of professionals) and showing the graphs to the team showing the progress she and her children made.

Key stakeholders, including consumers, should be invited to share results of the evaluation at local, state, and national conferences. I have co-presented several conference presentations with stakeholders. I have also coauthored published research with a key stakeholder (Brun & Giga, 1999). Student-faculty coauthored research and evaluation is also common (see, for example, Twill & Buckheister, 2009; Twill, Purvis, & Norris, 2011).

Define culturally sensitive integration of knowledge learned from the evaluation. Will the manner in which the results are shared with persons from different cultural groups respect those groups' values, attitudes, and beliefs? How will changes made on the basis of the evaluation be shared with persons from different cultural groups? How will different groups be able to respond to the findings of the evaluation? Reports are written for different audiences. Some stakeholders want brief reports that they can read in less than five minutes. Such reports are often called executive summaries. Other stakeholders may want to see the full statistical tables. For some stakeholders, seeing the tables is too overwhelming, and they will miss the important findings. For other stakeholders, it is important to remove jargon that is not understandable or relevant to them. I often adapt different presentations of the same evaluation to be respectful of my audience.

Inclusion has become a required item for most institutional review boards. The evaluator must demonstrate that the number of women participants is at least proportional to the population from which the sample is taken. The same must be demonstrated for inclusion of different minority groups. Also, some cultural groups are considered vulnerable groups and their participation must receive full IRB approval. Those vulnerable groups include the cognitively impaired, fetuses, pregnant women, and prisoners. Also, youth participants must have the consent of their parents or legal guardians.

EVALUATION OF THE EVALUATION

Thou Shall Evaluate the Evaluation.

How will you determine whether the evaluation is successful? This question guides practice and planning activities in an agency, so it makes sense that social service workers identify the criteria for a successful evaluation.

The evaluation decision-making questions asked at the beginning of each chapter can become the audit of the evaluator's activities and decisions. The audit can be the basis for evaluating the evaluator and the evaluation process.

Stakeholders should agree on the evaluators' tasks for each step of the evaluation and agree on how successful completion of these tasks will be measured. At specified times, measure whether the evaluator successfully completed the tasks. An example of an evaluation contract of activities is found in case example 13.

Case Example 13. Evaluation Agreement and Adherence to
Ethical Guidelines

The agreement reproduced below relates to the case example of the evaluation of out-of-home placements for African Americans in a public child welfare agency:

Proposed Assessment Plan between Carl Brun and the Agency Diversity Committee

Carl Brun will be working with the committee to carry out the diversity plan for fiscal 2001–2002. The proposed assessment activities for February 1–June 30, 2002, are as follows:

1. Analyze composite group data of a sample of children placed in out-of-home care for the time period 1996–2001. Look specifically at the relationship between race of children (African American or white) and characteristics such as type of maltreatment, length of time in care, and types of services received.

Procedures. Carl will be looking only at group data that have already been collected by the agency. He will not be analyzing individual case records. His contact person at the agency will be _____. Requests for data will be made only to this person. Carl will enter the data into an SPSS software program on his laptop computer. This computer will be kept in a locked office. The computer file can be opened only with his password.

Adherence to Confidentiality and Voluntary Participation. Carl will have no contact with individual clients. He will not have access to individual case folders. He will keep all statistical files confidential. Analysis of the data contained in a final report will be presented to the Diversity Awareness Committee.

2. Analyze the results from the recent staff surveys distributed by the Diversity Awareness Committee.

Procedures. A staff person from the agency will enter the results of each survey into an SPSS file according to the codebook developed by Carl. An identifying number will be assigned to each survey so that Carl will not know the name of the survey respondent. Carl will copy the SPSS file and perform frequency distributions and cross-tabulations of the group results.

Adherence to Confidentiality and Voluntary Participation. Carl will not have access to anyone's actual survey. He will have only the responses to each survey as coded by the designated staff member. He will keep all statistical files confidential. Analysis of the data will be presented to the Diversity Awareness Committee.

3. Facilitate the Diversity Awareness Committee retreat on February 22. The goal of the retreat is to arrive at further assessment activities between March and June 2002 related to the mission of the Diversity Awareness Committee. It is preferable that at least two parent consumers attend this retreat and serve on the Diversity Awareness Committee.

Procedures. Carl will prepare the agenda for the retreat with the committee cochairs. Carl will facilitate the retreat activities.

Adherence to Confidentiality and Voluntary Participation. All participants in the retreat will be asked to sign an informed consent form. The form will state that participation in the retreat is voluntary and confidential and that no negative consequences will occur to staff or clients for their comments or actions at this retreat. No deliberate verbal or physical harm to any participant will be tolerated.

4. Develop outcome measurements of the activities carried out by the Diversity Awareness Committee between March and June 2002. Provide a report of the results with recommendations.

Procedures. A more specific assessment plan will be developed on the basis of the discussions at the committee retreat. This assessment plan will be presented to the agency's Administrative Council before any further action is taken.

Adherence to Confidentiality and Voluntary Participation. The plan will be developed by the retreat participants. Participation is voluntary and confidential. The final report of the year's activities will be presented to the Diversity Awareness Committee.

In addition to completing the tasks, key stakeholders can evaluate other aspects of the evaluator. Was the evaluator professional in all interactions with stakeholders and participants? Did the evaluator explain the reasons behind evaluation decisions? Did the evaluator welcome input from stakeholders concerning evaluation decisions? Were the stakeholders overall satisfied with the activities of the evaluator?

CONFLICTS OF INTERESTS

Thou Shall Explore One's Own Values and Conflicts.

Some conflicts of interest between stakeholders deal with differences in personal values and worldviews. Wrestle with these issues in a reflective journal for your own use or to share with other members of the evaluation team. If you do differ philosophically with other evaluation stakeholders, respect their views just as you would the views of clients. Evaluators may overempathize, consciously or unconsciously, with some stakeholders. In reflecting back on the statewide evaluation of FSIs referenced throughout this book, I found myself being more understanding of direct-line social service workers than I did of administrative staff who countered the direct-line workers' views. I needed to put this bias in check.

Be open and honest about value conflicts with other stakeholders. Be genuine and respectful of all stakeholders in evaluation situations, just as you would in clinical situations. Confront persons when you are adamant about the methodology or protocol. Stick to your position when you feel that it is warranted. Although your views may create a conflict between your goals and those of other stakeholders, be explicit about those views, and do not conceal the conflicts. Conflicts can be resolved and negotiated much more quickly when people work through the differences openly and honestly.

I have been discussing a potential conflict of values, but IRBs are most interested in a conflict of financial interest. Evaluators should not receive financial or other gifts other than the compensation for their time to complete the evaluation. Evaluators should not have a vested financial interest in the agencies or schools that they are advising.

Some agencies though, as a result of budget constraints, do have their own staff conduct self-evaluations. Such evaluations are open to subjective biases that are controlled for by hiring outside evaluators. In self-evaluations, the evaluator needs to document potential conflicts of interest that may affect the evaluation process.

BENEFITS OF THE EVALUATION

Thou Shall Leave the Setting Better Than When Entered.

Properly evaluated settings are better settings than unevaluated practice. Many practice changes begin soon after the planning and implementing of an evaluation starts. A theme of this book is that evaluation is in itself an intervention. People change when they are involved in evaluation. That's intervention. At the same time, this does not mean that all evaluations are credible and systematic. A poorly conducted evaluation can actually lead to agency decisions that are more harmful than those made by an agency that has not been evaluated.

Evaluators can leave helpful reports behind. Reports that can be left with stakeholders and used long after the evaluation include evaluation training manuals, critiques of standardized instruments measuring results pertinent to the evaluation, annotated bibliographies, final reports, and published articles related to the evaluation. For a list of possible evaluation reports or other outputs that can be used by the agency long after the evaluation, see checklist 12.

MAJOR POINTS

Evaluation values reflect personal, agency, and community values. Evaluation stakeholders follow professional ethics, such as the NASW's (2008) *Code of Ethics* and professional standards such as the American Evaluation Association's (2004) *Guiding Principles for Evaluators*. Actual activities and stakeholder behaviors need to be clarified to demonstrate that agreed-on values are followed in an evaluation. Agencies should have an evaluation ethics review process. All evaluations being conducted for research purposes in conjunction with a university must have the process approved by an institutional review board (IRB). All participation in evaluations should be voluntary and confidential. Participants should be informed of the purpose of the evaluation and how the results will be used.

Checklist 13 combines the ethical guidelines discussed in this chapter and the value preferences discussed in chapter 3.

CRITICAL-THINKING QUESTIONS

1. Do you agree that all stakeholders need to approve the evaluation before the evaluation can begin? Under what circumstance would it be OK to not have agreement to evaluate?
2. Does your agency or school have an evaluation review process? Why or why not? Who must approve an evaluation before it begins? If you are a student, do you know the IRB procedures at your school?
3. Are there any times when an evaluation in an agency or school setting warrants that the evaluators use deception? Why?
4. Does your agency include a clause on its basic consent-to-services form that the client agrees that the agency may utilize his or her data for evaluation purposes or allow evaluators to contact the clients for potential participation in evaluations? Why or why not?
5. What are all of the components that should be in an informed consent form?
   a. Compare your answer to the list of federal requirements of the HIPAA law as captured in the document "Cover Letter/Consent Form Guidelines, at http://www.wright.edu/rsp/subjects.html.
   b. Review the consent forms in case examples 11 and 12 and determine whether they meet all criteria required listed in checklist 12.
6. Should participants in an evaluation of services provided in schools or social service agencies be compensated for their participation? If not, why not? If so, why? If so, what is a reasonable compensation for grade school students? High school students? College students? Adults and their families living in poverty? Middle-class families? Upper-class families?
7. IRBs define confidentiality as pertaining only to the protection of the identity of individual participants. Can you think of circumstances when an evaluator may argue that the confidentiality of systems, such as organizations or agencies, should also be protected? If a system's confidentiality cannot be protected, what steps should the evaluator take?

8. Is there any situation you can think of where the evaluator may not share all facts with the evaluation stakeholders? The evaluation participants? Explain.

9. What is your ethical representation for cultural inclusion if the population is homogeneous? For example, the population is 98 percent white.

10. List five different culturally competent ways to administer a survey. To conduct observations? To report the results?

11. If you are an evaluator, do you welcome feedback from stakeholders and participants about your evaluation? If yes, how would you solicit the feedback?

12. What items do you think should be included in an evaluation of the evaluator?

13. Think of an evaluation or research project you have been a part of in the past. What benefits did you personally receive by being part of the evaluation?

14. Do you agree that "evaluated settings are better than unevaluated settings"? Why or why not?

15. Read the NASW's *Code of Ethics* related to evaluation and research. Identify those provisions that you are currently prepared to follow. Identify those provisions that you need more time and knowledge to acquire. Identify those provisions that your agency needs more time and knowledge to acquire.

16. Select one of the resources listed in the "Further Resources" section of this chapter. How do the authors address some of the critical-thinking questions asked here?

FURTHER RESOURCES

U.S. Department of Health and Human Services. (1979). *The Belmont report.* Retrieved from http://www.hhs.gov/ohrp/humansubjects/guidance/belmont.html.

U.S. Department of Health and Human Services, Centers for Disease Control and Prevention. (2011). *U.S. public health service syphilis study at Tuskegee.* Retrieved from http://www.cdc.gov/tuskegee/index.html.

Checklist 12. Evaluation Outputs That Benefit a Setting

Check all items that will be outputs from the evaluation that will be helpful to the setting long after the evaluation is over:

___ The entire context of the original request for proposal (RFP)

___ The evaluation plan in the RFP

___ PowerPoint presentations of the evaluation plan

___ The evaluation plan available at a project website

___ Periodic evaluation reports

___ Literature review or annotated bibliography

___ Critiques of standardized instruments

___ Data-collection surveys and interviews constructed for the evaluation

___ Participant protocols developed for the evaluation, including consent to participate forms, procedures for recruiting participants, evaluation design, and other information required by an IRB

___ Written and electronic presentations of results, including statistical tables and narrative stories

___ Photographs taken as part of the data collection

___ Training materials developed from the evaluation

___ Program reports that incorporate evaluation results

___ Final evaluation reports submitted to various stakeholders

___ Evaluation results that are integrated into other agency publications (e.g., annual reports, brochures, advertisements)

___ Conference presentations related to the evaluation

___ Articles published in professional journals, newsletters, books, dissertations, or class assignments

___ Other

Checklist 13. Reaching Agreement on Activities Related to
           Evaluation Values and Ethics

Check all items that apply to a current evaluation at your agency or
practicum setting.

These values and ethics will be followed for this evaluation:
____ Ensure written, informed consent of all participants.
____ Ensure confidentiality of all participants.
____ Ensure anonymity of all participants.
____ Ensure that no physical harm will occur to any participant.
____ Ensure that no emotional harm will occur to any participant.
____ Ensure that all participation is voluntary.
____ Ensure that a participant is not denied services because of his or her
     participation or lack of participation in the evaluation.
____ Ensure that the results of the evaluation will be made available to
     all participants.
____ Ensure involvement from persons of all cultural backgrounds in the
     design, implementation, and participation in the evaluation.
____ Ensure involvement from all stakeholders in the design and imple-
     mentation of the evaluation.
____ Ensure that the results of the evaluation will be made available to
     all stakeholders of the evaluation.
____ Assure the participants and stakeholders that the results will be
     accurate.
____ The evaluation will be evaluated by another person or other persons.
____ Allow the participants to give feedback about the interpretation of
     their data.
____ Allow the stakeholders to give feedback about the interpretation of
     the evaluation data.
____ Allow the participants to help write the evaluation report.
____ Allow the stakeholders to help write the evaluation report.
____ Decide not to conduct the evaluation if a stakeholder deems the
     evaluation question and/or purpose unethical.
____ Decide not to conduct the evaluation if the stakeholders will not
     supply in writing a statement of how the evaluation will be utilized.
____ Decide not to conduct the evaluation if it is not feasible to answer
     the evaluation questions using the allotted resources.
____ Decide not to conduct the evaluation if there is no agreement
     among stakeholders on the evaluation question or purpose.
____ Apply the following ethical guideline(s) not listed above:

DOCUMENTATION TASKS

Complete a petition for approval of research involving human subjects. All of the following questions should be answered in the petition:

Do all stakeholders agree the intervention should be evaluated?

What is the ethical review process before any data can be collected in the evaluation?

Does the evaluation process cause any potential harm to participants?

Is there an informed consent form?

Are participants' confidentiality protected?

Is voluntary participation assured?

Are participants openly aware of all aspects of participating in the evaluation?

Are the evaluation procedures respectful of the cultures of all participants?

What are the procedures for evaluating the evaluation?

Have the evaluators openly discussed potential conflicts of interests or values?

What are the benefits of conducting the evaluation?

NEGOTIATING WITH STAKEHOLDERS

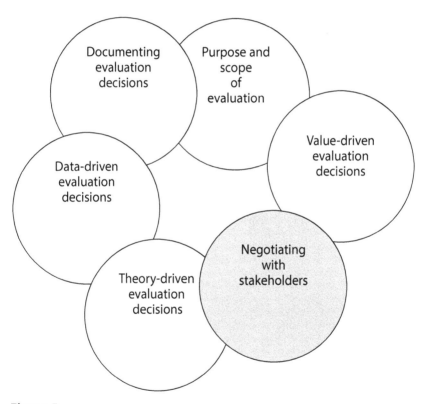

Figure 5.
Interactive model of evaluation: Negotiating with stakeholders

Politics of Evaluation

5

EVALUATION DECISION-MAKING QUESTIONS

Is this evaluation driven by internal stakeholders?

Is this evaluation driven by external stakeholders?

Is there a written evaluation plan agreed upon by all stakeholders?

Who are the stakeholders authorizing the evaluation?

Who are the persons on the evaluation advisory board?

Who are the members of the evaluation team?

This chapter can help social service workers involve key persons, called stake-holders, in the evaluation decision-making process. The range of persons iden-tified as stakeholders was discussed in chapter 1. Evaluations can be driven by internal stakeholders, those persons within the setting such as clients, stu-dents, teachers, direct-care workers, administrators, and boards of directors. Evaluations can be driven by external stakeholders, such as direct funding sources and indirect funding sources, such as county commissioners who over-see public funding or community groups. The concept of internal and external stakeholders is taken from Ginsberg's (2001) typology of internal and external evaluations.

The discussion in this chapter calls for a written authorization or contract from the key stakeholders and evaluation advisory board and a clear written statement of the work to be done by the evaluation team, including required written reports.

INTERNALLY DRIVEN EVALUATIONS

Internally driven evaluations are those initiated by stakeholders within the agency or those connected locally to the agency, such as a board of directors or a community advisory group. The motivation to evaluate may come from external sources, but the local agencies assume control over how the evaluation will be conducted. The persons taking on the main tasks of internally driven evaluations are often employees of the agency conducting the evaluation.

Examples of internally driven evaluations discussed in previous chapters are the following:

- The director of the strengths-based case management (SBCM) program wanted to describe client perceptions of the intervention to see whether those perceptions matched the intended goals of the program.
- The director of the children's grief support group wanted to describe the activities of the weekend camp to better understand what works and what does not in achieving the goals of the intervention.
- The chairs of the diversity committee of a public child welfare agency wanted to describe possible reasons why African American children were in out-of-home care disproportionately to white children in order to change the situations that created this disparity.

One goal of this book is for practitioners to proactively participate in internally driven evaluation activities in order to improve practice and to be accountable when externally driven evaluation activities are expected. Do you trust your practice, planning, and evaluation skills and knowledge enough to engage more in evaluations? Read the questions outlined in checklist 14 to assess your own comfort level with evaluation. Are you more comfortable now, after applying many of the concepts from this book than you were before you began reading this book, taking this class, or planning an evaluation?

Checklist 14. Self-Assessment of Evaluation Comfort Level

Social service practitioners, agencies, and professional organizations contain rich resources for conducting evaluations. Social service workers can begin each evaluation with a self-assessment at their own comfort level with the current evaluation by answering the questions outlined below.

Think of your answers as they apply not just to evaluations in general but also to a specific evaluation at your agency or practicum setting.

On a scale of 1–10, with 10 being the highest level, what is your overall evaluation skill and knowledge level? _____ Explain your rating.

List the classes you have taken on research or evaluation design and statistical analyses.

List the agency training or conference workshops you have attended that increased your personal integration of evaluation into daily practice.

List your skills that were helpful in past evaluations.

List the areas you need to improve to complete the current evaluation tasks.

List the textbooks from past classes that you need to dust off to refresh your research knowledge.

List the persons you can contact from past conferences as consultants for the current project.

A social service agency can be a place that supports and encourages staff to integrate evaluation into practice. One way to integrate evaluation into the daily operation of social service agencies is to encourage dialogue among the social service staff about evaluation. Evaluation language can become as commonplace as intervention and policy language. Dialogue about evaluation can occur informally in reading groups or current-research groups that meet over the lunch hour or after work to discuss research reported in the literature.

Every agency can benefit from an **evaluation advisory board**, those stakeholders overseeing the planning and implementation of an evaluation, whether it is required or not. Evaluation advisory boards can provide the following:

- Reinforcement of evaluation activities
- Guarantee of consumer representation in designing evaluations
- Resources, structure, and protocol for evaluations
- Feedback about important evaluation decisions

Evaluation advisory board members can help individuals bring their evaluations to fruition. They can also request progress reports, making available preliminary findings. Evaluation reports and other products of evaluation, whether they be verbal, electronic, tape-recorded, or video-taped, are important components of evaluation that tend to receive the least amount of attention. One reason is that evaluation products usually come at the end of an evaluation and people are tired—too tired to polish previous notes, memos, or preliminary findings.

Discussions during formal staff, board of directors, and agency committee meetings often generate ideas about evaluation, but workers do not always devote continued agency time to carrying out evaluations. Membership on these committees can include staff, board members, and consumers of services.

EXTERNALLY DRIVEN EVALUATIONS

Externally driven evaluations are those initiated by stakeholders outside the local agency, such as state or federal funding sources. In most externally driven evaluations, the persons assigned to the tasks of evaluation do not work for the agencies being evaluated and are often hired by the public funder.

Examples of externally driven evaluations described in previous chapters are repeated here. All the examples had an evaluation oversight committee at the state level and a separate institutional review board (IRB) for the evaluators, all of whom were employed at a public university. The role of IRBs in ensuring ethical evaluation procedures was discussed in chapter 4. In all the examples, program results were used to guide implementation of similar programs funded subsequently:

- Three different state funders collaborated on the statewide evaluation of thirty-eight family support interventions (FSIs). The purpose of the evaluation was to describe the desired results across all programs and to explain the impact of the programs on family functioning.
- The state Department of Jobs and Family Services (DJFS) oversaw the statewide evaluation of county outreach programs to enroll children in the Children's Health Insurance Program (CHIP). The purpose of the evaluation was to describe the successful outreach efforts and the obstacles to enrolling eligible children in the program.
- The state Department of Mental Health (DMH) oversaw the statewide study of competencies to be required of direct-care mental health workers. The purpose of this study was to describe the top five competencies agreed on by key stakeholders. These prioritized competencies would be the focus of future mandatory employee training.
- The federal Substance Abuse and Mental Health Services Administration (SAMHSA) oversaw the measurement of required measures according to the Government Performance and Results Act (GPRA) (Office of Management and Budget, 2013) for a school-district-wide implementation of a Safe Schools Healthy Students grant to reduce violence and substance use.

In each of these examples, the evaluators had a great deal of contact with social service workers even though staff from the local programs did not initiate the evaluations. Local social service workers and educators were able to utilize the interaction with the evaluation team to gain a better understanding of the programs from the information being collected and analyzed. It helped social service workers, teachers, and administrators to understand the objectives of the external evaluators.

The primary objective for external evaluators is to conduct an accurate and complete evaluation. The evaluator may come across as being rigid when it comes to making decisions about the evaluation design, sticking to the logic model, or implementing rigorous quantitative or qualitative approaches to data collection (all of which are described in later chapters). The reason for this rigidity may be that the evaluator wants to complete the task competently, just as practitioners want to deliver an intervention competently. The evaluator may follow the original program logic model since that is what is stated in the request for proposals (RFP) that funds the intervention and evaluation. Or he or she may follow specific data-collection procedures that were agreed on in the original contract. Understand that evaluators' decisions are based on their knowledge of the best ways to collect information for specific purposes. Also, view the relationship with the evaluator as you do any change-agent contract. *Negotiate.* Make sure the evaluator's objectives meet your objectives.

A second objective for external evaluators is to disseminate the knowledge gained from the evaluation. Thus, there should be a statement in a written evaluation contract about the authorship of any publications or presentations to emerge from the evaluation. Look back at the list of potential evaluation reports and outputs found in checklist 12 in the previous chapter. Consider these questions before beginning the evaluation:

• Whose names will appear on these reports?
• Who will hold the copyright on these reports?
• What permission is needed from the stakeholders to disseminate these reports?

A third objective for external evaluators is to ensure that ethical guidelines are followed during the entire evaluation process to protect participants' confidentiality and to identify potential conflicts of interest among persons involved in the evaluation. Roles of stakeholders often overlap in evaluations. For example, in some community-based evaluations, social service staff—because they are residents of the community or parents of children attending a community-based school program—may also be consumers of services. Clarifying any potential conflict of interest in these roles is an important part of those evaluations. Chapter 4 was devoted exclusively to upholding evaluation ethics.

Whether the evaluation is internally or externally driven, social service workers have the right to expect the following from evaluators:

- Evaluators should seek input from funders, social service providers, consumers, and community members in designing the evaluation.
- Evaluators should acknowledge the skills, knowledge, and underlying perspectives that they have followed in previous evaluations, both in a written résumé and, more important, in a pre-evaluation interview. For an example of an evaluator clarifying his perspective on evaluation to key stakeholders, see case example 13 from the previous chapter.
- Evaluators should provide reports on the evaluation process, results, and recommended changes on a regular basis, such as during face-to-face meetings held monthly or bimonthly and written reports issued every three to six months.
- Where there is an evaluation team, one person should be designated as the translator of the process. If the evaluation is being conducted through a contract with university faculty, the coordinator of the evaluation is often called the **primary investigator**, or principal investigator. That person has his or her name on the contract; thus, his or her reputation is on the line. Get to know that person well.
- Evaluators should be receptive to feedback. They should know whether clients are satisfied with the process, results, and products of the evaluation. Meet with the evaluator on a regular basis (e.g., every three months) to discuss your feedback. Specify the grounds for discontinuing or continuing the evaluation contract, for example, your satisfaction or the availability of resources.

EVALUATION STAKEHOLDER AGREEMENT

No evaluation happens in isolation. Evaluation activities are planned and delivered after much negotiation. Stakeholder evaluation agreement can be reached by following the seven points listed under section C, "Integrity/ Honesty," of the American Evaluation Association's (2004) *Guiding Principles of Evaluation*. These seven points parallel similar expectations social service workers are taught to follow in the worker-client relationship. They are discussed below and applied in case example 14.

Case Example 14. AEA Principles of Integrity and Honesty Applied during Evaluation Stakeholder Negotiation

The seven principles under section C, "Integrity/Honesty," of the American Evaluation Association's (2004) *Guiding Principles for Evaluators* are applied below to a family violence prevention planning grant.

1. **Negotiate the scope of the evaluation with stakeholders.** Many stakeholders needed to reach agreement on the activities to create the family violence prevention plan and on the activities to evaluate the planning process. Those stakeholders included the following:
   Representatives of the private foundation funding the grants, which were given to five separate awardees, each representing a different county or region in the state
   Directors of each of the five grant awardees
   Cross-site evaluators hired by the funder
   The director of the local county collaborative that received the grant
   Members of the steering committee to the local county grant
   Members of the advisory board to the local county planning grant
   The project director, the project planner, and an evaluator hired to implement the tasks of the grant

2. **Stakeholders and evaluators should identify any potential conflicts of interest.** As the evaluator, I was not directly involved in any of the stakeholder agencies. My university lay outside the county, so I also had no direct investment in the evaluation, nor was I aware of the different potential conflicts of interest among stakeholders. I did, however, have a direct investment in the focus of the project: preventing family violence. This area has been my primary practice and research area of interest. There may have been times that I advocated a little more strongly for certain approaches, such as systems collaboration, than I would normally—because of my prior knowledge and experiences.

3. **Record all changes made to the evaluation plan.** The funder required six-month reports that included the director's report and a separate evaluator's report. The original evaluation plan was contained in the first six-month report and updated in each subsequent report. The final report needed to show how the family violence

prevention plan was developed from information collected through the evaluation plan and other activities of the grant. Additionally, stakeholder feedback about the evaluation plan was recorded in the minutes of the steering committee and the advisory board committee.

4. **Be explicit about the interests of all persons involved in the outcomes of an evaluation.** At the midpoint of the two-year planning grant, a "State of Family Violence" report was printed that contained a summary of the information collected locally and from the research literature. This document contained target areas for the eventual plan. The advisory board held a one-day planning meeting to discuss the report and to guide the remaining planning activities. The evidence presented in the report became the driving force behind the strategies proposed in the final plan. All the members of the advisory board had explicit stakes in the final plan because proposed strategies potentially affected the constituencies they represented.

5–6. **Report results accurately, and do not misrepresent findings; and inform stakeholders if it is felt that certain procedures will produce misleading results.** Each of my reports was based on the county's logic model since the funder used each local grantee's logic model as the basis for feedback. I did not try to interpret the findings beyond their application to the local county logic model. I acknowledged limitations to the information collected and reported. For example, a survey was constructed collaboratively by me and other stakeholders and distributed to local social service providers to gain their perceptions of ways in which to prevent family violence. Using a standardized instrument proven valid and reliable in previous research would in some respects have been preferable. At the same time, the networking that arose during the course of survey administration elicited much positive support from the community for the final plan.

7. **Disclose to all stakeholders the financial support for the evaluation.** The budget for the planning grant was made public to all advisory board members. The annual budget was approximately $100,000, with about $10,000 allocated for evaluation activities. With the agreement of the stakeholders, my contracted time as the evaluator went as much toward facilitation and education as it did toward data collection and analysis. I was asked to attend monthly meetings of the steer-

ing committee; bimonthly meetings of the advisory board; monthly cross-site meetings or teleconferences with the funders; and biweekly meetings with the project coordinator, director, and planner. The majority of the budget went toward the project director's tasks and the planner's tasks. With the agreement of the stakeholders, I consulted on some data-collection tasks, such as helping construct the service provider survey. But the project director actually distributed the survey, and the planner analyzed the results. Thus, the roles of educator, facilitator, and evaluator overlapped among the primary persons coordinating the grant. The coordinator of the county grant was the director of the county women's shelter, and she spent much more time on the project than the agency was compensated for. Members of the steering committee and the advisory board also were given time off from their regular duties by their employers to participate in the grant activities.

First, negotiate the scope of the evaluation with stakeholders, just as social service workers negotiate the scope of an intervention or program with the client. Discuss the fees and agree on a budget. State the tasks that all stakeholders are expected to perform, the methods that will be used to gather information, and the expected uses of the evaluation. Have all persons who have a financial interest in the evaluation (e.g., the funder and those people contracted to conduct the evaluation) sign the contract. Give all stakeholders a written statement of the purpose, timeline, and activities, and obtain their approval. A statement of how the evaluation will be used should be clearly discussed during this negotiation process.

Second, stakeholders and evaluators should identify any potential conflicts of interest. Many conflicts of interest between stakeholders involve differences in personal values and worldview, differences that inevitably affect the intervention, planning, and evaluation processes. Be respectful of the views of evaluation stakeholders, just as you respect a client's right to differ with your views during an assessment and the development of a service plan. Also, in circumstances in which social service workers are involved in evaluations of their own programs, an analysis of agency weaknesses as well as agency strengths should be conducted. An evaluation that reports only agency strengths is one that has not been open to all the information collected from different critical vantage points.

Third, record all changes made to the evaluation plan and the reasons for those changes. The documentation of evaluation decisions can become the official document in which such changes are recorded, similar to the official case record for clients. Send a memo of any changes made to the appropriate stakeholders with a statement of when the changes were made, why, and the persons involved in approving them. In many cases, the original scope of the evaluation proposes an ambitious timeline and underestimates the amount of resources needed. To conduct a feasible evaluation, monitor changes that need to be made to the timeline and resources.

Fourth, be explicit about the interests of all persons involved in the outcomes of an evaluation. All stakeholders have something to gain and something to lose. Try to have all stakeholders in the same room at the beginning of an evaluation to state clearly their expectations, just as you might have a family or group share outcomes and processes expected of an intervention or program. If the evaluation is external and has been commissioned by a state agency to collect information from county social service workers, ask the state funders to write statements of the purpose of the evaluation and how they will use the information collected. Also, have a meeting at a central location with contact persons from all counties to answer questions about the scope of the evaluation. In negotiations with the funders, stakeholders can make clear their own interest in the evaluation, for example, a desire to increase collaboration between the university and the community or to add to the knowledge base by submitting articles based on the evaluation for publication.

Fifth, report results accurately, and do not misrepresent findings. Final reports should go through a rigorous review process. On submission, the report becomes a public document and may be used by some stakeholders long after the evaluation is over. Members of an evaluation advisory group should review reports. Seek someone who has no knowledge of the evaluation to review the reports, statistical analyses, and narrative analyses. Particular attention should be paid to the interpretations and recommendations of the findings. Do the reports show a clear connection between the findings and the interpretations? There is more discussion of report writing in chapter 12.

Sixth, inform stakeholders if it is believed that certain procedures will produce misleading results. That is, evaluators should inform stakeholders of the limitations of certain methodologies. While stakeholders will still be free to employ the methodologies they prefer, at least they will be choosing those methodologies knowledgeably. For example, one evaluator found herself involved in a situation in which the agency had already distributed surveys to staff. Her job was to help compile the results electronically and then report frequencies and percentages of responses. It turned out, however, that the survey method was not reliable and the results not valid and, therefore, that no inferential statistics could be calculated. Still, the evaluator was able to suggest other, more reliable standardized instruments, thus reinforcing this beginning attempt at evaluation.

Finally, disclose to all stakeholders the financial support for the evaluation. State the funding source and the amounts contracted for the different tasks. Staff time is an important resource. Social service workers may be asked to serve on an evaluation advisory board or even to help carry out the evaluation plan. How, if at all, will worker time be compensated? Is the worker expected to participate on his or her own time? Does the employer view evaluation activity as part of the employee's normal work responsibilities? The issue of making time to evaluate and being compensated for that time is an obstacle that many social service workers experience. The topic of budgeting and conducting evaluations feasibly was discussed in chapter 3.

EVALUATION STAKEHOLDER PLAN

A major theme of this chapter is that no evaluation is the work of one person. The collection of the information needed for an evaluation requires a cooperative effort—between direct-service workers and agency administrators and planners, in the case of external and internal evaluations, and between students and both faculty advisers and agency staff, in the case of class projects.

An **evaluation stakeholder plan** delineates the people responsible for overseeing and completing an evaluation. The plan includes the resources each stakeholder brings to the evaluation, the reports expected from each stakeholder, and the timeline on which the evaluation activities will be completed. A brief discussion and case application of each of the general stakeholder categories follows.

One group of key stakeholders is those persons authorizing the evaluation. Who is requiring the evaluation? What individual, group, or organization does this person represent? What evaluation questions does the authorizing person want answered? Individuals authorizing evaluations fall into three categories: (1) external funders overseeing grant awards to multiple agencies that have similar goals, programs, and results; (2) internal stakeholders wanting to answer local program evaluation questions; and (3) students and agency workers who want to answer local program evaluation questions.

Many examples have been given in earlier chapters in which an external funder initiated the evaluation. A challenge in those examples was to evaluate common desired results among programs while at the same time allowing local programs to develop unique interventions and results geared to their target populations. In the evaluation of family violence prevention planning, all five funded grantees reached the desired outcome of writing a strategic plan that was based on collaborative community involvement and information demonstrating the need for the proposed interventions. At the same time, the specific plans varied considerably among grantees. One grantee's strategic plan needed to account for the fact that its county was experiencing rapid population growth, which would likely increase the incidence of family violence during the time the prevention plan would be implemented.

The case examples so far in this text have been of internally initiated evaluations focused on exploratory and descriptive evaluation questions, whereas there was pressure in the externally driven evaluations to answer explanatory evaluation questions if possible. External evaluations in the case examples also had a defined time frame, ranging from one to two years, whereas the internal evaluation case examples had a more flexible time frame.

The student examples in this book covered exploratory, descriptive, and explanatory evaluation questions and also ranged from a ten-week class project to a two-year dissertation study. The challenge for students is to utilize the academic research to further their own education and at the same time contribute to agency interventions. Of the academic examples in this book, all were of projects that were conducted in consultation with agency workers and whose results were reported to agency stakeholders.

Who is overseeing the planning and implementation of the evaluation? Another component of the stakeholder evaluation plan is to form an evaluation advisory board. Members of an advisory team may be persons in addition to those authorizing the evaluation. An evaluation advisory team existed for most evaluation case examples given in this book.

For some external evaluations there was a general advisory board to the state funders. The funder communicated the desires of the advisory board to the other persons in the stakeholder plan. Such an arrangement characterized the statewide evaluation of FSIs and the statewide study of competencies for direct-care mental health workers. The advantage of this advisory arrangement was that the evaluator's time was better spent gathering information than engaging in long discussions of political issues related to program planning, practice, and evaluation.

At the same time, it was beneficial for at least one member of the evaluation team to be aware of how evaluation advisory team concerns affected the scope of the evaluation. In the evaluation of FSIs, the evaluation advisory team required that student performance outcomes be measured. In the study of direct-care mental health workers' competencies, the evaluation advisory team required that certain competencies appear on the survey distributed to mental health workers.

Local programs also had their own advisory boards in the external evaluation examples. The evaluators needed to be aware not only of the desires of the primary funders but also of the desires of the local monitors of the funded intervention. In the case of the FSIs, there was much variety in the interventions provided locally to reach the common goal of improving family functioning. In the case of the direct-care mental health workers' competencies, some local behavioral health organizations had special populations, such as youth or older adults that were not targets of the other behavioral health organizations.

The advisory board to the family violence prevention planning process had more than a purely advisory role. A subcommittee of the board was formed specifically to oversee the evaluation activities. The evaluator was very involved in discussions with the general advisory board and the evaluation advisory board about political issues shaping planning and evaluation.

Consumer representation was sought for the state and local evaluation advisory teams in all the case examples. Often, one or two consumers were on the boards. In the family violence prevention planning example, an agency stakeholder met separately with the youth consumers of prevention efforts to decipher the adult dialogues that occurred during the advisory board meetings. In the mental health competency example, client advocates rather than clients were on the advisory board—because the competencies being developed were for workers in agencies for persons with long-term mental illness. The stakeholders all agreed that client advocates, not the clients themselves, should be on the advisory board.

People initiating internal evaluations and students arranging to conduct evaluations or research for academic reasons sometimes lose sight of the fact that the evaluation still needs an advisory process. Minimally, all evaluations need to follow ethical guidelines. The role of institutional review boards in ensuring that such guidelines are followed is discussed in the next chapter, a discussion that applies to all evaluation and research conducted by university students and faculty. It was recommended earlier in this chapter that agencies have an IRB, if feasible.

Students and agency workers also commonly lose sight of the fact that, eventually, other stakeholders' support is needed either to carry out the evaluation or to implement the recommendations that emerge from the evaluation. In the internally driven evaluation of out-of-home placements of African American children, the workers were permitted to use work time to study and discuss the issue. Eventually, they needed administrative support to engage other persons in the case-review process and to follow up on the discoveries of the evaluation.

Who are the primary persons responsible for implementing the evaluation activities? Evaluations are best completed by an **evaluation team**. It takes a collaborative team to deliver social services to clients. It also takes a collaborative team to complete an evaluation in a timely and reasonable manner. Among the team is at least one person identified as the primary investigator or primary evaluator. This is the key person responsible for reporting directly to the funder of the evaluation and other key stakeholders. In some evaluations, there may actually be co–primary investigators. When students carry out evaluations or research projects, they are the co-investigators with the professor of the course or the person overseeing the evaluation.

Even when there is only one evaluator, that person still forms a team with the other stakeholders. In the evaluation of the strengths-based case management (SBCM) program, the evaluator formed a team with the program director and his staff to clarify the scope of the evaluation and to receive access to the clients, who became the primary participants in the evaluation.

In all the external evaluation examples used in this book, there were several persons involved in implementing the evaluation. In each example, one person was responsible for ensuring that all the evaluation activities were completed and reported in the manner agreed on by the stakeholders. In the larger evaluations, the primary evaluator became the person who met with evaluation advisory board members.

All of the components of an evaluation stakeholder plan discussed in this section are summarized in checklist 15, which appears in the "Documentation Tasks" section at the end of this chapter.

MAJOR POINTS

The following persons have a stake in the process and results of an evaluation and shape how the evaluation activities are negotiated: funders, social service providers, consumers of social services, students, community members, and evaluators. Evaluations can be internally driven by agency practitioners and administrators or externally driven by funders and policy makers, and driven by research interests. An evaluation advisory board of stakeholders can oversee all evaluation activities. A list of questions to ask potential evaluators was provided. The American Evaluation Association's seven points related to honesty and integrity of stakeholder negotiation were discussed and applied to a case example. Social service workers and educators who are responsible for conducting a program or practice evaluation can ask these questions at the very beginning of the evaluation: What is at stake for each stakeholder? What does each stakeholder have to gain? What does each stakeholder have to lose? What is each stakeholder willing to invest in the program and evaluation? This chapter concluded with a discussion of an evaluation stakeholder plan that delineates the provided resources and expected reports from key stakeholders within a specified time frame.

CRITICAL-THINKING QUESTIONS

1. Answer the following questions as they pertain to a specific evaluation you are planning or implementing:
   a. Which agency stakeholders are requesting the current evaluation? Why?
   b. Are there any conflicting tensions between agency stakeholders around the need for the evaluation? How will these tensions be addressed?

c. Are you internal to the agency or an external stakeholder? Being internal means that you report to the agency and thus the agency is liable for your actions. How does your status as "internal" or "external" affect your interaction with key stakeholders?

d. Is there a culture within the agency that values continuous evaluation and feedback to improve interventions? Why or why not?

e. Which external stakeholders are requesting the current evaluation? Why?

f. Are there any conflicting tensions between external and internal stakeholders around the need for the evaluation? How will these tensions be addressed?

g. If you are a student conducting this evaluation for a course or degree requirement, how do your requirements for the college or university complement or conflict with expectations from the agency or school setting? Is the agency cooperating with your requirement to get IRB approval before collecting data? Is the college or university liable for your activities as an evaluator?

h. Are the external stakeholders providing technical assistance and training to assist the agency or school in completing the evaluation?

i. Is there a written evaluation plan? Why or why not?

2. For any evaluation, what are the potential disadvantages of not having a written evaluation plan?

3. For a current evaluation, whose written consent do you need before you go any further with your evaluation?

4. For any evaluation, how can authorizing stakeholders help you get buy-in from other evaluation participants?

5. For a current evaluation, check your list of evaluation board members. Is any group missing? Sometimes, an advisory board member represents a population, such as consumers or workers. Sometimes, an advisory board member is a geographical representative if the evaluation spans several geographic regions or constituencies, such as different school districts.

DOCUMENTATION TASKS

Complete the evaluation stakeholder plan found in checklist 15.

Checklist 15. Evaluation Stakeholder Plan

Complete the information requested below.

The **authorizing stakeholders** for this evaluation are:

For each person listed above, provide the following information:

_____ agrees to complete the following tasks:

_____ agrees to complete the above tasks by _____
(specific date).

_____ agrees to provide the following resources:

_____ agrees to provide the following reports (include a deadline date):

The **evaluation advisory board members** are:

For each person listed above, provide the following information:

_____ agrees to complete the following tasks:

_____ agrees to complete the above tasks by _____
(specific date).

_____ agrees to provide the following resources:

_____ agrees to provide the following reports (include a deadline date):

The members of the **evaluation team** are:

For each person listed above, provide the following information:

_____ agrees to complete the following tasks:

_____ agrees to complete the above tasks by _____ (specific date).

_____ agrees to provide the following resources:

_____ agrees to provide the following reports (include a deadline date):

THEORY-DRIVEN
EVALUATION DECISIONS

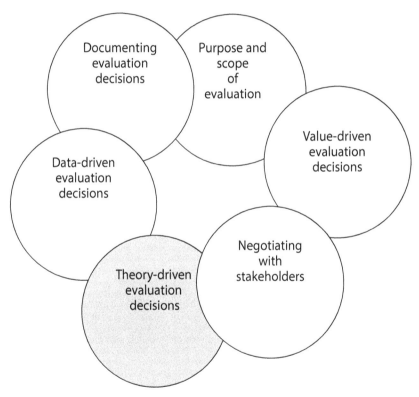

Figure 6.
Interactive model of evaluation: Theory-driven evaluation decisions

Developing a
Logic Model

6

Researchers complain that practitioners do not use the knowledge they generate, and practitioners complain that knowledge tastes like cardboard. Clearly, we need to better understand the process of knowledge utilization. (Marsh, 2003, p. 293)

Let us relegate theory to its proper role. It is neither essential nor necessarily desirable for research on social work practice to be theoretically driven. There are many negative consequences for our field's current insistence that dissertations be exercises in theory building. Rather than mandating that, by definition, a social work dissertation must be either theoretically based or contribute to theory, let us recognize the value of non-theoretical research contributions and not accord them secondary status. (Thyer, 2001, p. 22)

EVALUATION DECISION-MAKING QUESTIONS

Is theory necessary for this evaluation?
Will the evaluation build or test theory?
Is a logic model necessary for this evaluation?
If yes, is the logic model for a formative or summative evaluation?
Are all of the following components of the logic model included?

1. Goals
2. Strategies
3. Short-term results
4. Long-term results
5. Measures of reaching the short-term and long-term results

Are the goals, strategies, and results logically or theoretically linked?
Are the SCREAM values addressed in the logic model?

THEORY OF CHANGE

The discussion in this chapter and chapter 7 can help social service workers prioritize how theory, if at all, drives evaluation decisions. Theory, in general, is the connection between concepts to hypothesize a causal relationship or describe a noncausal relationship between concepts. Theory can be connected to past empirical research that tests or describes the relationship between those concepts. For example, a study can test a theory on the stages of grief that persons experience after a loss. Literature searches of evidence-based research on the application of theory is the topic of chapter 7. **Evidence-based practices** *are those programs or interventions (e.g., grief support group) that are implemented because the program has been demonstrated through empirical research to produce the hypothesized outcomes from the intervention. Evaluation is then conducted to analyze whether the hypothesized results occur from the intervention or program in the current setting.*

Some programs are grounded in logical assumptions made by stakeholders about the relationship between an intervention or program and desired results for clients or students, without necessarily having evidence to support the assumptions. This programmatic explanation of the connection between interventions and client outcomes is sometimes called **theory of change**. Once the theory of change is clearly applied in measurable terms, then research methods can determine whether the program theory in fact stands. For example, the theory of change may be that students participating in after-school social activities will improve on indicators of academic success (e.g., grades, progressing to the next grade level, graduating). One can collect data that measure academic success and then be able to attribute that success to the after-school program. Data collection and research designs are discussed in part 5.

The key stakeholders of an evaluation should be included when deciding the role that theory plays before, during, and after the evaluation is conducted. Given the decisions agreed on in the previous chapter, stakeholders may expect the application of some general theories, models, or perspectives throughout the entire evaluation. General theoretical models such as the strengths perspective, cultural competency, and systems theory guide the evaluation team to include certain processes and outcomes in the evaluation. Specific theories that apply to the intervention or program being implemented or planned also influence evaluation decisions.

A logic model and **literature review** are two tools that help social service workers connect theory to program planning, practice, and evaluation. The literature review helps social service workers and educators learn how other programs similar to their own applied theory to practice. The logic model helps social service stakeholders clarify their own program theory, which is the connection between the goals, the activities, and the desired results of their evaluated programs. The logic model is discussed later in this chapter. Conducting the literature review is discussed in chapter 7.

Theory and Values.

Theory connects research to practice. The previous chapter focused on how values drive evaluation decisions. This chapter focuses on how theories drive evaluation decisions. The difference is that values are what persons prefer or believe should be present, whereas theories are what they *think* should be present. Value priorities help evaluation stakeholders resolve ethical dilemmas by guiding them in choosing among a range of preferred ways to interact with others. Theories help evaluation stakeholders resolve theoretical dilemmas by guiding them in choosing among a range of approaches that make sense for evaluation stakeholders.

Ethical decisions are supported by documenting that specified value preferences were honored. For example, one would demonstrate that participants' and stakeholders' rights were respected and persons not harmed by documenting compliance with the mandates of an institutional review board. Theoretical decisions are supported by documenting the theories that guided practice, planning, and evaluation decisions. For example, one would reference and describe the theories that were applied to answer the evaluation questions, guide the methods used to answer the questions, and interpret the findings.

Program planning, practice, and evaluation involve values and theories. The two are intertwined. Stakeholders external to the program (e.g., funding sources) may establish value preferences about the program in the request for proposals (RFP) and in the required annual and semiannual reports. For example, a funding source may require that an evaluation carry out the following two values with or without documentation that theoretically connects these activities to client change: (1) collaborate on evaluation planning and implementation with multiple program stakeholders (e.g., clients, direct-care staff, administrators, community representatives) and (2) include measurements of client strengths in the evaluation.

It is important to acknowledge the opposing views concerning the place of theory in social services as captured in quotations at the beginning of this chapter. Patton (2012) argues that, in the past, too many evaluations were conducted without the results having been utilized to improve social service interventions. He states that no evaluation should be initiated until it has been determined how key stakeholders will utilize the evaluation. As Thyer (2001) argues, stakeholders may be more interested in the desired results of intervention whether or not the results can be theoretically connected to the interventions.

Marsh (2003) argues that helping workers connect theory to practice is a form of utilization of evaluation and research. In this text examples were given of the evidence-based research that demonstrates the desired results (e.g., academic success) of programs that support positive student behaviors. Many school districts across the country implement evidence-based and strengths-based interventions that have proved effective through empirical research. Three such interventions are Positive Behavior Intervention Systems (http://www.pbis.org), the Good Behavior Game (http://www.paxis.org), and Families and Schools Together (http://www.familiesandschools.org).

Testing theory can help social service workers solve client problems. Knowledge gained from evaluation is important, but helping clients achieve desired change is the priority. Social service workers and educators apply theories every day. Not all social workers are in the habit of consciously questioning whether those theories reduce client concerns or improve desired client or program results. Just because a social service worker's or teacher's applied theories do not appear in a journal does not mean that important knowledge was not gained from an intervention. Theory can be used to test the values that underlie interventions and evaluations.

Cycle of Theory Building and Theory Testing.

Theory building is the process of exploring or describing what one learns while gathering information. **Theory testing** is the process of gathering information to describe or explain the relationship between interventions and client change. The discussion of qualitative and quantitative approaches to gathering information is very much connected to theory building and theory testing. Data-collection methods are the focus of discussion in part 5. They are mentioned here because of the mutual interaction between theory and data collection.

For now, it is enough to know that a **qualitative approach** is an open-ended gathering of information to *build* theory to answer exploratory and descriptive evaluation questions. A **quantitative approach** is a closed-ended gathering of information to *test* theory to answer descriptive and explanatory evaluation questions and statements. For each type of evaluation question (exploratory, descriptive, or explanatory), there are specific types of research methods (qualitative or quantitative) that build or test theory (see figure 7).

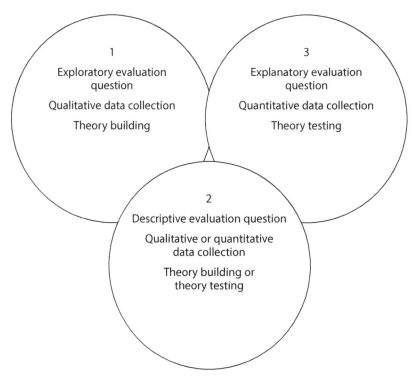

Figure 7.
Cycle of theory building and theory testing

To apply an example to figure 7, mental health workers in a school district wanted to build theory on how school principals, teachers, and counselors referred youth to mental health services. To do so, the workers visited thirty-seven schools and allowed the personnel at each school to discuss how they make mental health referrals and their desired results from the referrals. The collective program theory was the result of the data collected qualitatively from personnel at all thirty-seven schools (circle 1). A quantitative, closed-ended survey of an ideal mental health referral process can be developed from the qualitative data to test the results collectively described in the qualitative interviews (circle 2). Or qualitative and quantitative data can be collected at the same time (circle 3) to apply an evidence-based mental health referral process while at the same time exploring how the personnel actually make referrals. In all three examples, data collection, theory building, and theory testing overlap and inform different types of program decisions.

Theory building is often done during the program planning or formative evaluation stage. Stakeholders use the evaluation to collect data to determine whether there is a need for the program. Theory testing is done after the program is implemented during the summative evaluation stage. Stakeholders use the evaluation to test or to describe the desired results from the implementation. The stakeholders then change the intervention on the basis of the evaluation of outcomes. Stakeholders use the results and further exploratory data to then adapt or plan new interventions. This cycle is captured in figure 8. The cycle is always continuing, and there is always feedback to the stakeholders about how the results drive new program decisions.

LOGIC MODELS

A **logic model** is an agency's clarification of the connection between intervention and program goals, strategies, and expected results. It is a tool for developing program theory and adhering to that theory. It is difficult, if not impossible, to evaluate a program that has no clearly stated purpose and no clearly stated program goals and objectives agreed on by key stakeholders. The assumption is that one cannot evaluate a program if there is

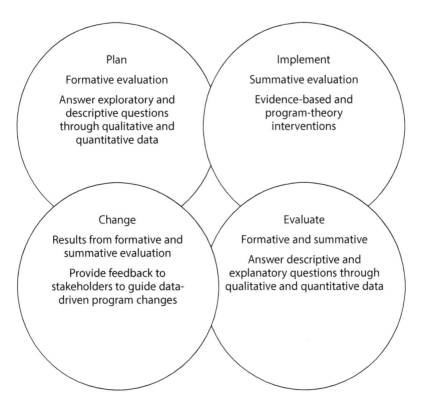

Figure 8.
Plan, implement, evaluate, and change cycle

not a clear plan for connecting the program to desired change. There is too much room for disagreement over the interpretation of the evaluation if stakeholders are not clear about the intended impact of the evaluation.

There are four basic components to a logic model: (1) **goals**, (2) **strategies**, (3) short-term **results**, and (4) long-term results. Some stakeholders add a component called inputs, which precedes the goals component. **Inputs** are the sources determining the logic model (e.g., needs assessment conducted with consumers and social service workers). Inputs can also include the resources required to provide the services such as staff training, funding, and stakeholder support. The rationale behind the inclusion of an input component is the demonstration of how the logic model was developed. In many cases, an entire report is necessary to document the process for determining the logic model.

Goals and Objectives.

Goals are general, abstract statements about the desired processes, outcomes, or results of an intervention or program. Three to five goals are usually preferred. Goals describe the underlying purpose, values, or theory of an intervention. Some persons may use the term *mission* or *vision*, although intervention goals are most often a subset of a larger mission or vision statement.

The key question to ask of goal statements is "Are these goals agreed on by the key stakeholders?" If you have the wrong goal statement, you will then have the wrong strategies and results. The correct goal statements are usually taken from the RFP or the final grant contract. If your goals differ from those outlined in those documents, add a written addendum signed by all stakeholders that the change in goals was approved.

Some persons add **objectives** to the goals. Objectives are measurable expectations that are necessary for reaching the goal. Objectives are usually a subset of goals and are written in measurable terms. Objectives should also have an expected time or date. Goals are deliberately abstract to allow for different means of reaching the same results. In this text, I use *objectives* synonymously with *results*, because objectives and results are measurable indicators that the goals were met.

An example of a goal and related objectives is taken from a formative, descriptive needs assessment for a county's application for state funding of pregnancy prevention programs in the schools. Persons from schools and government offices participated in focus groups and surveys asking for their objectives to reducing teenage pregnancy. The participants in this needs assessment expressed primarily conservative objectives. The goal was to reduce teenage pregnancies in South County. The objectives established from the needs assessment data were the following: (1) there will be a 2 percent decrease in the number of teenage pregnancies recorded at South Hospital within five years, (2) there will be an increase of students receiving pregnancy prevention programs in the school district this academic year, (3) there will be an increase in youth who abstain from sexual activities over a five-year period, (4) there will be a decrease in sexually active youth who do not use contraceptives over a five-year period.

Using this example, the same data collected in a different county may produce different objectives, such as the increase in the use of contraceptives, access to contraceptives, or increased knowledge and behavior related to protective sexual behavior. The reader can also see how values and theory easily overlap when establishing program objectives. One's value that abstinence is the preferred method for pregnancy prevention may direct persons to locate only evidence-based literature that tests abstinence-only interventions. An evaluator's role is to help persons consult the evidence-based literature, which is discussed in the next chapter, in guiding program objectives. At the same time, the evaluator cannot control if other stakeholders allow values to override evidence.

Strategies.

Strategies are the actual interventions employed to reach the stated goals. It is best to limit the number of strategies being evaluated. Two strategies are usually optimal. The reason is that the more strategies that are connected to the goals, the harder it is to demonstrate a causal connection between the strategies, goals, and desired results. For example, in the evaluation of the Safe Schools Healthy Students (SSHS) across an entire school district of seventeen schools, there were more than fifteen different interventions. An overall goal of the collective interventions was to reduce violence. It was difficult to pose an explanatory evaluation question to test that the specific combination of fifteen interventions resulted in a reduction of violence. That is, we could not *prove* that these specific fifteen programs reduced youth violence. It was possible to pose descriptive evaluation questions of each intervention that examined the relationship between that intervention (strategy) and the goal to reduce violence. That is, we could use data to determine whether there was a relationship between the implementation of the programs and a reduction in youth violence.

The other issue was that each strategy also had other goals and desired results. For example, the FAST strategy had a goal to improve the working relationship among teachers, parents, and students. The theory was that an improvement in working relationships between these groups would help all three groups work together to reduce violence among youth.

Strategies are sometimes called interventions, treatments, activities, or programs. As long as all stakeholders agree, alternative terms can be used. A more important issue is how specific the strategy needs to be. Examples of vague strategy statements are "Parental involvement programs," "Collaboration," and "Emphasis on positives rather than punishment." There are many evidence-based interventions that emphasize these goals, but the exact components of the strategy need to be clarified for the evaluation. For example, in the SSHS evaluation, the specific strategy that emphasized positives rather than punishment was the evidence-based program called Positive Behavior Intervention Systems (http://www.pbis.org).

The key question to ask about a strategy listed in a logic model is, "Is it logically connected to the goals?" For example, if the goal is "Develop a countywide family-violence prevention plan," then the strategies must be related to family violence prevention. This may seem simple enough, but it really is not. The place to start is to define the terms in the goal statement. For example, how is *prevention* defined? Prevention is often divided up into primary, tertiary, and secondary. Primary prevention is delivered to an entire community regardless of whether persons have experienced the identified concern. An example is a television ad emphasizing healthy relationships and describing signs of relationships that may become violent. Secondary prevention is targeted to at-risk populations. An example is providing services to adults who witnessed violence in the home but have not been victims of violence. Tertiary prevention is targeted to persons who have experienced the concern. An example is providing a safety plan to residents of a shelter for victims of domestic violence. So, if prevention is defined as delivering services to all members of a community who have not been victims of family violence (primary), then a shelter for victims of family violence would not be part of that plan (tertiary).

Results.

Results are the desired changes related to specific strategies. The term *results* is used to conceptualize change as being both **processes** and **outcomes**. Processes are how people do things, for example, "Changing the ways social service workers communicate with consumers of services."

Outcomes are what people do differently after receiving an intervention, for example, "Stop using alcohol and illegal substances." Some stakeholders may specify that persons list only outcomes and that the outcomes be measurable behaviors of the targeted group. The term *results* allows the evaluation question to shape whether processes, outcomes, or both are measured.

Another term that needs clarification is *desired changes*. In the planning stage, results are listed as the changes that stakeholders expect to occur. Since the intervention has not yet occurred, the changes have not yet occurred. During the implementation stage, these desired results are expected to become actual results. Some stakeholders require that the results be written in very specific terms: "55 percent of the young people participating in the program will report increased assets," or "The reports of child abuse and neglect will be reduced by 5 percent at the end of the five-year period." Results statements hold great weight because continuation of the intervention and evaluation can hinge on whether the stated results are met. It is important to clarify the consequences of the desired results not being met.

Another point about results is that there are often multiple systems at which change can be targeted, and stakeholders should agree on the systems to be targeted. For example, participants in the evaluation of family support interventions (FSIs) measured different results related to school readiness depending on the systems-level focus of intervention. School readiness was measured in terms of changes in the child (e.g., child passes educational marker level), changes in the family (e.g., parents help child with homework), changes in the school (e.g., the school is more "parent-friendly," providing transportation and inviting parents to participate in more school activities), or changes in the community (e.g., older adults volunteer as tutors). In such situations, stakeholder agreement on the systems level that you plan to measure as results is essential.

Distinguish between short-term and long-term results. Short-term results are those desired changes predicted to occur immediately after the intervention has been implemented. Short-term results are sometimes called program results because they are expected right after the program or intervention is delivered. The key question to ask of short-term results is, "Are they evidence that the goal has been achieved?" The simple fact that results have been achieved is not necessarily evidence that the goal itself has been achieved. Consider, for example, the goal statement "Reduce family violence in the county." One strategy related to that goal may be "Form a countywide coalition of social service agencies to coordinate efforts to prevent family violence." One short-term result of that strategy may be that the coalition is formed within a year of funding. But the fact that the coalition is in place is not evidence that family violence has been reduced; rather, it is simply evidence that the strategy has been implemented.

Long-term results are those desired changes predicted to occur after all strategies have been implemented. They demonstrate that the original goal has been reached. In most situations, it will take at least two years after the initial interventions are implemented for long-term results to become evident. Long-term results of program implementation are often called impacts or indicators because they are measurable evidence that the desired outcomes were reached.

There are two key questions to ask of long-term results: Are they connected to the overall goal? Are all the strategies and short-term results logically connected to the long-term results? Long-term results statements are a good reality check for the scope of a given logic model. For example, if it does not seem feasible to reduce the county reporting rates of child abuse and neglect, then which part of the logic model needs to be restated? Perhaps the results statement needs to be more realistic: for example, "Reducing incidences of child abuse only among families that received the specific intervention rather than using the county rate, which includes persons not receiving the intervention." Perhaps using child-abuse reporting rates is not the best indicator that child abuse was reduced because there are incidences of child abuse that go unreported.

The results should be the measurement of the objectives. Go back to the previous example of planning a teenage pregnancy intervention. Think of ways to measure the desired outcomes, that is, achievement of the objectives that were listed from that needs assessment:

Goal: Reduce teenage pregnancies in South County.

Objectives: (1) There will be a 2 percent decrease in the number of teenage pregnancies recorded at South Hospital over a five-year period. (2) There will be an increase of students receiving pregnancy prevention programs in the school district this academic year. (3) There will be an increase in youth who abstain from sexual activities over a five-year period. (4) There will be a decrease in sexually active youth who do not use contraceptives over a five-year period.

The first step is to **operationalize**, or define, the terms in the objective statements. What age range defines "teenage" for this study? "Pregnancy" seems to be defined as giving birth at South Hospital. Are the stakeholders content with knowing that this definition will not measure all pregnancies in the county? What confidentiality issues need to be addressed in using teenage birth records at a hospital as data? How will persons measure "the increase of students receiving teenage pregnancy prevention programs"? Is attendance of these programs kept? How will persons measure "youth will abstain from sexual activities" or "youth who do not use contraceptives"? Will they be asked? There are items on the Centers for Disease Control and Prevention's Youth Risk Behavior Surveillance System (YRBSS) that measure sexual risk behaviors (http://www.cdc.gov/HealthyYouth/yrbs). If the youth are asked, how will the evaluators know the data are accurate?

The point here is that writing a good logic model requires measurable objective and results statements. Checklist 16 provides a format to use when developing a logic model.

Case example 15 is an example of an evaluation plan to measure some practice behaviors for competency 1 of the Council on Social Work Education's (2012) Education Policy and Accreditation Standards using the logic model approach to assessment. According to competency 2.1.1, "[a] student will identify as a professional social worker and conduct oneself accordingly." The logic model language is changed in the following ways: goals become competencies, objectives become practice behaviors, strategies become courses, short-term results are the assignments in a specific course, and long-term results become the expectation of the student at time of graduation. The long-term results for the example are students' performance in the last term of field education and their discussion in a final portfolio paper of the growth they made throughout the program related to the specific practice behavior. This same logic model format can be used in any education setting to assess student performance of student objectives or outcomes.

Case Example 15. CSWE's (2012) Competency Logic Model Applied to Educational Policy Competency 2.1.1

Goal (Competency 1): Student will identify as a professional social worker and conduct oneself accordingly.

Objective (practice behavior)	Strategy (course title)	Short-term results	Long-term results
1. Advocate for client access to the services of social work.	SW 300—HBSE II—Macro	Student will complete a community assessment and community map assessing client access to social work services as evidenced by receiving at least a passing (70%) grade on the assignment.	In the final portfolio paper, student will describe his or her growth in reaching this practice behavior from the assignment in SW 301 to SW 401 to his or her performance of this practice behavior in Field Education I.
	SW 400—SW Practice II—Macro	Student will complete the agency access assessment and report agency changes implemented as evidenced by receiving at least a passing grade on the assignment.	Same as above.
	SW 450—SW Field Education I	Student will advocate for client access at the field placement as evidenced by the field supervisor's evaluation of a 2 or higher (on a 4-point scale, with 4 being the highest ranking).	Same as above.
	SW 460—SW Field Education II		Student will advocate for client access at the field placement as evidenced by the field supervisor's evaluation of 3 or 4 (on a 4-point scale, with 4 being the highest ranking).
2. Demonstrate professional demeanor in behavior, appearance, and communication.	SW 300—SW Practice I	Student conducts himself or herself professionally in the agency observation as evidenced by following the agency dress code, being prompt in all responsibilities, and interacting with all persons in a respectful manner.	In the final portfolio paper, student will describe his or her growth in reaching this practice behavior from the logs in SW 300 and 450 to his or her performance of this practice behavior in Field Education I.

Checklist 16. Logic Model Framework

Complete this logic model for an intervention you will be evaluating.

Goals	Objectives	Strategy	ST results	LT results
1.	a.			
	b.			
	c.			
2.	a.			
	b.			
	c.			
3.	a.			
	b.			
	c.			

Case Example 15. CSWE's (2012) Competency Logic Model Applied to Educational Policy Competency 2.1.1—*(continued)*

		SW 450— Field Education I	Student conducts him- or herself professionally in the field education as evidenced by following the agency dress code, being prompt in all responsibilities, and interacting with all persons in a respectful manner.	Same as above.
		SW 460— Field Education II		Student conducts him- or herself professionally in the field education as evidenced by following the agency dress code, being prompt in all responsibilities, and interacting with all persons in a respectful manner. Demonstration of this learning behavior means the student received a 3 or 4 on the final field supervisor's evaluation.
3.	Use supervision and consultation.	SW 300— SW Practice I	Student will come to weekly, one-hour supervision with a planned agenda.	In final portfolio paper, student will discuss how he or she utilized supervision and consultation throughout the program to improve generalist social work knowledge, skills, and values.
		SW 450— Field Education I	Student will come to weekly, one-hour supervision with a planned agenda.	
		SW 460— Field Education II		Field supervisor will rate student's use of supervision to improve the student's performance with a ranking of 3 or 4 (with 4 being the highest).

Logic models are negotiated just as is every process in the evaluation. Checklist 17 offers a guide to help students, educators, and social service workers address the political issues related to determining the goals, activities, and results of a logic model. This guide was used to help the staff in a university disabilities service office determine how to measure the success of their program.

This section closes with the reminder that the construction of a logic model is influenced by the values guiding an evaluation. Checklist 18 contains questions to consider when constructing a planning, practice, or evaluation logic model that takes account of the SCREAM values discussed in chapter 3. The SCREAM model focuses on (1) measuring strengths, (2) applying culturally competent evaluation procedures and measures, (3) conducting the evaluation within the resources one has, (4) following ethical guidelines, (5) seeking agreement on the evaluation from key stakeholders, and (6) measuring multiple systems levels.

FORMATIVE EVALUATION LOGIC MODEL

Evaluation was defined earlier as the systematic collection and analysis of information about one or more interventions with clients to improve practice, planning, and accountability and to contribute to knowledge building. What if the purpose of the evaluation is to develop a service that does not currently exist or to improve a program that does not meet some of the client or student needs? This is a formative evaluation for planning purposes. A needs assessment can be conducted to systematically determine what the needs are and then to develop and implement the evidence-based intervention that will meet those needs.

See case example 16, which contains three different formative evaluations discussed throughout this text. These are not complete logic models. Only two strategies for each program are listed. Notice that the logic model pertains more to the evaluation than to a specific program. There may be programs involved in collecting the data. There may also be an assumption that existing programs are related to the needs that become identified by the needs assessment. For example, the police data collected in the family violence prevention planning evaluation may lead the stakeholders to draw conclusions on how well or not well the current criminal justice policies and procedures decrease the occurrence of partner abuse.

Checklist 17. Negotiating Political Issues When Constructing a Logic Model

The handout reproduced below was distributed to the staff of the Office of Disability Services at a public university. The staff was constructing a logic model of their programs as the first step toward identifying outcomes and ways to measure those outcomes. Use this same checklist with stakeholders for an evaluation you are working on.

I. Program Information

Program name:
Interventions provided:

What I hope to achieve by these interventions:

The changes I will see in the students (clients) based on my interventions:

II. Evaluation

Have I met my goals? My goals:

How do I know? I will know the goals are met when:

Student examples:
Goal is to get into _____ major; I will know when I am accepted into _____.
Goal is to graduate; I will know when I receive my diploma.

III. Logic Model as a Tool

Statement of Goals, Objectives, Strategies to Reach the Goals and Results
Complete the information below:

Program Logic Model
Program Name:_____

Goals	Objectives	Strategies	Short-term results	Long-term results
1.	a.			
	b.			
	c.			
2.	a.			
	b.			
	c.			
3.	a.			
	b.			
	c.			

Beginning ideas of how to measure the results:

IV. Key Points to Consider about Choosing Goals

1. Do you have the "right" general goals?
   Do the goals fit your job description? If not, are your goals still considered relevant by OSD? By the Office of Student Affairs?

2. Do your goals contain a measurable outcome?
   How will you know your goal was reached?

3. Do your goals have a specific timeline?
   Example: I will graduate in five years versus I will graduate sometime.

V. Key Points to Choosing Strategies

1. There should be a logical connection between goals and intervention.
   Example: What would a person need to do to get accepted into a major? To graduate?

2. The logical connection between goals and activities needs to be "proved" by the following:
   a. The literature—research has been done to show that the activity is effective in reaching your stated goal
   b. Your own assessment.

3. No-longer-acceptable answers to the question, "Why do you do _____?"
   a. "It's common sense" or "It makes sense."
   b. "It's what I do best."
   c. "It's what we've always done."

4. A hard-to-swallow answer to the question, "Why do you do _____?" is "Because _____ made me"
   Sometimes policies are made without having a clear conceptual connection between the program and desired results.
   Answer: Test the approach and report the results.

VI. Results

After I do _____, this is how the student is different . . .

1.
2.
3.

VII. Key Points When Considering Results

1. There should be a logical connection among goals, interventions, and results.

2. Acknowledge that more than one intervention and/or program is connected to the results. Most results are due to a collaborative effort!

3. Results can be divided into long-term and short-term results. Example: Long-term goal of getting accepted into a major may have the following short-term goals: learn the acceptance criteria, take required courses, fill out the application.

   Allow enough time for long-term goals to feel the impact of your intervention. For example, if you implement a new program to improve graduation rates, allow three to five years to see a noticeable change.

Long-term results tend to be quantitative, measurable outcomes (e.g., number of majors, number of graduates).

Short-term results tend to be measures specific to the processes that led to the outcomes (e.g., improvement in grades after the intervention, improvement on a study skills survey).

4. Results can be processes or outcomes.
   Examples of processes to get accepted into a major: successfully completed a course on choosing majors, attended informational meetings within a department, or completed a career inventory. You must be able to "prove" the conceptual connection between the processes or short-term outcomes and the long-term outcomes.

5. Select reasonable long-term results.
   "Unreachable" results will look like the interventions didn't work. "Too easy" results will look like the interventions were not necessary.
   Result indicators become the benchmark by which your intervention is assessed.

VIII. The Hard Part Is Now Done!

1. The logic model determines the method of assessment.

2. Take sufficient time to write a clear logic model.

3. Be visual—draw a causality chart. Use only pictures—no words.

Checklist 18. SCREAM Analysis of a Logic Model

After constructing a logic model for an evaluation, answer the following questions.

___ Do the goals, activities, and results include an increase or maintenance of stakeholder **strengths**?

___ Do the goals, activities, and results include recognition of the diverse **cultures** represented by the stakeholders?

___ Are the goals, activities, and results realistic for the **resources** that are available?

___ Are the goals, activities, and results achievable within the boundaries of **ethical** conduct for evaluations?

___ Are all key stakeholders in **agreement** with the goals, activities, and results?

___ Do the goals, activities, and results measure impact on **multiple** systems levels?

Case Example 16. Logic Models for Formative Evaluations

Family Violence Prevention Plan

Goal	Strategies	ST results	LT results
Develop a countywide prevention plan.	a. Focus groups with workers at (1) Child Protection, (2) Adult Protection, & (3) Partner Abuse Services	Prioritize 5 family violence prevention strategies.	Develop a 5-year plan.
	b. Analyze domestic violence reports from (1) sheriff, (2) state patrol, & (3) city police departments.	Publish domestic violence data for past year.	Develop a 5-year plan.

United Way Five-Year Funding Priorities

Goal	Strategies	ST results	LT results
Develop a 5-year plan for funding priorities.	a. Analyze results of 4 recent needs assessments.	Identify 5 priority areas.	Develop a 5-year plan.
	b. Conduct focus group with current UW board members.	Identify 5 priority areas.	Develop a 5-year plan.

Teenage Pregnancy Prevention

Goal	Strategies	ST results	LT results
Develop a teenage pregnancy prevention plan.	a. Complete a literature review of evidence-based pregnancy prevention programs.	List of evidence-based programs	Develop a 5-year plan.
	b. Survey teens who are pregnant.	Results of teens' perceptions of effective interventions	Develop a 5-year plan.
	c. Knowledge and sexual behavior survey taken by teens.	Results of teens' knowledge & sexual behavior	Develop a 5-year plan.

All three examples posed descriptive evaluation questions. Those questions were based on these formative, descriptive evaluation questions: (1) What is the best family violence prevention plan for our county? (2) What are the five top-priority areas for our United Way funding? and (3) What are the best pregnancy prevention services for our county? The context of the logic models for each needs assessment was determined by the stakeholders of each evaluation. Other stakeholders in other communities may have developed very different data-collection strategies and thus would have different desired results.

The evaluation questions were not exploratory because the stakeholders had clear parameters for each of their evaluation questions. For example, the family violence prevention project had specific persons in mind for the focus groups and narrowed the secondary data to police reports of domestic violence. Thus, other agencies targeting family violence were not included and other evidence of family violence was not included. By the end of this evaluation, though, data of child abuse and neglect incidences and incidences of adult abuse and neglect were added to the results.

The evaluation questions were not explanatory because there was not a hypothesis that specific interventions affected the data collected. The needs assessment in all three examples did include a survey of all social service agencies targeting the needs being assessed. For example, a list of all agencies directly or indirectly working toward family violence prevention was gathered. The evaluators surveyed staff from these agencies on the services provided, any data the agency collected related to desired results, and the desired results of their programs.

SUMMATIVE EVALUATION LOGIC MODEL

A logic model can be also be constructed for summative evaluations to answer descriptive or explanatory evaluation questions of existing programs. The purpose of the data-collection methods is to measure the short- and long-term results of the intervention and to measure a relationship (descriptive evaluation) or causal impact (explanatory evaluation) between the strategy or intervention and the measured results.

See case example 17 for an example of two different programs within a university's Office of Disability Services (ODS). The overall goal of ODS is to offer services, programs, and activities that allow students with disabilities to participate in all facets of university life. Two programs offered by ODS to reach this goal are adaptive technology and academic support. Each program has its own set of goals. Each program has its strategies and desired results. Each program goal and results are logically connected to the overall goal of ODS that students with disabilities participate in all facets of university life.

Case Example 17. A Summative Evaluation Logic Model

Below are the logic models for two programs offered at a university office of disability services.

University Office of Disability Services—Program: Adaptive Technology

Goal: Students with disabilities will have access to all university learning venues.

Objective	Strategies	ST results	LT results
1. Ensure computer labs are accessible to all disabled students.	a. Purchase needed equipment. b. Educate students about the equipment.	a. Improve labs. b. Increase use of labs.	In 5 years, 90% of disabled students will be using computer labs.
2. Disabled students will improve their computer skills.	Train students to utilize technology.	Increase the skill level of students using the labs.	Over 5 years, 90% of disabled students using the labs will increase their skills.
3. Disabled students will generalize technology skills outside of campus.	a. Help students buy equipment. b. Train students in their off-campus homes.	a. Increase the number of students with equipment at home. b. Increase the skill level of those using equipment in their homes.	Over 5 years, 50% of disabled students will have equipment in their home. Over 5 years, 50% of disabled students will increase their computer skills with home equipment.

University Office of Disability Services—Program: Academic Support

Goal: Students with disabilities will have access to all university learning venues.

Objective	Strategies	ST results	LT results
1. To ensure that students who are deaf or hard of hearing have access to the same spoken class material as hearing students.	a. Sign-language interpreters b. C-print c. Real-time captioning d. Class notes	Accommodations made in every classroom situation.	Disabled students will have improved test scores & higher GPAs.

2. To ensure that visually impaired students have access to all required printed material for in-class and out-of-class work.	a. Provide required text material in alternative formats. b. Raised-line enhancement of maps, drawings, or use of talking globe. c. Reader or writers in classes such as math and science labs. d. Copies of classmates' notes, read or scanned.	Students with visual impairments will have access to print materials prior to each class.	Students will have improved test scores & higher GPAs.
3. To ensure that students with learning disabilities have access to all academic accommodations & support for which they are eligible.	a. Carefully review documentation and interview students to assess extent of learning disability and accommodations needed. b. Explain verbally and in writing how services are to be accessed. c. Explain how students are required to notify instructors and keep in touch with instructors. d. Remind students often and in as many ways as possible of their responsibilities as students.	a. Students with learning disabilities will know the services of ODS. b. Persons with learning disabilities will actively participate in class and all assignments, develop self-advocacy, time-management, and organization skills.	Students will have improved test scores & higher GPAs.

Some descriptive evaluation questions that may be formulated to evaluate the ODS program of academic support are the following:

1. How do disabled students experience the strategies listed in the logic model? This is a descriptive question that may rely on open-ended, qualitative data collection, such as conducting focus groups with disabled students and asking questions such as, "What is it like to have an interpreter in your class?" This evaluation question is considered a

process evaluation question because the focus is on how the service is interpreted rather than on the outcomes of the service. Another process question might be, "What is it like to receive time and a half to take tests?" This descriptive question may rely on closed-ended, quantitative data collection such as answering surveys that list the strategy and ask the participant to rate how helpful the strategy was for her or him.

2. Are the desired results of academic support reached? This is a descriptive, outcomes evaluation question. The focus is on the achievement of the results rather than on how the services are provided. The data-collection methodology will measure the specific results listed in the logic model. Achievement of the results can demonstrate that the change in the students was related to the academic support provided by ODS staff, but we cannot conclude that the changes were solely caused by ODS services.

Explanatory evaluation statements that may be formulated to evaluate the ODS program of Academic Support are the following:

1. The use of sign-language interpreters will result in hearing-impaired students increasing their scores on exams in each class.
2. The use of sign-language interpreters will result in hearing-impaired students increasing their overall grade point average (GPA).
3. The use of readers and writers will result in visually impaired students increasing their scores on exams in each class.
4. The use of readers and writers will result in visually impaired students increasing their overall grade point average (GPA).

The data-collection methodology to test the above hypotheses (statements of desired results based on the intervention) will need to contain the components of an experimental research design that is described in chapter 10. The components of random assignment to the intervention and having a control group are not feasible in an education setting and thus would not be feasible. Without the experimental design components, one would only be able to demonstrate a relationship between ODS and the changes in student outcomes without ruling out alternative explanations for the results.

Most evaluations of existing programs pose descriptive evaluation questions because it is not feasible or sometimes not ethical to implement an experimental design to test explanatory hypotheses. Descriptive evaluations are still very valuable to a program. Such evaluations help the program staff clarify their program logic model in measurable, observable terms. Stakeholders can have tangible data that demonstrate that the program logic model has been implemented according to design and has reached the desired results, or the results lead to changes in the underlying theories of the program and/or the implementation of different strategies to reach the desired results.

The Council on Social Work Education (CSWE, 2012) requires all social work programs to have clear mission statements, goals, objectives, and outcomes. Further, programs are required to implement an assessment plan that measures the success of the program in reaching the goals, objectives, and outcomes. The CSWE has provided a document that aids social work programs in implementing evaluations to measure the accomplishment of competencies and practice behaviors (Holloway, 2012).

MAJOR POINTS

Theory for evaluation purposes is not so much about building knowledge as it is about justifying the need for the intervention or making decisions about changing interventions. It is not uncommon to find the following questions in an RFP or in required reports for funders related to theory: What is the theory of change? What is the program logic model? How is the intervention supported by evidence-based theory? How is intervention based on best practices? What are the expected outcomes of the program? What all these questions have in common is that answering them requires connecting aspects of the program with desired changes in the targeted population. A logic model was the tool discussed in this chapter to answer the above questions. The logic model must contain goals, strategies, and results. The logic model can be applied to evaluate existing programs or curriculum or to guide the implementation of a needs assessment.

CRITICAL-THINKING QUESTIONS

1. Do you agree more with the quote from Marsh or Thyer that began this chapter? Why or why not? As a social service worker, educator, or student, do you utilize theory in your daily interventions with clients? Why or why not?
2. Does an evaluation need to be theoretically driven? Consult references at the end of this chapter to support your answer.
3. What are the theories of change that drive the interventions at your agency or school? How does your agency or school inform workers, educators, clients, or students of these program theories (e.g., mission statements, brochures, posters)?
4. Which is more important: theory testing or theory building? Consult the references at the end of this chapter to support your answer.
5. How does your agency or school seek input from key stakeholders to agree on a program's theory of change?
6. What are ways that your agency or school tests the efficacy of its program theory?
7. Is there a logic model in your current evaluation? Why or why not? If yes, how is the logic model used to direct evaluation data-collection methods? Are the SCREAM values reflected in the logic model?
8. Refer to case example 17 of two services provided to students with disabilities.
   a. Are there any circumstances in a university setting in which students with disabilities can or should be randomly assigned to ODS services or to no service in order to test the theory that the ODS services result in positive outcomes for disabled students?
   b. Are there any circumstances in a university setting in which students with disabilities can or should be assigned to a comparison group that does not receive the same services as ODS?
9. What are limitations of using a logic model for an agency evaluation? Consult references and resources at the end of this chapter to support your answer.

FURTHER RESOURCES

Centers for Disease Control and Prevention. (n.d.). *Healthier worksite initiative: Logic model.* Retrieved from http://www.cdc.gov/nccdphp/dnpao/hwi/program design/logic_model.htm.

Community Toolbox (n.d.). *Developing a logic model or theory of change.* Lawrence: University of Kansas. Retrieved from http://ctb.ku.edu/en/ tablecontents/sub_section_main_1877.aspx

Public Health Agency of Canada (n.d.). *Integrated strategy on healthy living and chronic diseases: Healthy living program component—Annex A: Logic models.* Retrieved from http://www.phac-aspc.gc.ca/about_apropos/reports/2008-09/ hlcd-vsmc/hl-vs/annex-annexe-a-eng.php.

University of Wisconsin Extension. (2010). *Program development and evaluation: Logic model.* Retrieved from http://www.uwex.edu/ces/pdande/evaluation/ evallogicmodel.html.

U.S. Department of Justice, Bureau of Justice Assistance Center for Program Evaluation and Performance Measurement. (n.d.). *Planning the evaluation: Developing and working with program logic models.* Retrieved from https://www.bja.gov/evaluation/guide/pe4.htm.

DOCUMENTATION TASKS

Construct a logic model for one to three interventions that will be evaluated with all of the following components of the logic model included:

1. Goals
2. Objectives
3. Strategies
4. Short-term results
5. Long-term results
6. Measures of reaching the short-term and long-term results

Are the goals, strategies, and results logically and theoretically linked?

Are the SCREAM values addressed in the logic model?

Conducting Literature Reviews

7

EVALUATION DECISION-MAKING QUESTION

Has a thorough literature review of evidence-based practice related to the interventions being evaluated been conducted?

LITERATURE REVIEWS

The main reason for completing a literature review is to learn from relevant evaluations and research conducted by others as the research relates to a current evaluation. The sources and methods for finding the right literature to review for a given evaluation are discussed a little later. First, I cover what to look for in the literature and how the literature can be helpful in making evaluation decisions.

Social service workers utilize the literature in the following ways:

- Evidence-based theory and practice reported in the literature can help workers in the planning stage select interventions shown to be the most effective under rigorous data-collection designs.
- Exploratory, descriptive, and explanatory evaluation and research reported in the literature can help social service workers make evaluation decisions appropriate to the questions they are posing in the current evaluation.
- Qualitative and quantitative data-collection approaches reported in the literature can help social service workers learn the best data-collection methods to use in their current evaluation.

In addition, social service workers and educators can locate literature that reports statistical or case-study evidence of problems or issues that require social service intervention (e.g., the incidence of family violence reported in a given region or nationwide). They can locate articles offering critiques of the literature. And they can locate editorials discussing experience, conceptual applications, or other criteria.

It is no wonder, then, that students and social service workers alike go in different directions in their evaluation decision making, depending on what they read before, during, and after the evaluation. Some literature will lead workers to certain data-collection decisions. Some literature will lead them to reconceptualize the problem or intervention. Findings can, of course, be contradictory, depending on the problems addressed, the interventions attempted, the data-collection methods employed, and the results obtained.

Even if specific findings are not adopted, the literature review will still have affected the evaluation decision-making process. Social service workers are expected to be critical readers of reported evaluation and research, as is clearly stated in the *Code of Ethics* of the National Association of Social Workers (NASW, 2008) and the Educational Policy Accreditation Standards of the Council on Social Work Education (CSWE, 2012). Critical social service workers are those who question the place of information in the decision-making process and are able to recognize what among the literature will be useful to that process.

A brief discussion now focuses on evidence-based practice and how theory is utilized at different stages to answer exploratory, descriptive, and explanatory questions. References will be made to qualitative and quantitative data-collection approaches, methods that are discussed in more detail in the next chapter.

EVIDENCE-BASED PRACTICE

The term *evidence-based* must be clarified for every evaluation, just as the reader was encouraged in previous chapters to clarify other terms such as *evaluation, stakeholders, strengths, culture, ethical guidelines,* and *multiple systems levels. Evidence-based theory* and *evidence-based practice* are terms that are appearing in many requests for proposals (RFPs), sometimes without any clear indication of how they are being applied in a given situation.

Evidence-based practice in social work has been advocated for a long time, especially in the writings of Gambrill and Gibbs (e.g., Gambrill, 2013; Gambrill & Gibbs, 2009; Gibbs, 2003). It is not my intent to summarize the sources that already exist on evidence-based practice. Interested readers can consult the "Further Resources" section of this chapter. Take the time to read an original source thoroughly if you are going to follow a specific author's application of evidence-based practice. Also, take the time to have stakeholders agree on the terms taken or adapted from the literature on this subject.

Evidence-based practices are the interventions that, on the basis of the most rigorous data collection feasible, have been demonstrated to be effective in the practice setting. Evidence-based literature should be consulted in the planning stage to guide the selection of intervention type. Even if an intervention has already been implemented, the literature can be utilized to help workers adapt or change the intervention.

Stakeholders may direct workers to consult specific sources for evidence-based theory and practices. One source mentioned later in this chapter is the Campbell Collaboration (http://www.campbellcollaboration .org), a literature database sponsored by the University of Pennsylvania. This database currently contains only reports of evaluations and research that were conducted using experimental or quasi-experimental data-collection methods and may contain qualitative data collection in future reviews. The reports are categorized by problem focus. The criteria for inclusion in the database are given on the website.

In all evaluations, decisions are based on some type of evidence, whether it be evidence reported in the literature or evidence gained during the course of conducting the current evaluation. Stakeholders should agree on what evidence is acceptable. Discuss the following issues:

- What are acceptable sources for locating literature as evidence?
- Must the evidence reported in the literature have been collected through specific data-collection methods?
- Will stakeholders accept evidence collected through qualitative approaches or quasi-experimental designs?
- What is unacceptable evidence?
- What are the guidelines for choosing or rejecting literature that is located through a search process?

THEORY BUILDING: EMERGING LITERATURE REVIEWS FOR EXPLORATORY STUDIES

Students and social service workers consulting the literature at the beginning of a project are most likely reading reports of work that has taken years to complete. They must, therefore, be careful to remember that, while they themselves are still wrestling with formulating the scope of their evaluation and making complicated decisions with regard to theory and data collection, the authors to whom they are turning for guidance have that all behind them. Published reports reflect not the early stages of negotiating with stakeholders, but the final stage, that at which negotiations have been concluded and the project itself completed.

Most published reports contain references to the literature the author consulted, which reinforces the point that social service workers and researchers are constantly testing past theories and building new ones. Get in the habit of understanding how the author of an article utilized past literature to guide the evaluation decisions and the inferences reported in the article. Authors sometimes discuss utilizing the literature differently depending on whether their reported evaluation or research was conducted to answer exploratory, descriptive, or explanatory questions.

Stakeholders ask exploratory questions when they want to know the experiences of persons connected to the social service system or when there is little published knowledge about a specific situation, setting, or stakeholder group. While those asking exploratory evaluation questions have usually formulated a working theory, they remain open to new theories encountered during the evaluation process, placing no limits on the scope of responses.

There are times in the program planning and formative evaluation stage when agencies are able to build theory and develop innovative programs based on exploratory evaluation questions. Examples of exploratory questions listed are the following:

- What is it like to have been an educator for more than ten years?
- What happens after clients are discharged from services?
- How do parents predicted to be at risk for child abuse and neglect successfully raise their children?

Take the exploratory question, "How do parents predicted to be at risk for child abuse and neglect successfully raise their children?" The agency logic model was the following: the strategy of providing in-home outreach interventions will result in a decrease in the incidence of child abuse and neglect. When conducting the open-ended, qualitative interviews, the student researcher never heard participants use the words *abuse, neglect,* or *at risk.* Instead, the six participants, all women, described the strengths they called on within themselves, their friends, and their formal supports to help them raise their children. Throughout the study, the researcher consulted literature that supported the effectiveness of the strengths described by parents. The Interactive Model of Coping with Life's Demands emerged from the parent stories and the literature. This model has been used to train social workers to support family strengths when providing in-home services (Brun, 1997).

The literature review occurred more during and after the data-collection process rather than before the data-collection process. The researcher did not want existing or a priori theory to foreground or influence the questions to the participants. The open-ended data-collection methods led to data in the participants' own words that were then compared to studies reporting similar results.

THEORY TESTING: LITERATURE REVIEW FOR EXPLANATORY AND DESCRIPTIVE STUDIES

Stakeholders ask explanatory questions to determine whether an intervention produced the results predicted by theories systematically tested in previous evaluations or research. Persons testing explanatory hypotheses rely on specific, preconceived theories as those theories apply to the current situation. During the testing process, much attention is devoted to replicating or repeating the implementation and evaluation of the intervention as it was reported in the literature. In such evaluations, explanatory statements or hypotheses are used rather than evaluation questions. In the case example of the evaluation of family support interventions (FSIs), a hypothesis tested was "Consumers of FSIs will significantly improve family functioning."

Explanatory evaluations predict that certain relationships between the intervention and changes in the consumers will be found, whereas descriptive evaluations make no such predictions. Explanatory evaluation questions not only target certain program characteristics but also pose answers to the question, "Why did the intervention produce the expected changes?" In the FSI example, methods can be employed to further assess how separate components of the FSIs improved family functioning. Examples of intervention components were assessment, treatment planning, referral, and goal setting.

For example, to test the hypothesis "Consumers of FSIs will significantly improve family functioning," the evaluators consulted the evidence-based literature and made the following data-collection decisions:

- The standardized instrument adapted and used to measure family functioning was called the Family Assessment Device (FAD) and was based on a substantial body of literature substantiating its validity and reliability (Epstein, Baldwin, & Bishop, 1982).
- The results of the implementation of the FAD were compared to those of other studies and included in the final evaluation report.
- The evaluators also conducted separate literature reviews to report the validity and reliability of instruments that measured child health, other measures of family functioning, and parent involvement with children's school performance.

Stakeholders ask descriptive questions when they are planning or implementing interventions based on some preconceived theoretical relationship between the intervention and desired changes in the targeted clients. Those asking descriptive evaluation questions limit the scope of responses by focusing questions. Sometimes they follow open-ended, qualitative approaches and allow participants to answer in their own words, and sometimes they follow closed-ended, quantitative approaches and give participants specific responses from which to choose.

Be clear which approach is being used in the literature you review and how that approach applies to your current evaluation. The case example of the evaluation of strengths-based case management (SBCM) with persons who had abused substances followed an open-ended, qualitative approach. The evaluators were open to the themes that emerged from the participants' responses. These themes were compared to the literature on similar interventions (Brun & Rapp, 2001).

The case example described earlier in this book of direct-care mental health workers' competencies followed a closed-ended, quantitative approach. Participants' responses were compared to the literature base from which the survey was constructed (Clasen, Meyer, Brun, Mase, & Cauley, 2003).

Sometimes, stakeholders may agree that conducting a thorough literature review of evidence-based practice becomes an output of the evaluation. In the evaluation of family resource centers and school-based family resource centers, the funders wanted to have a literature review of the most common measures of child and family outcomes. This literature review was later published (Smith & Brun, 2006).

CONDUCTING A LITERATURE REVIEW

Sources for the Literature Review.

For a list of sources for evaluations and research studies pertinent to your current evaluation, see checklist 19. A university library website is also a valuable resource, allowing you to access most of the sources. Many of the sources can be obtained electronically, which means that at least the initial search for relevant studies can be conducted from your home or office. Eventually, you may find some sources you need that are available only in print. Universities pay a fee to obtain the rights to the electronic sources. For this reason, some university electronic resources may be available only to current students and faculty. Access to literature resources is, thus, an important benefit of university-agency evaluation partnerships.

A common way to locate evaluations and research studies is by conducting a keyword search using an abstract database. An abstract database is a compilation of brief summaries, called abstracts, of published scholarship. The abstracts describe articles that appeared in academic sources (usually peer-reviewed journals), dissertations, and books. A peer-reviewed research article is one that is approved for publication by two or more researchers.

Each database lists the journals from which the abstracts were taken and the time period during which the journals were published. Since persons from different professions work collaboratively and across disciplines, it is best to use more than one database to conduct a keyword search. Some common academic databases used for social service evaluations are the following:

- Education Resources Information Center (ERIC), which contains published and unpublished papers, microfiche, and presentations related to education
- Lexis/Nexis Academic Universe, which contains state and federal legislation and analysis of legislation
- PsycINFO, which contains abstracts of research studies found in psychology
- Social Science Index, which contains abstracts of research studies found in sociology and social work
- Social Work Abstracts, which contains abstracts of research studies found in social work
- MEDLINE, which contains abstracts of research studies found in health and medicine

Depending on the abstract database, the indexed scholarship will usually include results from exploratory, descriptive, and explanatory evaluations and research. It can also include editorials, descriptions of interventions, policy analyses, and case studies. Some databases include

Checklist 19. Sources for a Literature Review

Check all sources used to conduct a literature search for a current evaluation at your agency or practicum setting:

___ University library services
___ University research services
___ Abstract databases
___ Academic journals
___ Reference lists appearing at the ends of published articles
___ National government offices
___ State and local government offices
___ Campbell Collaboration for Evidence-Based Research
___ Internet search engines
___ Organization websites
___ Requests for proposals
___ Funders' websites
___ Books
___ Conference papers
___ Conference proceedings
___ Statistical databases
___ Popular press and media
___ Local and federal policies and legislation

unpublished or non-peer-reviewed papers. Some include media and popular press sources. Clarify with all stakeholders which databases are acceptable.

Evaluation and research literature can also be located through the Internet. Some of the evaluation resources listed at the end of chapter 2 are private and public evaluation groups that include research and evaluation studies, both published and unpublished. There are several different search engines available with which to locate other sites not listed in this book that may relate to your evaluation. Popular search engines include Google and Yahoo. The main limitation to literature located on the Internet is that the studies and results may not have gone through a peer-review process. Again, be clear with stakeholders about the criteria for including or excluding literature located through the Internet.

Method for Conducting the Literature Search.

A keyword literature search is the process of locating abstracts by using the search function of an abstract database, online library-book catalog, or other computerized system in which published scholarship has been compiled and categorized. The search function in most academic databases is conducted by author, title, keyword, or subject. If you know the exact title of an article, then the search function will locate the abstract and publication information. The article itself may be available online through one of several, usually subscription, services. If it is not, or if you do not have access to the service carrying it, you will then need to locate it at a university library or obtain it from the publisher.

If you know the author of a published work related to your evaluation, the search function will locate all persons with that name, which should allow you to locate the correct author and article. The advantage to the author search is that you are likely to discover other, possibly more recent articles by that author that are related to your topic. An author search is more easily conducted through an academic database than through an Internet database. An author search on the Internet will result in literally hundreds, if not thousands, of hits, few of which are likely to be related to your focus.

The most patience and time is required when conducting a keyword or subject search. Enter the words into the search field that you think best describe the focus of your evaluation. The search function will look for the keywords anywhere in the abstract, including the article title. In the evaluation of the family violence prevention planning grant, there were several different subcategories of family violence. The keywords used in conducting a literature search were *family violence, domestic or partner violence, elder abuse, child abuse or neglect, rape or date rape,* and *dating violence.*

These keywords were also matched with the keyword *prevention.* Using the word *and* in a keyword search results in abstracts that contain both sets of keywords, for example, both *family violence* and *prevention.* There may be one thousand references to family violence and three thousand references to prevention but only one hundred references that contain both sets of words. The word *or* in a keyword search results in abstracts that contain either set of keywords, for example, either *child abuse* or *neglect.* There may be five thousand abstracts on child abuse and three thousand abstracts on child neglect, resulting in eight thousand abstracts that contain either set of words.

The *or* command allows you to expand the number of possible articles, whereas the *and* command to narrow the number. For the sake of feasibility, it is best to begin with a list of potential sources that is well under one hundred. Narrowing the search field to most recent years of publication will reduce the number. For other tips on conducting feasible literature searches, see the "Further Resources" section at the end of this chapter.

Case example 18 provides a description of the keyword search conducted in the evaluation of Children's Health Insurance Program outreach programs. The example provides a nice illustration of all the issues connected to conducting a literature review. The evaluators also stated why they used both academic and Internet search engines.

Case Example 18. Conducting a Literature and Website Review

This example relates to the evaluation of statewide outreach efforts to enroll eligible children in the Children's Health Insurance Program (CHIP). One of the products agreed to by stakeholders was a literature and website review. The procedures described here are excerpts from the final grant report (Meyer et al., 2001, pp. 6–9):

The goal of the literature review was to investigate the results from empirical evaluations of outreach interventions that have proved effective or ineffective in increasing child enrollment into public insurance programs.

Sources and Methods for Keyword Search. The databases for the electronic search were: MEDLINE, HealthStar, Cumulative Index to Nursing and Allied Health Literature (CINAHL), Lexis/Nexis Academic Universe, and PsycINFO. The search terms combined *Medicaid* and *CHIP* with *outreach, evaluation of research,* and *enrollment.* This search yielded more than fifty citations, the majority of which were not relevant to the narrow focus of the research. . . . Only three of the articles met the criteria of studies that had examined the impact of outreach strategies on child health insurance enrollment.

The Internet proved to be a much richer source of research data on this topic. Internet searches were performed to locate reports that had not yet been published in journals or books. Using similar terms as in the traditional literature review, we used major search engines including HotBot, AltaVista, Yahoo, Google, Lycos, and Excite. We also visited government websites, including the Centers for Disease Control, state CHIP sites, the Health Care Financing Administration, the Health Resources and Services Administration, and the U.S. General Accounting Office. We also included in the search academic and private health policy and research centers, foundation websites, professional associations, state associations, and child advocacy organizations. Links to other resources were followed at all sites and proved to be a valuable source of downloadable research materials.

Using this method, an additional seventy-five documents were located. Of these, forty are included in the final bibliography. A slight majority of the studies reviewed came from academic or private research centers (twelve), followed by government agencies (ten), foundation-sponsored studies (ten), child advocacy organizations (six), and professional or state associations (two).

Types of Evaluations Included. The authors excluded from the final bibliography those articles that had an overly broad focus on the topic or had general conceptual suggestions without some base of related research. In Internet publications we excluded articles that did not appear to come from a credible source. The bibliography did contain some studies that conveyed focus groups and structured interviews. Because outreach to engage populations not traditionally targeted is at such an early stage, it seemed important to include some of this qualitative research as a base for identifying hypotheses to be tested by outreach programs.

Final Literature Review Report. As mentioned earlier, the evaluators found the Internet to be a valuable resource for results and implications from credible evaluation and result studies. So much so that they wrote a website resource guide as part of the final bibliography. The guide begins with the top five websites, selected on the basis of the credibility of the sponsor, the relevance of the site's information on Medicaid and CHIP outreach, ease of use, comprehensiveness, currency, and value of links to other sites. Thirty-two other sites from the sources listed above were also listed. For each listing we provide information on the sponsor, the web address, the specific topic addressed at the site, a site overview, and a section describing application to Medicaid outreach.

SYSTEMATIC REVIEWS

A **systematic review** is an analysis of multiple studies conducted on the effectiveness of the same intervention. There are some published articles that are comprehensive reviews of the evidence-based studies. The important point is that the systematic review is of the best available research on the studied intervention. Some systematic reviews include a meta-analysis that statistically analyzes the strength of the results from the studies being reviewed. For example, Rapp (2011) conducted a meta-analysis of studies using strengths-based interventions with persons who have abused substances as part of his dissertation on strengths-based case management.

The Campbell Collaboration contains a library of systematic reviews of evidence-based interventions. The interventions fit under the following categories: "crime and justice," "education," "international development," "methods," and "social welfare." Plans for systematic reviews must first be approved by a panel. The criteria for a Campbell systematic review are as follows:

> Campbell reviews must include a systematic search for unpublished reports (to avoid publication bias). Campbell reviews are usually international in scope. A protocol (project plan) for the review is developed in advance and undergoes peer review. Study inclusion and coding decisions are accomplished by at least two reviewers who work independently and compare results. And, Campbell reviews undergo peer review and editorial review. (Campbell Collaboration, n.d.)

As mentioned earlier, the Campbell Collaboration is a good source for locating systematic reviews of interventions one is planning to implement or has already implemented.

CAVEATS ABOUT LITERATURE REVIEWS

Consulting the literature to make planning, practice, and evaluation decisions returns us to the overlap of theory and values. What do the current stakeholders value as being credible evidence: data collected by quantitative, qualitative, or mixed methods? What do current stakeholders value as credible sources of evidence: peer-reviewed sites, websites, and/or international sources? How does one evaluate the credibility of websites that publish evidence-based results?

The chapter started with a discussion of evidence-based practice and will end with an emerging concept of **evidence-informed practice**. Evidence-informed practice relies on evidence from empirical research and evaluation of theory of change conducted by practitioners and planners. It combines the theory-generating practices discussed in the previous chapter with the theory-testing literature discussed in this chapter. Nevo and Slonim-Nevo (2011) provide a good overview of evidence-informed practice with a comprehensive bibliography on the topic.

As more data are available through the Internet and social media, one must be disciplined in citing the sources. Not properly citing one's source of information is plagiarism. The *Publication Manual of the American Psychological Association* (APA, 2011) provides the correct methods for citing all forms of web-based literature and data.

There are other types of literature reviews besides reviews of empirical studies. There are theoretical or conceptual articles that support a theory of change without necessarily having empirical data yet on that theory. There are also reviews of standardized instruments. Some of these are studies of the reliability and validity of the instruments, which are discussed more in part 5.

Review checklist 20 on coming to agreement on the issues surrounding the use of literature reviews to inform a current evaluation.

MAJOR POINTS

The literature review is a tool to analyze research of evidence-based practice related to one's current evaluation. Literature reviews for exploratory evaluations are usually conducted after themes emerge from the open-ended data-collection strategies. Literature reviews for descriptive and explanatory studies are conducted prior to data collection and guide the evaluation question and evaluation methodology. Specific steps for conducting the literature review were discussed. A systematic review is an analysis of prior studies of a similar evidence-based intervention. The purpose of a systematic review is to analyze whether the data from rigorous research have shown a specific intervention to be effective in meeting the desired outcomes.

CRITICAL-THINKING QUESTIONS

1. You are a student intern or a new social service worker and you are asked to begin leading a focus group for children of divorced parents because your supervisor thinks it is a good thing to do. What are the concerns of beginning this group without first conducting a thorough literature review of evidence-based interventions with this population?
2. What are the reasons you think that social service workers, educators, and students do not take the time to complete a thorough literature review before implementing a new intervention?
3. Read an article about a quantitative, descriptive, or explanatory evaluation. Now, read a different article about a qualitative, descriptive, or explanatory evaluation of a similar intervention. What are the differences in how the authors connect the literature to the evaluation question, methodology, and results?
4. Read a systematic review of a similar intervention as you learned about in question 3. How is the systematic review different than the two articles you read for question 3?

FURTHER RESOURCES

American Psychological Association. (2011). *Publication manual of the American Psychological Association* (6th ed.). Washington, DC: Author.
Best Practices in Mental Health. [A journal published by Lyceum Books, Chicago.]
Briggs, H., & Rzepnicki, T. (Eds.). (2004). *Using evidence in social work practice: Behavioral perspectives.* Chicago, IL: Lyceum Books.
Corcoran, J. (2000). *Evidence-based social work practice with families: A lifespan approach.* New York, NY: Springer.

Checklist 20. Agreement on the Literature Review Procedures

Check all that apply for a given evaluation.

It is acceptable to utilize the following resources for the literature review:

___ Peer-reviewed journals

___ Government websites

___ Education websites

___ Agency websites

___ School websites

___ Internet search engines such as Google or Bing

___ Social media such as Facebook or LinkedIn

___ Studies that use qualitative methods

___ Studies that use quantitative methods

___ Other criteria

DOCUMENTATION TASKS

Conduct a literature review of evidence-based practice related to the interventions being evaluated.

List the sources used for the literature review.

List the keywords used for the literature search.

Compose a list of possible abstracts related to the evaluation.

Locate the full articles of those studies most relevant to the evaluation.
For each full article reviewed, provide a one-page summary that includes:

Proper APA citation

Research or evaluation questions posed

Research design: qualitative, experimental, quasi-experiment, single systems

Research protocol:

Sample: How selected? Sample size. Sample demographics.

Data collection: List the instruments used to answer questions, observe, or analyze secondary documents

Data analysis: Themes or statistical

Findings

Implications of this study to your evaluation

Corcoran, K., & Fischer, J. (2007). *Measures for clinical practice and research: A sourcebook* (4th ed., Vols. 1–2). New York, NY: Oxford University Press.

Cournoyer, B. (2004). *The evidence-based social work skills book.* Boston, MA: Pearson, Allyn & Bacon.

DeGennaro, M., & Fogel, S. (2010). *Using evidence to inform practice for community and organizational change.* Chicago, IL: Lyceum Books.

Donaldson, S., Christie, C., & Mark, M. (Eds.). (2009). *What counts as credible evidence in applied research and evaluation practice?* Los Angeles, CA: Sage.

Drisko, J., & Grady, M. (2012). *Evidence-based practice in clinical social work.* New York, NY: Springer.

Fischer, J. (2009). *Toward evidence-based practice: Variations on a theme.* Chicago, IL: Lyceum Books.

Franklin, C., Harris, M., & Allen-Meares, P. (2008). *The school practitioner's concise companion to preventing violence and conflict.* New York, NY: Oxford University Press.

Macdonald, G. (2001). *Effective interventions for child abuse and neglect: An evidence-based approach to planning and evaluating interventions.* New York, NY: Wiley.

O'Hare, T. (2005). *Evidenced-based practices for social workers: An interdisciplinary approach.* Chicago, IL: Lyceum Books.

Shaw, I., Briar-Lawson, K., Orme, J., & Ruckdeschel, R. (Eds.). (2010). *The SAGE handbook of social work research.* Los Angeles, CA: Sage.

DATA-DRIVEN
EVALUATION DECISIONS

V

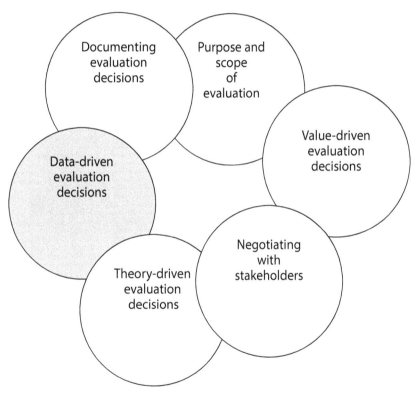

Figure 9.
Interactive model of evaluation: Data-driven evaluation decisions

Research Methods

8

What information is being transformed into data?

What is the research design?

Qualitative

Quantitative

Mixed methods

What is the research protocol for . . .

Selecting evaluation participants?

Selecting the data-collection method?

Analyzing the data?

Ensuring the credibility of the data-collection methods?

This chapter is about research. Go back to chapter 1 and notice the distinction between research and evaluation. Evaluation uses research methods to answer evaluation questions. The term research *is used throughout this chapter.*

This chapter can help social service workers, educators, and students select the best methods for collecting information and transforming that information into data to be used to answer the evaluation questions agreed on by key stakeholders. Ideally, key stakeholders should agree on the following decisions before data collection begins because these decisions influence how the data are collected and analyzed:

- Scope and purpose of the evaluation
- Evaluation stakeholder plan, including timeline
- Ethical and value guidelines
- Use of literature review and logic model

Evaluation is a fluid process that goes back and forth between each of the activities described in the previous chapters. Becoming more involved in the data-collection activities may result in adjusting some of the earlier evaluation activities. Knowing the amount of time needed, for example, to conduct and analyze open-ended and qualitative focus groups with large numbers of participants may influence stakeholders to ask more narrowly focused and descriptive evaluation questions rather than exploratory evaluation questions. Likewise, knowing the ethical dilemmas involved in utilizing a comparison group to increase the credibility of the administration of a closed-ended and quantitative written questionnaire may influence stakeholders to ask descriptive rather than explanatory evaluation questions.

TRANSFORMING INFORMATION INTO DATA

Social service workers and teachers collect information all the time: when they write case notes, when they write individualized education programs (IEPs), when they check a box on an intake form, when they enter numbers into a computerized management information system, and when they submit data for school records. **Data** are information systematically collected for specific evaluation and research purposes. The evaluation purposes discussed in this book are (1) planning new programs; (2) evaluating programs that have been implemented; (3) providing evidence that program characteristics do exist (e.g., for accreditation); and (4) answering exploratory, descriptive, or explanatory evaluation questions. The term *information* has been deliberately used up to this point in the book because the discussion has not yet focused on which information would be collected as *data* to answer specific evaluation questions.

Data collection is the last set of decisions in the evaluation decision-making process discussed in this book. Stakeholder agreement on the prior tasks in the evaluation leads to the selection of the most appropriate data-collection method. For example, clarifying the value "respect culture" as "include consumer participants from all racial backgrounds represented at the agency" may lead to selecting participants according to racial background rather than randomly from the population of all clients. As another example, choosing the theoretical model of implementing and evaluating evidence-based interventions will most likely lead to the application of quantitative and closed-ended data-collection approaches to test whether the intervention is effective in the current setting.

A vague evaluation question can lead to stakeholder disagreement about whether the question is exploratory, descriptive, or explanatory. Some may assume that the purpose of the evaluation is to test the impact of an intervention (i.e., answering an explanatory evaluation question). Others may assume that the purpose is to report different aspects of the intervention without testing its impact (i.e., answering a descriptive evaluation question). The assumption that the evaluation is for explanatory purposes could lead to decisions to end an intervention if the findings are that it did not achieve the expected changes in client outcomes. In contrast, the assumption that the evaluation is for descriptive purposes could lead to changes in the intervention but not necessarily the decision to end it.

Stakeholders should clarify their definition of *data*, just as they are encouraged to clarify other evaluation terms previously covered in this book. Stakeholders come into an evaluation with different knowledge and experiences of evaluation. For this reason, the discussion here briefly covers some common myths about data. These myths are summarized in checklist 21.

Myths about Data.

Myth 1: *Data* is synonymous with the term *survey*. It is common for social service stakeholders to ask, "What is the best survey to evaluate our program?" Collecting information or data by conducting a survey is only one of three basic data-collection methods. The three basic data-collection methods are the following:

1. Asking questions through interviews or surveys
2. Observing people, places, and objects
3. Analyzing data collected and documented by someone other than the current evaluators

Even if a written survey is used to collect data, there are many different ways of asking questions: conducting individual interviews, allowing a participant to answer a mailed survey, and so on. In addition, the results from data collection have more meaning for the stakeholders and are more credible if similar findings are obtained from at least one other data-collection method. Implementing multiple data-collection methods is called **triangulation.**

Myth 2: *Data* is synonymous with the term *focus groups*. Focus groups are becoming a popular method of engaging key stakeholders (e.g., clients, agency workers, persons from the community) as evaluation participants because more than one person can be interviewed at a time. Again, focus groups are only one type of data-collection method. As is explained later, focus groups, interviews, and written questions can be designed according to a closed-ended, quantitative format or an open-ended, qualitative format. Each approach produces different types of results.

Myth 3: *Data* is synonymous with the term *statistics*. Statistical analysis is one method of analyzing data. Data analysis is making sense of and obtaining meaning out of the information gathered in an evaluation. Statistical analysis converts information into numerical values in order to reduce large amounts of information into a format that can be more easily understood and applied. There are different types of statistical analysis. **Descriptive statistics** are the numerical meanings attributed to the distribution of quantitatively collected data. **Inferential statistics** are the numerical meanings attributed to the relationship between quantitatively collected data. A **theme** is the meaning attributed to the narrative data collected qualitatively.

Checklist 21. Clarifying Myths about Data

Check the data myths that are being followed in a current evaluation at your agency or practicum setting:

1. *Data* is synonymous with the term *survey.*
2. *Data* is synonymous with the term *focus groups.*
3. *Data* is synonymous with the term *statistics.*
4. *Data* is synonymous with the term *objective.*
5. *Data* is synonymous with the term *outcomes.*
6. Data alone drive evaluations.
7. Data are utilized only if they are valid and reliable.
8. Data are invisible until there is an evaluation.

Learning basic methods of quantitative statistical analyses is a Council on Social Work Education (CSWE) requirement for undergraduate and graduate programs. There are excellent social work research texts that cover statistical analysis in easy-to-follow and easy-to-apply contexts for students and social service workers. Some of those texts are listed in the "Further Resources" section of this chapter.

Myth 4: *Data* is synonymous with the term *objective*. Just because data were collected for evaluation purposes does not mean that they were collected in an objective, impartial way. Some evaluators begin with the assumption that the collection, analysis, and interpretation of data are of necessity biased by the subjective experiences of the evaluators and the other stakeholders involved in the evaluation process. Evaluators can document how they construct the evaluation process in the midst of the different influences on the evaluation decisions.

Myth 5: *Data* is synonymous with the term *outcomes*. A repeated theme of this book is that the process of evaluation and data collection is as important as the measured results. This is so for several reasons. First, stakeholders who actively participate in making evaluation decisions are prepared to take more control in future evaluations. Second, knowledge and insight obtained during the evaluation process can be applied immediately, long before the entire evaluation process is completed and the results finally analyzed and interpreted. Finally, results are just one component of an evaluation and do not necessarily drive program planning and practice decisions. From the current evaluation process stakeholders can learn reflectively and procedurally how to ensure that future evaluations are better utilized.

Myth 6: Data alone drive evaluations. Clarifying the scope, values, and theories of an evaluation with key stakeholders was discussed first because, in many evaluations, decisions are influenced as much, if not more, by those components. In every evaluation it is ideal to take the time necessary to do the following:

1. Clarify the problem, focus, or evaluation questions
2. Conduct a search of the literature to learn how others have approached similar questions.
3. *Then, and only then*, determine the best data-collection methods to resolve the questions.

A related myth is that data drive agency decision making. The discussion at the beginning of this book pointed out that evaluation is only one tool for influencing agency planning, practice, and policy decisions. Many agency decisions are made without consulting evaluation data. At the same time, the more social service workers use evaluation to improve practice and accountability, the more evaluation can be used to influence agency decisions in the future.

Myth 7: Data are utilized only if they are valid and reliable. The terms *validity* and *reliability* have specific meanings for quantitative approaches to data collection. The term **credibility** is used in this book because it can be applied to quantitative and qualitative data collection. Credibility is the rigorous and systematic collection of qualitative and quantitative data according to the most widely accepted procedures cited in the research and evaluation literature. The credibility of the evaluation results depends on the credibility of the evaluation planning and implementation process.

The results of evaluations that employ credible quantitative approaches reduce the threats to validity and reliability. **Validity** refers to describing or explaining the intended concepts and generalizing from the sample to the larger population. **Reliability** is the consistent measurement of the same concept.

The results of evaluations that employ credible qualitative approaches reduce the threats to the trustworthiness of the data. **Trustworthiness** is the accurate description of the concepts and realities as intended by the participants in the evaluation. The established norms for ensuring the trustworthiness of qualitative data are discussed later in this chapter, as are those for ensuring the validity and reliability of quantitative data. The "Further Resources" section at the end of this chapter contains several references on ensuring the credibility of data collection.

Myth 8: Data are invisible until there is an evaluation. Potential data are everywhere. Numerical data exist in agency management information systems, consumer responses to standardized assessment tools and satisfaction surveys, and communitywide databases. Narrative data exist in workers' case records, consumers' verbal or written goal statements, and agency and community meeting minutes.

As social workers integrate evaluation more routinely into daily interactions with consumers and other stakeholders, the roles of information and data will become interchangeable. Only the data that answer specific evaluation questions should be collected and reported for a specific evaluation. Avoid getting bogged down with information that is not relevant to the specific evaluation questions. Make sure that the important stakeholders are involved in selecting the right evaluation questions since those questions are what will guide planning and practice decisions.

Exploratory questions build theory through qualitative means. Descriptive questions build and test theory through qualitative and quantitative means. And explanatory questions test theory through quantitative processes. The following discussion expands on qualitative and quantitative data-collection approaches.

RESEARCH DESIGNS

The evaluation question is the real transformer of information into data. The evaluation question drives the data-collection process, connecting the current data with theory learned from other studies. Take a few minutes to go back to the discussion in chapter 2 that distinguished exploratory, descriptive, and explanatory questions. Look at figure 2 in chapter 2, which shows the continuum of the type of evaluation question, theory building and theory testing, and the use of qualitative and quantitative approaches.

The entire data-collection process is conducted differently from qualitative and quantitative designs. **Research design** refers to the conditions for collecting data in the most rigorous manner appropriate to the research or evaluation question being asked. The research design is the procedural map for collecting data. Purely exploratory evaluations rigorously follow empirical qualitative approaches. Purely explanatory evaluations rigorously follow empirical quantitative approaches. Descriptive evaluations can follow qualitative, quantitative, or both approaches. See figure 10 for an outline of the data-collection method decisions that are connected to each type of evaluation. These decisions are discussed later in this chapter and in chapters 9–11.

As you begin to develop the evaluation, you can use the table in figure 10 to identify the method decisions you need to make on the basis of the type of evaluation question being asked. Circle the evaluation question being asked and then circle the appropriate methods from that column. Research and evaluation *always* begins with the question!

Evaluation method	Explore	Describe	Explain
Evaluation type	Formative	Formative or summative	Summative
Research design	Qualitative	Qualitative or quasi-experimental	Single-systems experimental group
Participant selection	Purposive	Purposive	Random
Data-collection approach	Qualitative	Qualitative or quantitative	Quantitative
Data-collection method	Asking questions Observation Secondary data	Asking questions Observation Secondary data	Asking questions Observation Secondary data
Data analysis	Themes	Themes or statistics	Statistics
Data credibility	Qualitative methods: Prolonged engagement Member checking Peer debriefing Theme redundancy Audit trail Reflective journaling	Qualitative or quantitative	Quantitative methods: Standardized tests Comparison groups Random selection Inferential statistics Other controls for validity and reliability
Theory	Triangulation Theory building	Triangulation Theory building or theory testing	Triangulation Theory testing

Figure 10.
Data-collection decision-making table

Research protocol refers to the following steps for implementing the research design: selecting the participants, collecting the data, analyzing the data, and ensuring the credibility of the data. The research protocol must be appropriate for the type of evaluation or research question being asked.

It is possible for an evaluation to ask more than one type of evaluation question, but it is important that those questions are not methodologically, philosophically, or theoretically opposed. For example, it is difficult, if not impossible, to ask an explanatory and exploratory question of the same intervention. The explanatory question calls for quantitative, data-collection methods to test the hypothesized relationship between the intervention and client outcomes. The exploratory question calls for emerging themes that may not be related to the intervention or predetermined outcomes.

The terms *qualitative approach* and *quantitative approach* are used rather than the terms *qualitative method* and *quantitative method*. The term *approach* connotes how decisions are made throughout the entire evaluation process. The terms *qualitative method* and *quantitative method* often refer to only one component of the entire evaluation, that is, the information-gathering process, more often called data collection. The term *method* implies a practical, procedural process devoid of underlying values and theoretical premises shaping the planning, practice, and evaluation decisions.

Before discussing each data-collection step, I briefly cover the general differences among qualitative, quantitative, and mixed methods approaches to data collection. **Mixed methods** refer to the use of both quantitative and qualitative data-collection approaches in the same evaluation.

Qualitative Research Designs.

Qualitative research designs refer to the gathering of information in an open-ended manner to answer exploratory or descriptive evaluation questions. As mentioned in the previous chapter, qualitative approaches are used to answer exploratory or descriptive evaluation questions. They are used primarily in formative evaluations. Stakeholders want to know the experiences of persons connected to the program or are seeking information about a specific situation, setting, or stakeholder group on which very little has been published.

In qualitative approaches, stakeholders are open to the responses given in the participants' own words and spend much time planning the best way to systematically and rigorously capture the important characteristics that emerge from the participants. The participants—including consumers of services, because consumers know best their own perceptions of the intervention—become the experts on the evaluation question. In the dissertation study discussed throughout this book (Brun, 1997), only the perceptions of parents were collected as data, whereas in the strengths-based case management (SBCM) program, perceptions of clients and workers were collected as data. Be clear in qualitative approaches how the data, including the literature reviewed, lend authority to the interpretation of results.

Qualitative approaches generate new or affirm current program theory on the basis of the information gathered. Theory generated from qualitative approaches to data collection was discussed in chapter 6. Qualitative approaches to answering exploratory questions are open to theory that is learned throughout the evaluation. Qualitative approaches to answering descriptive questions already have some beginning theoretical framework. The open-ended responses to the qualitative focus groups with family support intervention (FSI) stakeholders were grouped according to the following predetermined, targeted systems for change: individuals, families, the agency, and/or the community.

There is a large range of theoretical paradigms that apply qualitative research methods. Several resources are contained at the end of this chapter to refer readers to more in-depth discussions about the different theoretical frameworks that utilize qualitative methods.

Quantitative Research Designs.

Quantitative research designs refer to the gathering of information in a closed-ended manner to answer descriptive or explanatory evaluation questions. As mentioned in the previous chapter, some evaluations are conducted to determine whether an intervention produced the results predicted by theories empirically tested in previous evaluations or research. They are used primarily in summative evaluations. In such evaluations, explanatory statements or hypotheses are used rather than evaluation questions. In the evaluation of FSIs, one hypothesis tested was "Consumers of the FSIs will significantly improve family functioning."

In quantitative approaches, stakeholders predetermine the closed-ended responses that the participants can choose during the data-collection procedures. The process of narrowing the foci of the evaluation through quantitative processes before collecting information from participants results in different evaluation decisions than are made in qualitative designs. In quantitative approaches, much time is spent planning the best evaluation to systematically and rigorously measure predetermined characteristics.

Recall the discussion in chapter 6 of logic models. Quantitative logic models describe or test program theory that already exists before collecting more information. The experts guiding explanatory evaluation questions are most often the authors of the theories that have been tested in other settings. The research literature becomes the basis for designing the evaluation and intervention. Social service workers are held accountable for carrying out the intervention and evaluation according to the theorized relations supported by prior research. The evidence-based research literature takes priority over the social service workers' and consumers' experiences. The range of different quantitative designs are discussed in chapter 10.

Mixed-Methods Research Designs.

Many advocate the application of a mixed-methods research design, that is, both qualitative and quantitative data collection, for evaluation. Four reasons for the use of mixed-methods data collection are discussed here. The discussion ends by noting the confusion that can occur when mixing qualitative and quantitative approaches to answer more than one type of evaluation question.

First, a mixed-methods approach is used because narrative responses from qualitative, open-ended data-collection methods can affirm responses from quantitative, closed-ended methods. In the descriptive evaluation of direct-care mental health workers' competencies, the responses to the qualitative focus-group questions matched some of the same competencies prioritized in the quantitative mail survey. Many evaluations use direct quotes from participants to illustrate the results presented in statistical terms. The qualitatively collected direct quotes emphasize the qualitatively collected findings.

Second, responses to open-ended questions on a qualitative data-collection instrument can shed light on unexpected responses to closed-ended questions on a quantitative instrument. For example, in the evaluation of FSIs, a telephone survey using a standardized instrument to measure family functioning was used to test the explanatory evaluation hypothesis that consumers receiving FSIs would see significant improvement in family functioning compared to those not receiving FSIs. The expected results were not obtained. Responses by staff to open-ended interviews conducted in the same evaluation demonstrated that stakeholders from the various FSIs did not necessarily conceptualize the term *family functioning* or the underlying program theory in the same way. Such variation could explain why there were no significant changes in the quantitative measures.

Third, the combination of both qualitative and quantitative approaches helps bridge planning, practice, and evaluation. Qualitative approaches were administered in the evaluation of an SBCM intervention that had previously proved effective through quantitative methods. One of the findings of the qualitative interviews was that some participants did not trust the case worker's focus on strengths. This finding sparked the practice question, "How can we implement the SBCM in such a manner as to identify this possible obstacle?"

Fourth, quantitative approaches can be used to verify qualitative findings. Data collected through open-ended approaches can be quantified. For example, one can count how often a similar theme was repeated. Often, in descriptive evaluations using open-ended questions, one can quantify the responses to those open-ended questions. For example, on a survey to teachers, there was the following open-ended question: "What do you think are the five most occurring mental health concerns for students in your school?" The evaluators counted the responses. Going into the study, the project directors thought that bullying would be the number-one concern. Instead, depression was listed the most across all participants.

Mixed data-collection methods can provide comprehensive information to answer descriptive evaluation questions. Both quantitative and qualitative approaches were used in the descriptive evaluation to determine core competencies for direct-care mental health workers. In this evaluation, the following stakeholders completed a closed-ended-format survey that listed twenty-six competencies formulated on the basis of the literature and the evaluation advisory group: administrators, direct-care workers, supervisors, and consumer advocates. In that same evaluation, follow-up, open-ended focus groups were conducted with representatives from the same constituencies. The open-ended focus-group questions allowed the participants to explain in more detail the meaning of the prioritized competencies. Future required training of mental health workers in the participating agencies was based on the selection of the top five competencies and the comments from the focus groups.

Mixed data-collection methods may not be appropriate in an evaluation that contains both exploratory and explanatory questions. It is difficult to rigorously apply the methods for both approaches at the same time. For example, how can practitioners explore multiple emergent possibilities (i.e., teachers identifying depression as the top mental health concern for youth) and at the same time test a predetermined hypothesis (i.e., predicting that bullying will be the top concern)? Mixed data-collection methods allow one to be in a theory-building and theory-testing stage simultaneously.

RESEARCH PROTOCOL

The discussion moves now from overall research design to the research protocol. Go back to figure 10 to see the list of the different data-collection protocols according to qualitative and quantitative approaches and according to the type of evaluation question asked: exploratory, descriptive, or explanatory. Reference will be made to how each step of the research process is done differently from a qualitative, quantitative, and mixed-methods approach. More detail is given about the research protocol from each of these approaches in chapters 9–11.

Participant Selection.

The first data-collection decision is, who will be invited to participate in the evaluation and why? Evaluation participants are those persons from whom data are collected for research or evaluation purposes. The use of the term *participants*, rather than the research term *subjects*, illustrates that people, not objects, are the source of information. Even when the sources of information are secondary documents such as case records, the documents are about human behavior. The term *participants* is also a reminder that there are special ethical considerations in social service evaluation because it involves human subjects.

As discussed in chapter 5, stakeholders can advise the evaluation process and also be participants from whom data are collected. In the needs assessment conducted for the purpose of developing a countywide family violence prevention plan, social service directors of family violence prevention agencies served on the planning and evaluation advisory board. Some of these same persons became participants when they completed a provider survey about the services offered at their agencies. Stakeholders, including the funding source, were aware of this dual role of some stakeholders. In final reports, and even in media accounts of the information collected during the planning process, the sources of information were clearly acknowledged. There was never an intent to hide the overlapping roles that some persons played in advising and providing data for the planning and evaluation process.

Purposive selection means that the participants were chosen on the basis of specific criteria addressed in the evaluation question. Purposive selection is used for all exploratory questions and some descriptive questions. For example, in many evaluations, educators and social service providers want to collect data from students, clients, or consumers of one or more courses or interventions. Those participants are selected because they utilize the service or are in the class. In several evaluations described in this book, different service providers (agency directors, program managers, supervisors, and direct-care staff) were selected in order to understand the implementation of a program from their perspective. The results of the evaluation can be **generalized** only to the persons selected for the evaluation. Thus, a rich and thick description of the **context** pertinent to the participants allows readers of the evaluation results to determine if other persons with similar contexts may have similar results.

Random selection means that any person in the larger **population** has an equal chance of being selected to participate in the evaluation. Random selection is used for all explanatory questions and some descriptive questions. Population refers to the group to which the results can be generalized. For example, if one wants to assess the impact of an undergraduate social work program on the 300 majors and that evaluation uses random selection to collect data from 150 of those majors, the population is the 300 majors and the **sample** is the 150 selected. Random selection means that all 300 majors have an equal chance to be in the evaluation. Sometimes, a stratified, random-sampling method is used to attempt to select participants from subgroups represented proportionally to the population demographics. For example, if the breakdown of the 300 majors is 100 sophomores, 100 juniors, and 100 seniors, a stratified random-sampling method would randomly select 50 students from each group: sophomores, juniors, and seniors.

Data-Collection Methods.

The three general ways to collect data are (1) to ask questions through face-to-face interviews or self-administered surveys and instruments; (2) to observe people, places, and objects; and (3) to collect secondary documents, that is, information and data collected, analyzed, and reported by someone else. All three data-collection methods can be implemented through qualitative or quantitative approaches. The discussion here makes no assumptions as to which approach readers are implementing in their current evaluation.

Questions can be asked through a face-to-face interview with one or more persons. Individuals can answer written questions handed to them, mailed to them, asked of them over the phone, or asked of them via the Internet. The questions can have set, predetermined answers (quantitative), or they can be the type that respondents can answer in their own words (qualitative). The results can be reported individually by question (qualitative or quantitative) or collectively for all questions (quantitative). Responses can be reported as statistics (quantitative) or as themes and actual quotes (qualitative). The evaluators and local stakeholders can write the questions (qualitative or quantitative), or a standardized instrument can be implemented (quantitative). Many evaluators construct surveys that combine questions from standardized instruments with questions of local interest.

It is important to understand the different data one will receive when asking open-ended, qualitative questions as opposed to closed-ended, quantitative questions. For example, write a one- to two-paragraph answer to the open-ended question, "Why are you taking a class on evaluation?" Now, go back and complete the closed-end survey from checklist 1, "Why People Evaluate." How did your answers from each approach vary? What was captured differently? What was captured the same?

Observations of a person's behaviors can be self-reported, reported by a person familiar with the person observed, or reported by a person who has no relationship with the participant. Observations can also be made of places and objects. For example, persons conducting a home visit often routinely record their observations of the physical environment. The observational documentation could take the form of a written, open-ended narrative description based on general categories (e.g., cleanliness, safety, neatness) or no categories (qualitative approach) or of a closed-ended observation sheet on which boxes are checked off (quantitative approach).

To understand the difference between qualitative and quantitative observations, think of the overall descriptive evaluation question, "Will social service and education students be able to conduct an evaluation in a rigorous and systemically correct way?" A person conducting a qualitative observation would watch a student perform evaluation tasks and write all that he or she sees the student do in the evaluation. A person conducting a quantitative observation will check the appropriate boxes from a list of evaluation tasks expected of the student. In the first example, the observation may include skills not on the quantitative list.

Secondary documents are sources of information recorded by someone else prior to the current evaluation that are used to help answer the current evaluation questions. Secondary documents are not restricted to written materials. They can include video and audio recordings, photographs, images on a website, dance, music, theater, and other expressions of thoughts and feelings. Secondary documents need not necessarily contain an analysis of the information. An agency annual report that includes evaluation outcomes is one document, and another person's written critique of that report is a separate document.

In a qualitative evaluation, the documents selected for analysis emerge from the participants, whereas in a quantitative evaluation, the evaluation stakeholders select documents for analysis. Think of the same descriptive evaluation question as stated earlier: "Will social service and education students be able to conduct an evaluation in a rigorous and systemically correct way?" From a qualitative approach, the evaluator may ask students to provide the documents that they utilize to conduct an evaluation. The documents could be evaluation texts, lecture notes, or documentation notes. From a quantitative approach, the evaluator may have a checklist of items needed to conduct an evaluation, and then the evaluator would check whether or not the evaluator used those documents. The qualitative approach may result in learning about documents used by the student that were not predicted on the predetermined list. At the same time, from a qualitative approach, the student may omit documents that were predicted to be present from the quantitative, closed-ended checklist.

As discussed earlier, triangulation is the process of implementing multiple data-collection methods in the same evaluation. Methodologically, triangulation increases the credibility of the results because the same evaluation questions are answered by more than one data-collection strategy. This increased credibility is a big reason that there have been calls for mixed-methods evaluations. Examples of evaluations that used multiple data-collection methods and both qualitative and quantitative approaches are provided in chapter 11.

Data Analysis.

Data analysis is the process of making sense and meaning of information gathered in an evaluation. Data analysis is first a process of reducing the original information into a form that can be more easily managed and understood within the theoretical context of the evaluation. Once the original information is reduced, data analysis becomes a process of interpreting the connection between the findings and the evaluation questions.

Open-ended, qualitative data are reduced to themes, whereas closed-ended, quantitative data are reduced to **statistical analyses.** Some open-ended interviews or focus groups may contain hundreds of pages of transcriptions and notes related to the participants' answers to the questions. Stakeholders would rather have a summary of the important themes and content. The process of rigorously and systematically reducing open-ended data to themes is discussed in chapter 9. Similarly, survey data from hundreds of participants result in hundreds of pages of data. Rather than reading all of the answers from each participant, stakeholders would rather read the statistics that describe the overall response to each question and statistics that help stakeholders draw conclusions about the relationship between the answers to two or more questions. The process of rigorously and systematically reducing closed-ended data to statistics is discussed in chapter 10.

Now that the original data are reduced to manageable themes or statistics, how are the results interpreted and connected to theory? In very general terms, qualitative approaches to data analysis are open to the theories that emerge from the data and are not limited to analyzing the data from predetermined theories. In the quantitative approach to data analysis, there is a specific theoretical relationship between intervention and client or student change that is tested (explanatory evaluation) or described (descriptive evaluation). There is a constant cycle connecting the evaluation question, theory building, and theory testing, on the one hand, and qualitative and quantitative approaches, on the other hand.

In a mixed-methods evaluation, data analysis can be different than the approach used to collect the data. The results of open-ended focus groups (qualitative approach) can be organized into predetermined categories on the basis of a specific theory or model (quantitative approach). Similarly, documents that participants select and choose to give to the evaluators (qualitative approach) can be analyzed by category on the basis of a specific theory or model (quantitative approach). Surveys that contain closed-ended questions (quantitative approach) often also contain open-ended questions (qualitative approach). The data analysis can compare the answers that were narrowly focused by the evaluators (quantitative approach) to the answers that emerged from the participants (qualitative approach). Except for purely exploratory and purely explanatory evaluations, the entire evaluation process can be a combination of qualitative and quantitative approaches.

The data analysis process is less cumbersome when persons collect only information relating to the evaluation questions. This avoids the presence of data that distract from the original questions. Keeping the focus narrow is always difficult because of natural human curiosity.

Keeping the focus narrow is even more difficult in qualitative approaches. A goal of qualitative data collection is to learn what is relevant or important to the participants. The possible boundaries or categories are not exhausted until the practitioner has had prolonged engagement in the natural setting of the participants, that is, until the researcher has observed and interviewed the participants to the point of theme redundancy. Those themes narrow the focus from the wide range of possible foci that were present when the researcher or evaluator first entered the setting.

The focus in quantitative approaches is on answering descriptive and explanatory questions and is already narrowed down to certain specified categories. Thus, the data collected should be pertinent to the characteristics already identified in the literature and by key evaluation stakeholders. The evaluation becomes the place to test whether those characteristics are present in the current setting.

The data analysis procedures must also match the evaluation questions being asked. Thus, qualitative approaches to data analysis will not answer explanatory questions, and quantitative approaches will not answer exploratory questions. The middle-ground descriptive questions can be answered through qualitative and quantitative approaches.

Data Credibility.

There are many techniques that the evaluator can employ to increase the credibility of the data-collection and analysis process. **Credibility** is the rigorous and systematic collection of qualitative and quantitative data according to the accepted procedures cited in the evaluation and research literature. Literally, can the results be believed? In qualitative approaches, steps are taken to ensure that the evaluator has captured the participants' stories and concepts accurately in the view of the participants and within the contexts captured by all data. In other words, do the participants believe the conclusions being made from their data? If not, why not? In quantitative approaches, steps are taken to reduce external influences of the results, including **biases** of the evaluator and other stakeholders. The purpose of collecting the data is to determine whether there is a believable connection between the intervention and desired results when ruling out external influences. If there isn't, why not?

The research design and research protocol directly affect the credibility of the data. In qualitative approaches, credibility is achieved through techniques that increase the trustworthiness of the data, that is, the accurate description of the concepts and realities as intended by the evaluation participants. The techniques for reaching credibility of qualitative data are described in chapter 9 and include prolonged engagement, member checking, peer debriefing, theme redundancy, audit trails of evaluation decision making, reflective journaling, and triangulation of data-collection methods.

In quantitative approaches, credibility is achieved through techniques that increase reliability and validity of the data collection and results. Reliability refers to the data being collected consistently and in the same manner. Validity refers to collecting data that are pertinent to the evaluation question and items being evaluated. Both reliability and validity are achieved through the research design (experimental or quasi-experimental), participant selection (random), data collection (using reliable and valid instruments), and data analysis (descriptive and inferential statistics). The goal of reliability and validity is to rule out external explanations for the presumed relationship between program and desired results. More discussion on quantitative methods of credibility is provided in chapter 11.

MAJOR POINTS

The ultimate learning outcome for part 5, "Data-Driven Evaluations," is for the reader to develop and implement a data-collection plan for an evaluation in her or his agency or field education setting. Selecting the appropriate methods for transforming information into data to answer evaluation questions builds on all the decisions that have been discussed in the previous chapters. The discussion in this chapter included myths about data and how information is transformed into data during the research process. The overall process that guides data collection is called the research design. Within the research design is the research protocol for selecting participants, collecting data, analyzing the data, and assuring the credibility of the data. The discussion throughout the entire chapter illustrated that qualitative and quantitative approaches can be used exclusively or together in the same evaluation. Each of these approaches (qualitative, quantitative, and mixed methods) is discussed in more detail in chapters 9–11.

CRITICAL-THINKING QUESTIONS

1. What are your reactions to the myths about data discussed at the beginning of the chapter? Do you agree with any of the myths? Do you feel that some of them should actually guide evaluations?
2. What are your reactions to the discussion about qualitative and quantitative approaches to data collection? Which approach do you favor and why? What skills or knowledge do you need to better master either or both approaches?
3. Which methods of participant selection—random or purposive—do you support more and why?
4. What data-collection methods discussed in this chapter do you want to learn more about? Set a contract with yourself to read one of the books cited in this chapter related to those methods.
5. What data analysis methods discussed in this chapter do you want to learn more about? Set a contract with yourself to read one of the books cited in this chapter related to those methods.
6. Do you feel that evaluators can control the setting and, thereby, remain objective and keep their biases from influencing the evaluation? Do you feel that evaluators always influence the evaluation participants and results? Which methods of obtaining evaluation credibility do you have the most confidence in?

DOCUMENTATION TASKS

What information is being transformed into data?

What is the overall research design?

    Qualitative
    Quantitative
    Mixed methods

What is the overall research protocol for?

    Selecting evaluation participants?
    Selecting the data-collection method?
    Analyzing the data?
    Ensuring the credibility of the data-collection methods?

7. Everyone in the classroom write a one- to two-paragraph answer to the question, "What is it like to be in an evaluation class?" Go around the room and hear everyone's answers. Develop categories in which all of the answers can be grouped. Now, develop a closed-ended survey that lists the specific categories based on the answers from you and your peers.

FURTHER RESOURCES

Creswell, J. (2012). *Educational research: Planning, conducting, and evaluating quantitative and qualitative research* (4th ed.). Boston, MA: Pearson.

Creswell, J. (2013). *Qualitative inquiry and research design: Choosing among five approaches* (3rd ed.). Los Angeles, CA: Sage.

Creswell, J., & Plano Clark, V. (2011). *Designing and conducting mixed-methods research* (2nd ed.). Los Angeles, CA: Sage.

Mertens, D. (2010). *Research and evaluation in education and psychology: Integrating diversity with quantitative, qualitative, and mixed-methods.* Los Angeles, CA: Sage.

Patton, M. (2012). *Essentials of utilization-focused evaluation* (5th ed.). Thousand Oaks, CA: Sage.

Plano Clark, V., & Creswell, J. (Eds.). (2008). *The mixed-methods reader.* Thousand Oaks, CA: Sage.

Qualitative Research Designs: Exploratory Evaluation Questions

9

EVALUATION DECISION-MAKING QUESTIONS

Are the evaluation conditions appropriate for a qualitative exploratory research design?

How are the participants purposively selected?

How are data qualitatively collected?

    ___ Individual interviews

    ___ Focus groups

    ___ Written surveys

    ___ Observation

    ___ Secondary documents

How are data qualitatively analyzed?

    ___ Audiotaped

    ___ Videotaped

    ___ Transcription procedures

    ___ Theme-analysis procedures

How is the credibility of the data qualitatively ensured?

    ___ Member checking

    ___ Peer debriefing

    ___ Evaluation audit

    ___ Triangulation

EVALUATION CONDITIONS APPROPRIATE FOR A
QUALITATIVE RESEARCH DESIGN

In this chapter and the entire text, I discuss research design from a practical, procedural perspective rather than a specific, theoretical perspective. Qualitative methods are interdisciplinary. They are used in education, nursing, psychology, social work, sociology, and anthropology. Rigorous, agreed-on procedures have been developed that cross all of those disciplines. Those common, qualitative procedures are the focus of this chapter.

Qualitative methods are often described theoretically as following a **post-positivist** paradigm or framework. A **positivist** paradigm views the world as being measurable and predictable. In very general terms, a positivist worldview is to objectively measure causal relationships. In evaluation terms, that would be to measure the effectiveness of an intervention on desired client or student change. A positivist approach is to control the evaluation setting to rule out alternative explanations for the desired outcomes. Post-positivists begin with the assumption that one can never be totally objective. We, as human beings, can never be totally objective. We are subjective and selective beginning with choosing what we plan to evaluate. These two worldviews, positivist and post-positivist, guide the procedures that are discussed in this and the next chapter.

Within a post-positivist paradigm, there are many other theoretical frameworks that utilize qualitative methods. Feminist theory supports a post-positivist paradigm because many theories of human development were based on positivist theories conducted by men on men but then generalized to women. A post-positivist feminist approach values the voices of each participant in helping develop themes that emerge from the data. Constructivist approaches place importance on how the researcher becomes part of the data. We all construct reality from our own experiences and views. Thus, a constructivist approach values the procedures for documenting researcher biases throughout the research process. There are several resources at the end of this chapter that provide much more in-depth discussion of the different theories and paradigms that use qualitative research methods.

PURPOSIVE PARTICIPANT SELECTION

In evaluations that answer exploratory questions, participants who best fit the experiences specified in the question are selected. In an exploratory study with parents, the overall question asked was, "How do parents predicted to be at risk for child abuse and neglect successfully raise their children?" This exploratory question was chosen because there was minimal empirical research literature on this specific question. **Empirical** research refers to the published, peer-reviewed dissemination of the results of studies that applied credible data-collection methods. Empirical research includes credible qualitative and quantitative approaches.

Practitioners should be critical of authors' interpretations of evaluations found in reports, conference presentations, and journal articles, including connections made between the results of an evaluation and the empirical literature. For items that should be included when reporting the results of qualitative approaches, refer to the "Further Resources" section at the end of this chapter.

Most of the empirical research consulted for the study with the parents mentioned above that related to risk factors for child abuse and neglect concentrated on social service workers' and researchers' conceptualization of the causes of child abuse. Some of those theories focused on parent characteristics (e.g., parent was abused as a child, parent abuses substances, parent has a mental illness) as the primary cause of abuse and neglect. Some focused on environmental characteristics (e.g., the family lives in poverty, the family lives in a high-crime neighborhood). The study's final research question focused on how parents who were identified as at risk for child abuse and neglect perceived their own parenting skills. The obtained data—parents' experiences related in their own words—were then compared to the existing empirical literature.

Purposive participant selection means that participants were selected on the basis of specific criteria addressed in the evaluation question. The participants are not randomly chosen as in explanatory and some descriptive evaluations. The procedural journal is where the evaluator can offer important proof that participants were purposively selected. Keeping a record of evaluation decisions—why specific data-collection methods were chosen, whether procedural changes were questioned, the negotiation process by which such questions were resolved—ensures the credibility of qualitative approaches.

The purposive sample reached in the study of parents was a homogeneous sample of six women raising children: some alone and some with a partner. All participants were receiving preventative services from the same agency. Fathers and mothers were invited to participate, but none of the fathers chose to participate.

Alternative selection decisions by other researchers could have resulted in a different group of participants and, thus, different results. Some of the alternative decisions that could have been made were (1) to invite participants from one or more agencies, (2) to select participants in such a way that diversity was ensured in terms of gender and age, or (3) to solicit participants from the general public through advertisements run in newspapers or posted in public places such as doctors' offices, social service agencies, grocery stores, and Laundromats.

Another important decision made in this example was who *not* to select for information gathering. The researcher chose to interview only parents. He deliberately chose not to interview social service workers because he did not want their perceptions to deflect attention from the experiences of the parents.

The results of the research were reported in a doctoral dissertation and at the national Head Start conference, from which an article was published (Brun, 1997). All of these reports discussed the fact that the participant selection process resulted in a sample—six women, five of whom were African American and all of whom were between the ages of twenty-one and thirty-five—that was small and not necessarily representative. Still, however, the reports were useful because of the rich, contextual information about participants that each supplied. A separate chapter offering detailed case studies of all participants appeared in the dissertation. Connections were also made between common themes expressed by the participants and the discussion, or lack thereof, of these same themes in the empirical literature. Readers of these reports could be critical of the interpretation of results and determine whether the findings apply to consumers of their social services.

Another example of a purposive sample is from the evaluation of veterans who were in strengths-based case management (SBCM) to prevent further substance abuse. The overall evaluation question was, "How do consumers experience SBCM?" Prior empirical research reported in the literature and obtained from evaluations previously conducted at the agency demonstrated the effectiveness of SBCM with substance abuse populations. The results of the new evaluation could provide experiences from the consumers' perspective that may or may not support the effectiveness of the SBCM. The participants gave information about areas of SBCM not analyzed in prior empirical research.

The participants were purposively selected because a key stakeholder, the director of the intervention, wanted to limit the evaluation to persons currently participating in SBCM. Because of limited available funding, only persons referred to SBCM within a six-month period were invited to participate in the evaluation. The stakeholders agreed that the evaluator would interview the three caseworkers who delivered the services to assess the match between the workers' and the consumers' perceptions of the intervention.

The interpretation of the results from this evaluation appeared in a final report, a presentation given at a national conference, and an article published in a peer-reviewed journal (Brun & Rapp, 2001). The authors noted the limitations imposed by the small sample size but noted the high percentage of participants who participated in all three interviews. The results—presented as common themes with brief social histories given about some of the participants—offered information not reported in previous research (namely, the consumers' mistrust of the approach) as well as consumers' descriptions of the positive impact of SBCM. Approximately one-third of the participants reported no substance use during the six-month evaluation period, a result that matched the findings of prior research in this same setting. Persons attending the presentation or reading the reports must assess the results critically to determine whether the knowledge gained from the evaluation can be applied to the stakeholders to whom they provide similar services.

This example also demonstrates the importance of **outlier** data. *Outlier* means that the response was not similar to any other participant. In the SBCM study, one African American man stated that he did not trust the strengths-based approach. He was the only participant who had a negative perception of the approach. His reasoning was that in his past, the only time anyone ever said something good to him was because they wanted something from him, usually money for substances. Learning more about his contextual situations allowed the caseworkers to understand how others may also feel manipulated by hearing positive comments. So, instead of ignoring the outlier, qualitative approaches seek an understanding from outlier data.

How many participants are needed in evaluations using qualitative approaches? Methodologically speaking, qualitative and quantitative approaches differ in terms of the number of participants needed to answer the evaluation question. When the approach is qualitative, participants are selected until theme redundancy is reached. **Theme redundancy** is when conceptual patterns or themes will be repeated if persons possessing the same characteristics are selected. In the study of parents considered to be at risk for child abuse or neglect, the dissertation committee and additional peer reviewers agreed that theme redundancy had occurred across the six women interviewed because of the similarities in their backgrounds and experiences. Had the researcher chosen to change the research focus to comparing mothers' and fathers' perceptions of parenting, then he would have had to purposively include fathers in the research. Still, the exclusion of fathers was not itself purposive. The researcher began the selection process without limiting his focus to women. But, while there were fathers in the homes of five of the six women interviewed, none chose to participate.

In the SBCM evaluation, no new themes were reported from men selected in the third month of the evaluation period compared to the first two months. Throughout the evaluation period, no women were referred to the program, in which only about three women annually participate.

Checklist 22 is a summary of the points to consider when selecting participants through qualitative, purposive, and nonrandom approaches.

QUALITATIVE DATA COLLECTION

Asking Questions.

Qualitative, face-to-face interviews can be conducted with individuals or groups to answer exploratory or descriptive evaluation questions. Qualitative individual interviews were conducted in the research study that answered the exploratory question "How do parents predicted to be at risk for child abuse and neglect successfully raise their children?" Qualitative individual interviews were conducted in the evaluation that answered the descriptive question "How do consumers experience SBCM?" In both examples, the participants were purposively selected in consultation with key stakeholders because their backgrounds fit the exploratory question.

The interviews took place in the participants' **natural setting**, that is, a place that was familiar to the participants and, thus, not distracting. In the first example, all the interviews took place in participants' homes at a time they chose. In the second example, the first interview took place when the SBCM participants were in a residential facility and had not yet begun SBCM. This facility served as a thirty-day transition from the hospital where they received substance abuse detoxification treatment to their eventual independent or semi-independent housing in the community. The second interview took place in a private office in the SBCM care manager's building. The third interview took place in participants' community residences.

In both examples, the same person asked the questions of each participant and followed the same **interview guide**, which is a set of general questions that allow participants to describe their experiences about a subject in their own words. See case example 19 for the list of questions asked in the three interviews with parents.

Case Example 19. Exploratory, Qualitative, Face-to-Face Interview Guide

The following interview guide was used in the exploratory study with six parents.

To be covered in the first interview:

____ The purpose of my interview is to learn in your own words the experiences you have had as a parent. Parenting is often defined by the researchers rather than the parents. I want this interview to be a mutual effort where we both choose the topics to talk about.

____ If it is OK, I would like to turn on the tape recorder now in order to get all of the information from the interview.

____ The study is for parents age 21–35, with three or fewer children living with them. The children are eleven years old or younger, and they have not had a finding of child abuse or neglect report.

____ Next, let me go over the details of the interviews by going over the consent form.

____ The report will be in the library and will be read by other social workers and researchers.

____ Let me start by asking you, "How has it been to raise your child(ren)? What has it been like to be a parent?"

____ What has been enjoyable about being a parent?

____ How would you have liked to do things differently?

Checklist 22. Purposive Participant Selection

Complete this checklist for a current evaluation. Examples are given after each item.

___ 1. Write the *exploratory evaluation question.*

_____

_____

_____

Examples of exploratory, qualitative questions are the following:
a. What is it like to have worked in one's job for more than ten years?
b. What happens after you are no longer a client?
c. How do parents predicted to be at risk for child abuse and neglect successfully raise their children?

___ 2. Think of all the possible *contexts* that surround the question. State why you want to include persons with certain backgrounds. You should have an answer grounded either in the literature or in the agency purpose for the evaluation to justify your decisions to purposively include persons with specific characteristics.

_____

_____

_____

Below are examples of contextual decisions to make related to purposive sample selection. If the evaluation is of multiple agencies, how do you select which agencies to include? For example, do you want to make sure there is representation of rural and urban agencies? From one agency, who do you select: administrators, direct-line staff, clients, board members, and/or client advocates? Do you want persons who have similar demographics? Do you want men and women, older and younger persons, or persons from different cultural backgrounds? What other characteristics should the participants possess? Be able to answer why for each contextual decision made.

___ 3. How will you *purposively select* persons who meet your contextual definition in step 2?

_____

_____

_____

Selection decisions to consider are the following: Will you invite participants from a particular intervention? Will you select persons who are involved in the intervention for a certain time period? Will you advertise for persons by posting announcements in the agency or in other public places? Will you ask participants to recommend other persons to participate (this is called a snowball sample)? What other methods will you use to invite participants? Be able to answer why for each contextual decision made.

___ 4. How will you ensure the voluntary and confidential participation of the participants?

_____

_____

_____

Remember that agency personnel cannot give you identifying information of potential participants without prior, written permission from the potential participants. Since you will be asking open-ended detailed questions, how will you include contextual information and direct quotes without disclosing a participant's identity?

___ 5. How will you decide that theme redundancy has occurred and that there is, therefore, no need to invite more participants?

_____

_____

_____

You should be able to convince stakeholders that persons with the same contextual background as the persons selected in steps 2 and 3 will result in no new themes.

___ How have you changed since becoming a parent?
___ What does it mean to be a successful parent?
___ What tips would you give a new parent?
___ What has influenced you the most as a parent? Who are the persons who have influenced your parenting?

In the second interview, the focus was mainly on follow-up questions from the first interview and/or topics that arose from the participants:

___ How have things been since I saw you last?
___ Is there anything you thought of that we talked about when I was here last?
___ Is there anything from the transcription of the last interview that you wanted to talk about?
___ How was it for you growing up?
___ How was it during your pregnancy with your child?
___ How have you handled child care?
___ How have you handled finances?
___ How has it been to raise your children in this neighborhood? What is your neighborhood like?
___ How does being African American affect taking care of your children?
___ Would you talk more about the children's father?

In the third interview, the beginning questions asked were the same as at the beginning of interview 2. The main part of this last interview was to go over material from the first interviews. I read the parents my summary of this material and asked them if they had anything else to add. Then the following questions were asked because they were relevant themes across participants from the first two interviews:

___ How would you like your story told?
___ Whom would you like to read it?
___ Has alcoholism ever been a problem in your family?
___ Has child welfare services ever been involved with your children?
___ How would you define "child neglect"? How would you define "child abuse"?
___ What else would you like to talk about?
___ Do you have any questions for me?
___ Do you have any suggestions for when I meet other parents?
___ How has it been to do the interviews?
___ I will mail the third transcription with follow-up questions.

The questions in the interview guide in case example 19 were asked in a conversational manner to help the parents feel comfortable discussing any and all aspects of parenting. After the first interview was conducted with all six participants, a follow-up set of questions was developed to address themes that arose during the previous interviews but were not previously discussed with all participants. The second and third interviews allowed the interviewer to clarify the content of previous interviews, a process called **member checking** (discussed later in this chapter).

Focus Groups.

Focus groups are interviews conducted with more than one person at a time. The term *focus groups* has become one of those evaluation terms that many stakeholders use generically without specifying whether the method will be qualitatively or quantitatively implemented. Qualitative focus groups follow a general, open-ended interview guide. Focus groups require special practical considerations, considerations that set them apart from face-to-face interviews. For example, two evaluators should conduct the focus groups, one to facilitate the interview and the other to record the information gathered.

The facilitators should follow a script that contains the following:

1. Introductions of the evaluators and a statement of the purpose of the focus group.
2. Conditions of informed consent stated verbally with each person asked to sign the written permission-to-participate form.
3. An explanation of the format of the focus group (e.g., "I will give each of you a chance to answer a question before I go on to the next one," "Please save all of your questions for me until the end").
4. The actual interview guide questions.
5. Instructions to leave time for questions from the participants and then to thank them and let them know how they can request the results of the evaluation.

The two evaluators should establish a protocol for how they will work together. The recorder may ask follow-up questions based on his or her observation of the focus group. For an example of a qualitative focus-group protocol, see case example 20. This particular example is of a descriptive, qualitative question, as the consumers of the social service were asked to discuss their experience with being enrolled in the service. A true exploratory focus-group interview guide would allow the participants to discuss their experiences without the specific prompts contained in case example 20.

Case Example 20. Qualitative Focus-Group Interview Guide

Consumer Focus-Group Questions

Introduction (five minutes)

The following is an informal checklist of items to cover before starting the focus groups. Cover the content in the words that work best for you.

Introductions

___ My name is _____. I'll be asking the questions today.
___ My name is _____. I'll be taking notes today.

Details about the Consent Form

___ This focus group discussion is part of a two-year study _____ evaluating the outreach efforts of counties to enroll children who are eligible for the Medicaid expansion program commonly called Healthy Start or CHIP.
___ This focus group will be taped. Please talk slowly and clearly so my colleague can take good notes.
___ Your participation is voluntary and confidential. Also, please respect the confidentiality of the other persons in the room. Do not repeat their comments to anyone else outside of this room. Please take time to read the consent to participate form before we go any further.
___ At the end of this interview, you will receive a $15 gift certificate to _____ grocery.
___ The entire focus group will last no longer than one hour.
___ Are there any questions?
___ If not, please sign the consent form if you agree to participate in this focus group. If you do not agree with the form, you do not have to participate in this focus group.

Format of the Focus Group

___ I will read one question at a time. Each person will have the chance to answer the question. Please, only one person respond at a time. I may need to limit how much time we give to each question.
___ I understand it may be difficult to hold your responses, but I need to structure the responses so that I can record them accurately. We have provided you with paper and pencils to write down your thoughts

while waiting to respond so that you don't forget the important points you want to say.

___ If there is something you did not have a chance to say, we will have a few minutes at the end of the focus group to go over your responses.

___ Any questions before I go on?

Consumer Focus-Group Questions

The interviewer will ask each question with one person at a time. (Allot fifteen minutes.)

1. How did you first find out about the health insurance program for your children called Healthy Start or CHIP? For example, did you hear about Healthy Start from a caseworker? Health advocate? Hospital staff? Friends or family? Advertisements? How did you apply for Healthy Start (or CHIP)? What persons helped you apply for Healthy Start (or CHIP)? Was your child accepted into the program? If no, why not? Is your child still in the program? If no, why not?
2. What or who helped you the most to enroll your child(ren) in Healthy Start? (Allot five minutes.)
3. What were the obstacles to enrolling your child(ren) in Healthy Start? (Allot five minutes.)
4. Are you aware of specific outreach efforts in your area to enroll minority groups in Healthy Start? (Allot five minutes.) (If yes, the interviewer lists the strategies and the target minority group on the flip chart.)
5. Were there any posters, billboards, or flyers you saw describing Healthy Start? (Allot ten minutes.) If yes, what and where were they? Did these flyers influence you to call Healthy Start? Were there any commercials you heard describing Healthy Start? If yes, what and where were they? Did these commercials influence you to call Healthy Start? Were there any _____ (other efforts in the plan that have not yet been discussed)? If yes, what and where were they? Did these efforts influence you to call Healthy Start?
6. Were you part of an evaluation of _____? (Allot five minutes.) If yes, please explain.
7. That covers all of my questions. Do you have anything else to add about Healthy Start or CHIP and your outreach strategies? (Allot five minutes for questions 7 and 8.)
8. Do you have any questions for me?

Thank you for your participation!

If practitioners audiotape the focus group, the facilitator may need to instruct participants to speak slowly and clearly and, at times, repeat their statements. Transcribing an audiotape is very difficult, especially if persons' voices or tones are similar. Sometimes, the facilitator can announce that a new person is responding to the question to aid the person transcribing the interview. Videotaping the focus group helps in keeping observational notes, especially if one wants to capture participants' nonverbal reactions. The transcriber needs to enter initials or other symbols onto the transcription for each respondent on the tape. More discussion about transcription occurs later in this chapter. The transcriber needs to also ensure in writing that all information will be kept confidential.

It is helpful to display key words via a flip chart or a projection device of some sort so that all respondents can see the collective responses. If one expects detailed notes from the evaluator who is serving as the recorder, then do not have the recorder also be the scribe for the flip charts. It is nearly impossible to facilitate and scribe at the same time. To ensure their full participation in the focus group, do not expect one of the participants to serve as scribe. The flip-chart sheets of paper peppered with permanent marker words can be a source of information to compare to the recorder's notes and later transcriptions.

Train all persons who are conducting focus groups to increase the consistency and reliability of data collection and reporting, especially when more than one team of evaluators is conducting the focus groups at different sites. Training should cover points such as the following:

- How directive should the facilitator be?
- Is the audiotape the main source of data or a support to the notes of the recorder?
- How should the facilitator respond to questions about the purpose of the evaluation?

Provide a checklist of items for all teams to have before they jump in their cars and travel to the focus-group site. Train all evaluators regarding the format of and depth of information to include in the summary of the focus group.

Krueger and Casey's (2009) book on focus groups is an excellent resource for conducting qualitative focus groups for exploratory and descriptive purposes. The authors conceptualize the qualitative focus group as an interactive, flexible, open-ended interview process. They provide suggestions for preparing and conducting the interviews as well as recording the information collected during the interviews.

Written Surveys.

Participants can be asked to answer written, qualitative questions on a survey. A survey or questionnaire is a set of questions developed by the evaluation stakeholders to collect locally specific information. The entire survey can contain only qualitative, open-ended questions, or it can contain both qualitative and quantitative questions.

One common way stakeholders use surveys is as part of a needs or assets assessment to determine respondents' perceptions of areas that need an intervention. Provider surveys are surveys sent to representatives of a social service agency asking questions about the services delivered.

Another common way in which stakeholders use surveys is to get feedback about an event, intervention, or program. The instruments employed for this purpose are called satisfaction surveys. Satisfaction surveys help persons adapt the intervention but do not provide data about whether the intervention created the desired results.

The following is a list of ways in which to administer surveys. Methods are listed in the order most likely to produce the best response rates, from highest to lowest. Ways in which potential participants are missed are listed, too:

1. Hand deliver a survey and wait for it to be completed. Examples of potential participants missed: persons not present due to illness or some other reason; persons who are present but do not like to answer surveys; persons who do not give serious thought to their answers; and persons who do not understand the questions, a possible occurrence for persons from cultural backgrounds different from the evaluators.

2. Conduct a telephone survey. Examples of potential participants missed: same as method 1, as well as persons without phones; persons not home when the phone call is made; and persons who have caller ID or screen calls for solicitors or phone surveys.

3. Conduct an Internet survey. Examples of potential participants missed: same as method 1, as well as persons without access to the Internet and persons who do have access but do not like to answer Internet surveys.
4. Mail a survey and request its return. Examples of potential participants missed: same as method 1, as well as persons without a mailing address; persons who moved without a forwarding address; and persons who do not like to respond to mail surveys.

There are many online survey tools available to all persons that are usually free. Using online surveys can help increase the return rate for those persons who do not have a telephone line or do not answer their telephone.

Observation.

The purpose of the open-ended, qualitative recording of observations is to provide rich, contextual descriptions surrounding the evaluation and research questions. In the exploratory study with parents, the researcher recorded open-ended observations of the environment in which each interview occurred. Five of the six interviews took place in participants' homes, and the sixth took place in the office of an agency worker.

The observations were hand recorded immediately after each interview and included descriptions of the following:

- The participant and any other persons present (adults and children).
- Items in the home that related to experiences the parents shared. One parent described how her faith helped her raise her child in a positive way. The observation notes included descriptions of religious items in the home.
- Observations of the parents' nonverbal behavior. It was noted that one parent established eye contact with the child by getting down on the floor.
- Observations of the surrounding neighborhood. One day's case notes were: "The home was located on a street with high traffic. The home was a two-story, four-unit apartment building that was part of a larger apartment complex."

- Observations of the researcher's behaviors that were not evident on the audiotape. It was noted that "the researcher turned off the tape recorder during the time Ms. Smith received a telephone call."

The researcher also took verbatim notes of a parenting support group that he attended with one of the participants. The purpose of observing the group was to experience an activity at the suggestion of one of the participants. The parent perceived the group as a positive support. The researcher's observation affirmed that the participant and other parents in the group offered support and advice to one another.

The qualitative observation approach in the evaluation of the SBCM program was similar. Observational notes were taken of the interview settings. The first two interviews took place in an agency setting; the last in the participant's home. The evaluator also documented his observation of an Alcoholics Anonymous group in the transitional living program and an SBCM assessment and case-planning session. The purpose of the observations was to observe events that the participants experienced. The evaluator's observations were triangulated with the participants' descriptions of the same events.

The main difference between qualitative and quantitative observations is that in qualitative evaluations, the evaluator tries not to have predetermined categories to frame the notes. The evaluator is open to noting all events rather than following a closed-ended checklist of items for the notes. Thus, themes emerge from the qualitative observation in the same manner that themes emerge in a qualitative interview.

Secondary Documents.

Secondary documents are sources of information recorded by someone else prior to the current evaluation that are used to help answer the current evaluation questions. In qualitative approaches, secondary documents are conceptualized as contextual descriptions of the experiences being explored or described. In the exploratory study with six parents, each participant was asked the question "Was there anything you read that helped you as a parent?" The answers to this question became one source of documents collected for this study. One parent provided posters she was given by the doctor at a local health clinic. The posters contained information on proper pre- and postnatal care. Another parent directed the researcher to a book she had read on Christian child raising. Another provided handouts from a parenting class. Qualitatively, these documents showed the range of materials that had shaped the way these parents raised their children.

There were two examples used earlier in this book in which secondary documents were qualitatively collected during agency site visits: (1) to describe the perceived success of family support interventions (FSIs) by staff and clients and (2) to describe the perceived success of the Children's Health Insurance Program (CHIP) outreach efforts. In both examples, the participants decided which documents were presented to the evaluation team. The evaluation team was open to all documents the participants chose.

Examples of secondary documents provided in the foregoing two examples are the following:

- Agency-written material, such as a mission statement as it appeared on a web page or in an agency brochure
- Agency promotional material distributed at community health fairs, such as pens, buttons, and other items carrying the agency name and services
- Media accounts of an event or situation, whether from newspapers, journals, or telecasts
- Reports from self-evaluations
- Data collected for annual reports, such as the number of consumers served or results from satisfaction surveys
- Curriculum used for community presentations

From a qualitative approach, the listed documents reflected the participants' perceptions of evidence of success. Reviewing the list, however, the reader can see that the documents included descriptions of the intervention as well as possible outcomes. Some reading the final evaluation report may, therefore, not agree that the documents do, in fact, demonstrate actual success. Data about how many consumers use an intervention, for example, reflect usage but not necessarily client change. The same is true for client satisfaction data. At the same time, the evaluators now have a preliminary view of how participants view program success. They and other key stakeholders can help participants collect data more in line with descriptive and explanatory evaluation questions.

The major disadvantage of using secondary documents as data is that the documents were written to meet goals different from those of the current evaluation. For example, a local United Way provided the reports of four separate needs assessments as the basis for an evaluation to determine the priority target areas when writing a five-year strategic plan. Each report was based on different evaluation questions, data-collection procedures, and foci. The difficult task for the evaluation team was to compose a data-analysis scheme (described later in this chapter) that applied across the different reports.

QUALITATIVE DATA ANALYSIS

The qualitative approach to data analysis can be applied to data collected and recorded in all three methods discussed earlier: (1) asking questions, (2) making observations, and (3) collecting secondary data. The goal of qualitative data analysis is to reduce the large amounts of open-ended narrative data into manageable codes, categories, and themes that credibly capture the experiences and descriptions of the participants and settings. The examples given in this section relate specifically to transforming interview data, but they can also apply to reported observations and secondary documents.

All ethical guidelines for the protection of participants must be followed during all parts of the evaluation process. The analysis of qualitative data can involve the selection of direct quotes that appear in final reports or journal articles. The evaluator needs to notify participants of this possibility and assure them that confidentiality will be maintained. No identifying information should be provided in final reports. It should not be possible to trace any direct quotes back to their sources. The only exception to this policy is when permission is given for reports to contain identifying information.

The several case examples reported earlier followed the procedures for reducing the data generated by open-ended interviews:

1. The interviewer tape-recorded the interview.
2. The interviewer wrote notes on the interview guide, highlighting points to closely review later.
3. After the interview was over, the interviewer recorded his comments about the interview in the reflective journal. Within one to three

days, he typed up his handwritten notes, taped post-interview comments, and any other insights he had about the interview.
4. The interviewer, or a person hired by him, transcribed the tape-recorded interview verbatim.
5. The transcription was organized by themes and corresponding quotes.

The important point to note is that each of these steps resulted in a transformation of the original information (i.e., the words spoken by the participants in the interviews). In theory, the verbatim transcription should be just that: verbatim. In actuality, transcribers make mistakes, which are influenced by their own predispositions, theoretical or otherwise. The following sections include some tips to consider about the mutual influence between evaluator and participants in each of the steps listed above. For more detailed discussion of qualitative approaches to data reduction and analysis, consult the texts on qualitative methods in the "Further Resources" section.

Tape Recording.

Buy, borrow, or rent a quality tape recorder. It should be one that has a microphone sensitive enough to capture the words of persons sitting far away. It should also be one that can be battery operated so that it can be used in those situations without access to an electrical outlet. Practice operating the recorder before the interview. Position the microphone away from such distracting sounds as a blaring television, a crying child, traffic, sirens, and loud voices. If distracting sounds cannot be avoided, ask to move to another location, or politely rearrange the interview time. Ask people to repeat their answers if needed. Some persons choose to videotape interviews. The main reason to videotape is to include observational data. If you plan to use only the words spoken, then video recording inundates you with information, more information than you need. A poor-quality tape recording affects all the remaining steps of the interview.
    Interviews can be videotaped also. Videotapes capture nonverbal responses not captured on an audiotape. That means there is much more data also on videotapes. Be clear of which medium is feasible for your evaluation. Most of this section can apply to video- or audiotaped interviews.

Note Taking.

Be clear about the purpose of taking notes during the interview. Are the notes the primary source of recording the data, or are they serving as a secondary method of collecting data or as a reliability check? Notes can serve as cues to double-check specific themes when reviewing the tape or transcription. Tape-recording the interview allows the evaluator to give the participant all his or her attention and not be distracted by the note-taking process. If practitioners are not able to tape-record the interview, then they may need to take more extensive notes.

Reflective Notes.

Take notes after an interview to reflect on issues, values, biases, and reactions that arise during the interview. The reflective journal is an important vehicle for identifying how your thoughts and actions intertwined with the participants' words. The awareness thereby attained helps the evaluator get out of the way of the participants and make the final interpretation a close approximation of their experiences. The analogy to direct practice is that the reflective journal serves a similar purpose as process notes. Both are used to analyze the interviewer's (e.g., the evaluator's, the therapist's) role in the interviewee-interviewer dialogue.

Transcribing.

Typing the recorded words of a person is no easy task! A one-hour verbatim-transcribed interview will consume twelve to fifteen typed pages. Buy, borrow, or rent a quality transcribing machine. It should be able to play back the tape through both headphones and speakers. The tape recording is sometimes easier to hear using the speaker, but if you must transcribe the tape in a public place (e.g., your office), it is essential that you use headphones, to protect the participants' privacy. The transcribing machine should also have a foot pedal that allows you to stop, rewind, and go forward on the tape. With practice, practitioners hope to achieve the ability to type at the same pace one is able to stop and forward the tape without rewinding. Finally, the transcribing machine should have speed control. This allows practitioners to adjust the speed of the tape to the point that one can type while listening to the tape. A slower speed also allows one to better understand words that may be hard to hear at regular speed.

Establish clear guidelines for yourself or others you hire to type the transcriptions. Not every transcription needs to be typed verbatim, although it is best to transcribe the first one or two interviews verbatim until you become familiar with the topics of the interview. Write down rules about the following:

- Typing utterances (e.g., *uh*, *oh*)
- Whether to retype a statement if the participant repeats him- or herself
- What to paraphrase if you are not transcribing verbatim
- Having clear indicators of which statements were made by the interviewer (e.g., *Int:*) and which by the respondent (e.g., *Res:*)
- Putting the participants' actual words in quotation marks to distinguish them from paraphrasing
- Having guidelines of when to start new paragraphs (e.g., when a person switches to a new topic)
- Numbering the pages and, sometimes, the lines

Enter the transcription into computer software that is compatible with the theme-analysis software you plan to use. For example, some types of qualitative software require the transcription to be in rich-text format. Most qualitative software applications have a process to convert files into a format appropriate to that application. Practitioners may be able to save valuable time if they enter the transcribed data directly into the software application to be used for the theme analysis.

Have someone other than the transcriber conduct a reliability check of the transcribed data. Reliability here refers to the accuracy and consistency of reducing and interpreting the data. In one evaluation, reliability was reached by having a second person listen to the taped interview while reading the transcription. The purpose of the reliability check was to ensure accuracy of transcription. In another evaluation, instead of reviewing the entire tape, the second person listened to one-minute snippets of the tape at fifteen-minute intervals. Major discrepancies between the transcription and the tape would indicate that the evaluator needed to compare the entire transcription against the tape.

Theme Analysis.

Theme analysis reduces the transcription to codes, categories, and themes. In qualitative processes, **codes** are symbols or labels given to words or phrases that compose a single idea. In the exploratory study of six parents, *GM* was the code given to references that participants made to their grandmothers. **Categories** are the labels given to groupings of codes addressing similar topics. In the same study, two categories were "advice" and "family." Statements coded *GM* could fall under both of these categories. Themes are more general, conceptual ideas that capture related categories. In the interactive model of parenting that emerged from this study, the five general themes were "spirituality," "slogans for change," "agencies in my way," "agencies that were supportive," and "knowing my child" (see case example 21). Conceptually, these themes were the common strengths on which the participants relied to raise their children. The words coded *GM* may have fallen under the themes "spirituality" and "slogans for change."

Case Example 21. Themes Emerging from Exploratory Research Questions

Interactive Model of Coping with Life's Demands: Common Themes across the Six Parents Interviewed in the Exploratory Study with Six Parents

Fighting oppression and/or facing discrimination

Being the target for blame	The children's father
Balancing work, school, and child care	Being African American
	Being young
Being on welfare	Strong women role models
Choice about pregnancy	

Relying on inner drive	*Meeting the child's needs*
Spirituality	Child's behavior
Slogans for change	Special needs
Recovery	Protecting them
	Discipline
	It's different from abuse

Experiencing feelings associated
with being a parent   *Sorting out advice*
Mixed feelings   Wanted advice
Depression   Unwanted advice
Conflicting advice

Negotiating resources
Supportive social agents
Social agents in the way

You can create codes and categories directly on the transcription. Use different colored pens to write different categories or themes in the margins. Save the original transcription as your raw, untouched data so that an outside person can see the original words before coding. Coded hard copies of qualitative transcriptions can be quite colorful. The originally straightforward dialogue of the transcription is transformed into multiple shades of highlighter pen with strange coded words or combinations of letters and numbers in the margins. Arrows can be drawn connecting codes and sentences to each other. Categories can be crossed out, and new labels can replace old ones. Drawing an accompanying flowchart or theme chart helps lend some order to the seemingly chaotic array of words and symbols. There are many software programs to assist with the qualitative coding process.

Exploratory and descriptive evaluation questions that follow primarily qualitative data-collection and data-analysis processes contribute to new knowledge through the process of the evaluation as much as the final product does. The evaluator and, one hopes, other stakeholders constantly move back and forth between gathering information and making critical assumptions about the interpretation of that information. Multiple interpretations are sought, including the analysis of the participants and the evaluator. Connections are made to relevant theories and empirical findings reported in the research literature. This notion of being critical of emerging and existing theories throughout the data-analysis process is adapted from the grounded theory approach (Corbin & Strauss, 2008).

Writing down coding rules in the procedural journal is essential to the reliability of the coding process. An example of a coding rule is "Each time a person describes any member of his or her family, place that coded group of words into the category titled 'family.'"

Entering the coded data into a computer software package is the next step for qualitative analysis. Qualitative analysis software packages allow you to move data out of the transcribed form into new files arranged by themes. You can then compare the similar themes and provide direct quotes that reflect those themes. There are many additional analyses that you can conduct with qualitative software, including frequency counts (how often codes appear) and the graphic display of themes, interactive PowerPoint presentations of the thematic data, and mapping of results reported in client narratives.

Take the time necessary to research the different qualitative software programs available before you begin to collect information. There are conceptual and practical considerations involved in choosing the software. The manual coding step is not always necessary. It is possible to code transcribed data as you read it on the computer screen. Some persons, myself included, keep the manual coding process to feel more in control of the comparative-theory coding process. Some feel confident that they can meet the same rigorous, grounded-theory process without manually coding hard data.

In summary:

- Have a data-management protocol.
- Decide where the evaluators send the tapes, notes, and summaries.
- Decide who summarizes the collective data and conducts the theme analysis.
- Decide where the data-analysis notes will be kept.
- Decide how these notes are then entered into a qualitative software package and by whom.
- Decide how the final themes are then developed.

Remember, the idea is to keep such detailed notes that an outside person can audit your steps backward—from the interpretations in the final report all the way to the original words spoken by the participant. The evaluators are the keepers of the raw data (e.g., field notes, transcriptions, software files), but the stakeholders have the right to know how the raw data were transformed.

DATA CREDIBILITY

The previous discussion of qualitative approaches to data collection emphasized that data go through multiple transformations. The methods used to increase the trustworthiness of the data during these transformations are summarized in checklist 23. These methods were used in the qualitative approach to answering the exploratory question "How do parents predicted to be at risk for child abuse and neglect successfully raise their children?" and in the qualitative approach to answering the descriptive question "How do consumers experience SBCM?" Trustworthiness means remaining true to the original source of data. All the methods in checklist 23 were implemented to keep the researcher and/or evaluator focused on the original evaluation purpose, which was to learn the participants' experiences.

The methods used in checklist 23 demonstrate how one evaluator's interaction with the collected information produced the interpretations reported. Another person conducting the same evaluation will mostly likely interpret the findings differently. The reality is that two people following identical procedures will not necessarily arrive at identical interpretations. In the exploratory study with parents, the researcher was a white man and all six participants women, five African American. The participants would have interacted much differently with an African American female researcher than they did with the white male researcher. The cultural differences between the researcher and the participants produced results specific to the participants and the setting.

The major benefit of collecting information systematically through rigorous qualitative approaches is that participants' experiences can be credibly reported to stakeholders. Findings from qualitative approaches are more than just "This is what the client said," or "This is what the workers think," or "This is what I, as the evaluator, claim." They are the collective knowledge about program decisions that is gained through a systematic analysis of all collected data, including the empirical results of other research reported in the literature.

Another way to reach data trustworthiness is to employ a procedure called member checking. This is the feedback from the participants about the evaluator's reporting, and in some cases interpretation, of the information collected. In the exploratory study with parents, the researcher made the decision that, to best be true to the participants, he should give each one the full fifteen pages of transcribed interviews. Thus, at the beginning of the second interview, he gave each participant a copy of the transcription of her first interview. This process was overwhelming for all the participants. As one participant said: "I never thought I talked that way." She was referring to her observation that the transcribed interview contained many unfinished sentences and repeated remarks and appeared to her to be unorganized. Verbatim conversations do not have the luxury of being edited for grammar or clarity.

Learning from this experience, before conducting the third interview, the evaluator prepared for each participant two-page summaries of the main topics discussed in the previous two interviews. He first read the summaries to the participants and then gave them hard copies to keep. The participants found the summaries much more manageable. Similarly, in the exploratory study with parents, the researcher gave each participant her final story as it appeared in her dissertation.

The purpose of the member checking in both examples was to ensure the accuracy of the data reported. If a point was inaccurately reported (e.g., a wrong age, location, event), participants corrected the researcher-evaluator, who noted any differences of interpretation between the evaluator and the participant.

If practitioners and evaluators use member checking, consider the following three decisions prior to conducting the interviews:

1. What written document, if any, are you going to give to the participants (e.g., full verbatim transcription or a summary of the interview)?
2. How are you going to use the participants' feedback about the information?
3. How will you protect the confidentiality of the participants in the final report and other publications? If possible, show the participants how you reworded background information to ensure their confidentiality.

Yet another way in which to reach data trustworthiness is **peer debriefing**. This is consultation about the evaluation process from persons

Checklist 23. Procedures to Increase Credibility of Qualitative Approaches to Data Collection

Check the qualitative data-collection approaches to assure credibility of the data that you followed in a current evaluation at your agency or practicum setting.

___ 1. Received approval from an institutional review board that ethical considerations are addressed.

___ 2. Conducted open-ended, almost conversational interviews.

___ 3. Conducted the interviews in the participant's natural environment.

___ 4. Selected the participants purposively on the basis of the experiences that are being explored or described.

___ 5. Triangulated at least three different data-collection strategies.

___ 6. Documented, in a reflective journal, the evaluator's influence on the data-collection process.

___ 7. Documented, in a procedural journal, the evaluation decisions made and the reasons for making those decisions based on stakeholder input and following rigorous procedures recommended in the research and evaluation literature.

___ 8. Established prolonged engagement with the participants and in their natural setting, to the point that theme redundancy is reached.

___ 9. Followed rigorous methods to identify emergent themes from the participants' experiences.

___ 10. Connected the emergent themes to empirical theories reported in the literature.

selected for their expertise. In the exploratory study with parents, three different African American women who were doctoral classmates of the researchers served as peer debriefers at three different times in the research process. The first debriefer read selected transcriptions of the first interviews and provided suggestions for improved interactions in the second and third interviews. The second debriefer provided literature references specific to African American families from an Afrocentric perspective. The third debriefer reviewed the final six stories that would appear in the dissertation and suggested edited, non-verbatim quotations from the interviews in which there were no grammatical errors to distract from the meaning behind the words. All the feedback from the peer debriefers was incorporated into the final dissertation.

Triangulation is the implementation of more than one data-collection method to answer the same evaluation question. The ideal would be to collect data by asking questions, through observation, and through the analysis of secondary documents, all in relation to the same focus. For example, in the parent survey, participants were asked open-ended questions about parenting, the evaluator took open-ended notes about his observation of parent-child interactions, and the evaluator collected documents that the parents stated helped them parent. Together, these three methods provided more trustworthiness of the interpretation of the data.

Data trustworthiness can also be achieved by conducting an **evaluation audit**, a review of the evaluation decisions by a person not connected to the evaluation. Minimally, the reviewer can conduct a procedural audit, commenting on whether the evaluator followed rigorous and accurate qualitative data-collection approaches. The evaluator, stakeholders, and auditor should agree on whether there are any other points that should be the focus of the audit.

Objectivity is the process of identifying evaluator biases and influences that distort the data-collection process. Qualitative and quantitative approaches address evaluator bias differently. Evaluator bias cannot be completely controlled. Evaluators are human beings who have views and biases that guide their decisions. Qualitative evaluators and researchers can document these biases in a reflective journal and report the actions taken to reduce the risks to the credibility of the final results (e.g., member checking, peer debriefing).

MAJOR POINTS

In evaluations that rely solely on qualitative research designs to answer exploratory questions, the evaluator's early goals are to learn what is important to gather from the participants and to have this information guide all other decisions, including the role of theory from other evaluations and research. There is an interplay between learning new information from data one collects and comparing that information to old and new theories read during the evaluation. Participants are selected purposively on the basis of the specific focus of the evaluation question. Data can be collected by asking open-ended questions, conducting observations with open-ended categories, and conducting an open-ended contextual analysis of secondary data. Data are analyzed by allowing repeated and outlier themes to emerge from the data rather than having preconceived theories about the data. Credibility of the data is reached through the following procedures: member checking, peer debriefing, triangulation, and evaluation audits.

CRITICAL-THINKING QUESTIONS

Utilize one or more of the references from the "Further Resources" section to justify your answer to the following questions:

1. Do you agree with the statement, "No evaluator can be totally objective and remove all bias from an evaluation process"? Why or why not?

2. If evaluator subjectivity or bias is always present, what should the evaluator do with this bias?

3. There are two hundred students taking four different sections of an evaluation course throughout a given year, and the professor wants to answer the overall exploratory question, "What is it like to be a student taking this evaluation course?"

   a. Knowing that the professor has the resources to interview only up to twenty persons, what are some ways the professor can purposively select the evaluation participants?

   b. Develop an interview guide with no more than five questions that the professor may ask participants.

DOCUMENTATION TASKS

Answer the following questions for any exploratory question being asked in this evaluation:

Are the evaluation conditions appropriate for a qualitative, exploratory research design? Why?

How are the participants purposively selected?

How are data qualitatively collected?
____ Individual interviews
____ Focus groups
____ Written surveys
____ Observation
____ Secondary documents

How are data qualitatively analyzed?
____ Audiotaped interviews
____ Videotaped interviews
____ Transcription procedures
____ Theme-analysis procedures

How is the credibility of the data qualitatively ensured?
____ Member checking
____ Peer debriefing
____ Evaluation audit
____ Triangulation

List any other qualitative methods used:

c. Should the professor ask these questions in a face-to-face interview or by giving the students the questions on paper to answer and turn in? Why or why not?

d. When conducting a member check of the professor's summary of each person's interview, should the professor allow the participant to review the verbatim transcript, the professor's summary of the interview, or the summary of themes from the interview? Why or why not?

4. Does following the procedures discussed in this chapter come easily to you? Why or why not?

FURTHER RESOURCES

Bazeley, P. (2007). *Qualitative data analysis with NVivo.* Los Angeles, CA: Sage.

Bogdan, R., & Biklen, S. (2007). *Qualitative research for education: An introduction to theories and methods* (5th ed.). Boston, MA: Pearson.

Denzin, N., & Giardina, M. (Eds.). (2006). *Qualitative inquiry and the conservative challenge.* Walnut Creek, CA: Left Coast Press.

Krueger, R., & Casey, M. (2009). *Focus groups: A practical guide for applied research* (4th ed.). Los Angeles, CA: Sage.

Lapan, S., Quartaroli, M., & Riemer, F. (Eds.). (2012). *Qualitative research: An introduction to methods and designs.* San Francisco, CA: Jossey-Bass.

Morse, J., Stern, P., Corbin, J., Bowers, B., Clarke, A., & Charmaz, K. (2009). *Developing grounded theory: The second generation.* Walnut Creek, CA: Left Coast Press.

Padgett, D. (Ed.). (2004). *The qualitative research experience.* Belmont, CA: Wadsworth/Thomson Learning.

Patton, M. (2002). *Qualitative evaluation and research methods* (3rd ed.). Thousand Oaks, CA: Sage.

Qualitative Inquiry. [A journal published by Sage, Thousand Oaks, CA.]

Qualitative Social Work. [A journal published by Sage, Thousand Oaks, CA.]

Richards, L. (2009). *Handling qualitative data: A practical guide* (2nd ed.). London, UK: Sage.

Richards, L., & Morse, J. (2013). *Readme first for a user's guide to qualitative methods* (3rd ed.). Los Angeles, CA: Sage.

Scott, S., & Garner, R. (2013). *Doing qualitative research: Designs, methods, and techniques.* Upper Saddle River, NJ: Pearson.

Quantitative Research Designs: Explanatory Questions

10

Are the evaluation conditions appropriate for explanatory questions?

How are the participants randomly selected?

How are data quantitatively collected?

   ___ Individual interviews

   ___ Focus groups

   ___ Written surveys

   ___ Observation

   ___ Secondary documents

How are the data quantitatively analyzed?

   ___ Outcomes were measured at the ordinal, interval, or ratio levels

   ___ Codebook of variables and values is kept

   ___ Inferential statistics demonstrating a causal relationship between intervention and outcomes were calculated

How is the credibility of the data quantitatively ensured?

   ___ Experimental group design

   ___ Random selection to intervention and comparison group

   ___ Controlling for threats to reliability

      ___ Consistency of data-collection methods

      ___ Using standardized instruments with high reliability

___ Controlling for threats to validity

___ Measurement of extraneous variables

___ Using standardized instruments with high validity

___ Following an experimental group design

EVALUATION CONDITIONS APPROPRIATE FOR EXPLANATORY QUANTITATIVE QUESTIONS

This chapter provides a very brief overview of quantitative research methods used to answer explanatory evaluation questions or hypotheses. In evaluations, a **hypothesis** predicts the causal relationship between a program or intervention and desired student or client outcomes. Entire research books in education and the social services cover the detailed and thorough analysis of quantitative methods that I only summarize in this chapter. The purpose here is to introduce the reader to these important methodological discussions and to direct the reader to the research texts that provide more information about the specific method used for your evaluation.

Quantitative methods follow a positivist paradigm view that the world is measurable and predictable. Causal relationships between phenomena, called **independent variables**, and outcomes, called **dependent variables**, can be isolated and measured. For formative evaluations, this means that needs or strengths (dependent variables) can be objectively measured and used to create interventions and programs (independent variables) theorized to reduce those needs and reinforce the strengths. For summative evaluations, that means that the causal relationship between an intervention or program can be connected to expected results and outcomes.

A positivist paradigm for social service and education research is adapted from quantitative methods used in the traditional STEM disciplines: science, technology, engineering, and mathematics. In those disciplines, literally life-and-death decisions are based on objective, measurable research that explains the causal relationships between the presence of objects or events and their consequences. For example, the isolation of viruses that lead to illness can result in treatment to eliminate the virus and thus the symptoms. Another example is the discovery of mechanisms that can allow persons with physical challenges to have the same mobility as persons without those challenges.

Quantitative methods are valued in the social sciences and education because the methods measure the effectiveness of evidence-based interventions to improve educational outcomes and outcomes of social service interventions and programs. At the beginning of this book one of the reasons stated for conducting evaluations was based on accountability to funders and the general public to demonstrate that interventions have the desired impact on individuals, families, groups, and communities.

To test the hypothesized relationship between interventions or programs, alternative explanations or biases must be ruled out. This chapter focuses on the procedures to objectively measure the impact of programs throughout the research process: from participant selection to data-collection methodology, data analysis, controls for reliability, and validity of the data.

This chapter focuses on explanatory evaluation questions whereas the next chapter focuses on descriptive evaluation questions. Explanatory questions measure causal relationships between interventions and programs and desired outcomes and use only quantitative methods. Descriptive evaluations analyze a possible relationship between interventions and programs and desired outcomes but are not able to *prove* that the intervention or program solely caused those outcomes. Descriptive questions can be answered by qualitative or quantitative methods or a combination of both. The discussion of quantitative methods in this chapter applies to some descriptive questions covered in the next chapter.

RANDOM PARTICIPANT SELECTION

In quantitative approaches, when the target population is too large to be sampled in its entirety, participants are selected randomly so that their responses will be generalizable or representative. Selecting a random sample, also called a probability sample, is based on the theory that a sample chosen systematically and randomly from a larger population will represent that larger population accurately. Random selection means that every member of the larger population has an equal chance of being selected.

Consider, for example, a population of ten thousand people from among whom a 10 percent random sample of one thousand is to be selected. According to probability theory, 95 percent of those thousand participants will report results consistent with those of the larger population of consumers. The reasoning here is based on the theory that results obtained from large populations will be naturally distributed along a bell-shaped curve. In a normal distribution, 95 percent of responses should fall within a range that runs from two standard deviations above to two standard deviations below the average or mean. Standard deviation refers to how dispersed the results are from the average.

Also according to probability theory, 5 percent of those thousand participants will report outlier results, results that are not consistent with 95 percent of the larger population of consumers. In quantitative designs, stakeholders view outlier data as nontypical of the expected results. In contrast, in the previous chapter there was a discussion of outlier data sometimes being the focal point of qualitative research.

Because of the value placed on generalizing the results from the sample to the population, there are pressures to use random sampling, especially on state or federal programs. Some stakeholders may desire a **stratified random sample** selection process. Persons from each of the identified demographic groups (e.g., the same percentage of women and men as is found in the population list) are randomly selected. For example, in a needs assessment to determine whether a federally qualified health clinic would benefit the county, the primary stakeholder wanted to conduct a random sample of the two cities that had the lowest median household income. Thus, the two communities were purposively selected. Neighborhoods identified by zip code within the communities were selected randomly. Heads of the households from each of the stratified, randomly selected neighborhoods were selected for door-to-door, closed-ended, quantitative interviews.

In the evaluation of direct-care mental health workers' competencies described earlier in this text, the quantitative evaluation question was answered by inviting the entire studied population (approximately 3,500 employees) to participate in the mail survey. Stakeholders and evaluators agreed that the resources were available to invite all of the workers to participate in the evaluation. All employees were given the data-collection instrument along with their monthly pay stub. An accompanying letter encouraged them to complete the survey and return the survey in the self-addressed envelope. Ultimately, 438 surveys were returned, for a response rate of 13 percent.

The limitations of the participant selection process in the foregoing example were stated in the final report. While the response rate was low, surveys were received from employees at each of the nine participating behavioral health organizations and in each of the job categories and education levels. Sixty-five percent of the respondents had worked in mental health for more than ten years (Clasen, Meyer, Brun, Mase, & Cauley, 2003, p. 12). The prioritized competencies in this evaluation matched the findings of prior empirical research. This evaluation contributed to future empirical research by constructing a valid and reliable instrument that other persons can implement to prioritize mental health competencies. This evaluation described the competencies. The purpose was not to test a relationship between possessing the competencies and achieving desired consumer results. Critical readers of the published evaluation must determine for themselves whether the results apply to the mental health setting in which they work.

As mentioned before, evaluations that answer explanatory questions begin with a hypothesis, which is a statement predicting a causal relationship between the intervention and desired results. In the evaluation of family support interventions (FSIs), the explanatory hypothesis tested through quantitative approaches was "Consumers of the FSIs will significantly improve family functioning." The hypothesis was based on the following goal in the logic model that was contained in the request for proposals for all the funded programs: "A goal of the family support interventions is to strengthen family functioning." The general functioning scale of the Family Assessment Device (Epstein, Baldwin, & Bishop, 1982) was selected to measure the outcome family functioning.

The original evaluation plan was to randomly select persons from each of the thirty-eight evaluated programs who were consumers of a program during a specified six-month period. There was sufficient funding to conduct telephone interviews with up to one thousand consumers and one thousand persons from a comparison group at three different times. The predicted sample size was based on the assumption that many more than one thousand consumers would be available across the thirty-eight programs.

It turned out that the number of potential consumers was actually much smaller for several reasons. First, each FSI had different operational definitions of consumers. Some programs considered consumers to be those individuals or families who received direct services. Others considered consumers to be all members of the community because the programs targeted community-level change. In these community-level programs the number of potential participants was much lower. Some agencies did not have intake information such as names, addresses, and phone numbers for recipients of community-level interventions (e.g., health fairs, presentations at a hospital).

Second, none of the FSIs included a consent form for participants to provide their names for possible evaluations. The agency directors wrote a letter explaining the evaluation and asking permission to release contact information to the evaluators. Once a consumer signed and returned the letter, his or her contact information was turned over to the evaluators. The telephone interviewers then contacted the consumer and sought verbal informed consent before proceeding to administer the questions on the family-functioning scale.

Third, many of the potential participants could not be reached by telephone. Unfortunately, only telephone interviews could be conducted because the expense of traveling to each of the thirty-eight sites and interviewing a sample of consumers was beyond the budget.

Efforts were made to reach the entire population of FSI consumers. Of the 1,261 telephone numbers provided by the FSI staff, 626 were usable at time 1, resulting in an initial clean rate of 49.6 percent. A clean sample rate is the number of participants who can be contacted (626) divided by the total number of participants on the original sample list (1,261). At time 1, 533 of the FSI participants on the cleaned list were interviewed, a response rate of 85.1 percent. The **response rate** is the number of persons who complete the survey (533) divided by the number of persons who were given the survey (626). Of those 533 participants, 318 were retained at time 2 and 205 at time 3, for a final retention rate of 38.5 percent. The **retention rate** is the number of persons who continued to participate in all three surveys (205) divided by the number of persons originally given the survey

(626). The number of FSI participants responding to all three surveys also represented 32.7 percent of the cleaned FSI population (205 of 626).

A sample of persons in a comparison group also completed the survey. A **comparison group** is made up of persons who do not receive the intervention, in this case, persons who were not consumers of FSIs. Ideally, explanatory evaluations use **random controlled trials** (RCTs), in which participants are randomly selected into the intervention (treatment group), **control group** (persons do not receive an intervention), or a comparison group (persons receive an intervention that is different from the treatment group).

An RCT was not feasible for the evaluation of FSIs because it would mean withholding interventions from persons in need of the intervention. The procedure for the random selection of the comparison group was as follows:

1. In each of the thirty-eight sites, the zip codes of persons answering the telephone survey were obtained.
2. Phone numbers for the appropriate area codes were purchased from Survey Sampling Inc., a company that provides this service for large-sample-size studies.
3. The evaluators entered those names into a computer software program that randomly selected for the comparison group the same number of persons who participated in the consumer interview.
4. The evaluators checked to make sure that none of the persons in the consumer interviews was also in the comparison group.

For the FSI comparison group (FSIC), 549 persons were contacted at time 1, of whom 333 were retained at time 2 and 248 at time 3. The retention rate for the number of original FSIC participants who completed all three surveys was 45.2 percent (248 of 549).

The interpretation of the results was provided in a final report, at a state-level conference, at a national conference, and in a manuscript submitted for publication in a peer-reviewed journal. In these presentations and reports, the authors stated the limitations of their sampling procedures. They claimed that, despite these limitations, the results from the sample could be generalized to the original population, which was all consumers of the thirty-eight evaluated FSIs.

The authors provided possible explanations for why there was not a significant change in family functioning for the consumers. One explanation was that family functioning was not conceptualized consistently across evaluated programs. The instrument selected from past research may not have been the best measure of all evaluated programs. Readers of these reports should be critical of the methodology and determine whether the interpretation of the results can apply to their own settings. For criteria to use when reading findings of quantitative evaluations reported in journals, see Thyer (2002).

The desired participant size and response rate should be agreed on prior to beginning data collection. First determine the population size, following the steps outlined in checklist 24. The evaluators of the FSIs erred by writing into the evaluation contract that they would interview one thousand consumers, not anticipating the problems that they would encounter. They were, however, able to negotiate the number of participants with the funders. In retrospect, it would have been better to state a percentage of the total population rather than an arbitrary number based on limited knowledge of the setting.

QUANTITATIVE DATA COLLECTION

Asking Quantitative Questions.

Quantitative survey questions have predetermined answers from which the respondent is asked to choose. The predetermined answers may be based on theory or practical administrative program needs. For example, the twenty-six competencies listed in the quantitative survey about mental health competencies were written by the evaluators on the basis of theories described in the literature and course syllabi about mental health competencies. The underlying theory was that workers possessing certain competencies deliver effective interventions to mental health clients. Closed-ended questions were also asked about the respondent's preferences for training on these competencies, such as whether he or she preferred receiving college course credit for the training or taking the courses on the weekend. These types of questions are common for quantitative needs assessments that are used to develop program planning, in this case training of mental health competencies. For the quantitative survey developed in this evaluation, see case example 22.

Case Example 22. Quantitative Survey

	How *important* do you think it is for a direct-care mental health worker to have the following skills and/or knowledge?					How much would you (or the workers you supervise) *benefit* from additional education in the following?				
	Not important	Somewhat important	Important	Very important	Extremely important	Definitely not important	Probably not important	Don't know	Probably benefit	Definitely benefit
1. Treating clients with respect, dignity, and as equal partners in their treatment.	①	②	③	④	⑤	①	②	③	④	⑤
2. Including family members and other supportive people/ groups in the client's treatment.	①	②	③	④	⑤	①	②	③	④	⑤
3. Knowing the symptoms/ characteristics of mental illness.	①	②	③	④	⑤	①	②	③	④	⑤
4. Responding to cultural, racial, and gender issues that affect clients.	①	②	③	④	⑤	①	②	③	④	⑤
5. Knowing the uses and side effects of psychiatric medications.	①	②	③	④	⑤	①	②	③	④	⑤
6. Knowing the biological nature of mental illness.	①	②	③	④	⑤	①	②	③	④	⑤
7. Knowing and using the best types of therapy for general mental illness.	①	②	③	④	⑤	①	②	③	④	⑤
8. Knowing and using the best types of therapy for people with a forensic status.	①	②	③	④	⑤	①	②	③	④	⑤
9. Knowing and using the best types of therapy for people with a substance abuse/mental illness (SA/MI) diagnosis.	①	②	③	④	⑤	①	②	③	④	⑤

Checklist 24. Quantitative Participant Selection

To select a participant group that represents a larger population, follow the steps below. Check off each step you have completed.

____ 1. Clarify who composes the population.

____ 2. Compose a population list of all persons who fit the clarified definition.

____ 3. Clean the list by removing persons whose name appears more than once or persons whom it is not feasible to contact (e.g., persons without addresses or phone numbers).

____ 4. Choose whether to conduct a random or purposive sample. If conducting a random sample, follow the appropriate steps to increase the power of statistical analysis (see Potocky-Tripodi & Tripodi, 2003).

____ 5. Contact all persons selected from the "clean list." Record how many of these persons respond. This number will now become the response rate of the persons chosen to be in the random sample (e.g., if 250 persons are contacted from the clean list and 125 respond, the response rate is 50 percent).

	How *important* do you think it is for a direct-care mental health worker to have the following skills and/or knowledge?					How much would you (or the workers you supervise) *benefit* from additional education in the following?				
	Not important	Somewhat important	Important	Very important	Extremely important	Definitely not important	Probably not important	Don't know	Probably benefit	Definitely benefit
10. Knowing and using the best types of therapy for people with a mental illness/mentally retarded (MI/MR) diagnosis.	①	②	③	④	⑤	①	②	③	④	⑤
11. Knowing and using the best types of therapy for children/adolescents affected by severe emotional disorders (SED).	①	②	③	④	⑤	①	②	③	④	⑤
12. Knowing and using crisis interventions.	①	②	③	④	⑤	①	②	③	④	⑤
13. Knowing and using recovery principles.	①	②	③	④	⑤	①	②	③	④	⑤
14. Developing and putting into practice Individual Service Plans (ISP) and Individual Treatment Plans (ITP).	①	②	③	④	⑤	①	②	③	④	⑤
15. Using community resources effectively.	①	②	③	④	⑤	①	②	③	④	⑤
16. Being a client advocate.	①	②	③	④	⑤	①	②	③	④	⑤
17. Knowing about legal issues, client rights, and ethical issues.	①	②	③	④	⑤	①	②	③	④	⑤
18. Working well as a member of an interdisciplinary team.	①	②	③	④	⑤	①	②	③	④	⑤
19. Working in a professional way.	①	②	③	④	⑤	①	②	③	④	⑤
20. Evaluating one's own work performance.	①	②	③	④	⑤	①	②	③	④	⑤

	How *important* do you think it is for a direct-care mental health worker to have the following skills and/or knowledge?					How much would you (or the workers you supervise) *benefit* from additional education in the following?				
	Not important	Somewhat important	Important	Very important	Extremely important	Definitely not important	Probably not important	Don't know	Probably benefit	Definitely benefit
21. Keeping accurate work records.	①	②	③	④	⑤	①	②	③	④	⑤
22. Knowing and being able to use first aid, CPR, and other ways to keep clients and workers safe.	①	②	③	④	⑤	①	②	③	④	⑤
23. Providing basic nursing care, including taking vital signs and helping clients use the bathroom.	①	②	③	④	⑤	①	②	③	④	⑤
24. Using different ways to reduce worker stress.	①	②	③	④	⑤	①	②	③	④	⑤
25. Knowing basic facts of good nutrition.	①	②	③	④	⑤	①	②	③	④	⑤
26. Using computer technology.	①	②	③	④	⑤	①	②	③	④	⑤

Standardized Instruments.

Standardized instruments are evaluation and research data-collection tools that were tested and reported in the literature for high validity and reliability. Corcoran and Fischer (2007) provide a two-volume set of actual instruments used most often by social service workers in clinical settings. The authors begin the first volume with an overview of the issues to consider when choosing a standardized instrument. In the first volume they provide additional sources for locating published instruments and discuss questions to ask when reviewing instruments. Royse, Thyer, and Padgett (2010) and Bloom, Fischer, and Orme (2009) provide a discussion on the use of standardized measures and include selected instruments.

During the course of the literature review, you will locate journal and website references that contain either actual instruments or reviews of instruments. During the evaluation of FSIs, reviews of family and child instruments were consulted. Authors often publish articles demonstrating the reliability and validity of standardized instruments in evaluation and research journals.

When reading reviews of specific instruments, look for the following information:

- General description of the instrument
- Description of the theory underlying the instrument
- Evidence of the instrument's validity and reliability
- Evidence of the instrument being used across different cultural groups
- Results of using the instrument
- Procedure for implementing and scoring the instrument
- Information on how to obtain the instrument, including costs
- Reports of using the instrument with diverse populations, including different translations of the instrument

Stakeholders may prefer using quantitative instruments rather than qualitative surveys, arguing that quantitative instruments are more efficient, credible, and accountable. From an efficiency standpoint, someone else has already done the hard and laborious work of constructing the instrument. It does take a lot of time to construct a well-thought-out, closed-ended set of questions. Finding an instrument that measures exactly what one wants to describe or explain is a great time saver. Make sure that the instrument does address the stakeholders' evaluation questions. In the evaluation of FSIs, it turned out that each FSI had a different conception of how its interventions affected family functioning. Thus, in retrospect, the evaluators may not have used the most valid instrument for the concepts tested.

From a credibility standpoint, evidence can be found that an instrument is valid and reliable. Validity in this sense means that the instrument measures the intended concepts. The General Family Functioning questions of the Family Assessment Device (Epstein et al., 1982) administered in the evaluation of FSIs were based on systems, role, and communication theories. There was extensive evidence available in the literature that this instrument did measure the theorized concepts as well as related concepts contained in other standardized instruments (Sawin, Harrigan, & Woog, 1995). Reliability here means that the instrument measures these concepts consistently and repeatedly across participants.

When reviewing the literature, look for descriptions of the validity and reliability of the instrument across different populations. Ask yourself the following questions: Has it been used with different cultural groups? Do its concepts have the same meaning across cultures or across genders? Has it been translated into different languages? Has it been normed for different cultural groups? Does a particular score have the same meaning for different groups?

Instrument Development.

Instruments are used in quantitative approaches to test theories that guide the planning and implementation of interventions. The closed-ended format of a quantitative instrument allows responses to be entered into a computer software program for analysis. The process for developing the Competency Assessment Tool—Mental Health (CAT-MH) was discussed earlier in the chapter covering the literature review process. Twenty-one competencies were selected on the basis of a thorough review of the theoretical and empirical literature available about mental health worker competencies. The evaluation advisory group added four competencies related to specialized populations (e.g., people with a substance abuse and/or mental illness diagnosis) and one related to the ability to apply computer technology in their jobs.

This instrument was developed because the evaluators could not locate a standardized instrument measuring mental health worker competencies. Once the competencies were agreed on, the evaluation team consulted with a statistical service that developed the actual Scantron survey. A Scantron survey allows participants to circle one answer to each question. Once the completed surveys are electronically scanned, numerical responses to each question by each respondent can be calculated and analyzed. "The instrument was piloted with twelve mental health employees for comprehension, readability, understanding, content validity, and clarity" (Clasen et al., 2003, p. 12). For the final instrument, see case example 22.

Statistical analyses of the returned instruments allowed the evaluators to assess the reliability of the two subscales for the instrument. For each question, the respondents were asked, "How *important* do you think it is for a direct-care mental health worker to have the following skills and/or knowledge?" This was called the "Knowledge" subscale. For each question, the respondents were asked, "How much would you (or the workers you supervise) *benefit* from additional education in the following?" This was called the "Benefit" subscale (Clasen et al., 2003, p. 12). The authors reported internal reliability for the two scales using a statistical analysis called Cronbach's alpha. They also reported correlation between items on the knowledge and benefit scales. "These correlations were conducted to determine if respondents thought a skill or knowledge was important, they would also think training in that area would be beneficial. Every correlation was significant" (Clasen et al., 2003, p. 13).

Whether an instrument is reliable and valid is important information for persons who intend to replicate that instrument in another evaluation or research setting. "Since all the competencies were rated by respondents as important, it seems clear that the CAT-MH successfully identified core competencies needed by mental health care workers. . . . In addition, assessments of the importance of a competency were significantly correlated to the benefit of training for that competency. The focus groups gathered narrative information that supported the validity of the constructed instrument. The competencies that ranked highest on both subscales were confirmed in the focus groups" (Clasen et al., 2003, p. 13). Future evaluations can test the reliability and validity of this instrument, and its validity can be compared to other instruments that measure either or both subscales.

Focus Groups.

Closed-ended questions can be asked of individuals or groups. Quantitative focus-group questions require more than one respondent to select closed-ended responses. In the evaluation to prioritize mental health competencies, the focus-group respondents were asked to answer the survey that some members had already completed individually. This format was followed partly to observe whether the focus-group responses would be reliable, that is, consistent with the results from the written survey. Besides prioritizing competencies from a predetermined list, the only discussion was meant to ascertain participants' descriptions of other competencies deemed important and preferences for training on the competencies.

The major difference between a qualitative and quantitative focus group is that in quantitative focus groups, the questions are closed-ended and predetermined. Qualitative focus groups allow for an open-ended, more flowing, participant-guided discussion than occurs in quantitative focus groups. The facilitator takes on more control of the quantitative focus group making sure that the answers stay focused on the specific questions being asked. The facilitator is aware of time limits and keeps the interview moving to ensure that all questions get asked. The advantage of the quantitative focus group is that the data are relevant and valid to the predetermined questions. Quantitative focus groups save time and can be more efficient than qualitative focus groups. The major disadvantage is that the participants may have important data to share that are outside of the scope of the interview questions. That is why it is helpful to conclude the focus group with at least one open-ended question, such as "Is there anything you would like to add that we have not covered?"

The discussion in chapter 9 about different ways to ask questions also applies to quantitative surveys and instruments: face-to-face, mail, telephone, and Internet. In a recent evaluation of mental health networking in schools, a survey was conducted of teachers, intervention specialists, counselors, and support staff in different schools throughout an entire county school district. The principals of each school sent an e-mail to every employee asking them to participate in the survey electronically. The memo from the principal contained a link to the survey. This method resulted in a 25 percent response rate.

Observations.

The purpose of the closed-ended, quantitative recording of observations is to provide valid and reliable measures of the desired results needed to answer descriptive and explanatory evaluation and research questions. In the research study of a parent behavioral modification intervention, a closed-ended observation tool was developed that allowed the social service worker to measure specific behaviors of the two parents and their two boys. An observation instrument was also developed that allowed each parent to measure desired (e.g., playing without hitting) and inappropriate (e.g., hitting) child behavior.

The first step in developing this observation tool was to operationalize the target behavior for change, in this case, hitting. The parents and the social service worker identified all hitting behaviors (e.g., pushing, biting, tripping, punching). They also defined different parent responses to the hitting (e.g., yelling, hitting, ignoring, placing in time-out). The process of defining the observed behaviors itself led to the desired outcome of less hitting because the parents became aware of their responses that actually increased the hitting.

The second step was to agree on the observation procedure. The parents agreed to record their children's behavior during the following thirty-minute intervals because these were the times the children fought the most: (1) 7:20–8:00 a.m.; (2) 2:30–3:00 p.m.; and (3) 7:30–8:00 p.m. They placed a sheet of paper on the refrigerator door for each boy that listed both appropriate behavior (playing without hitting) and what constituted hitting. Each time period was broken down into five-minute intervals. A check was placed in any interval in which any hitting behavior by either boy occurred, a star in any interval in which no hitting behavior occurred. This interval observation procedure was chosen because it was easier than recording frequency (i.e., every single time one boy hit), because the fighting was occurring so often, and also easier than recording duration (i.e., how long the hitting lasted) because the length of hitting bouts varied.

The third step was to ensure the reliability of the observation procedures. **Intrarater reliability** is achieved when an individual observer follows observation procedures consistently, and **interrater reliability** when all observers follow observation procedures consistently. In this case interrater reliability was achieved in two ways. First, each parent recorded the children's behaviors at the same times for a two-week period and then compared measurements. Once there was consistency (i.e., 80 percent agreement) in their ratings, then either parent could reliably record the child's behavior alone. The social service worker also conducted several observations of the children during the 2:30–3:00 p.m. time slot and also achieved agreement with the parents' ratings.

Intrarater reliability was checked only through self-reporting. No outside observer took measurements frequently enough to enable comparison with the parents' measurements. The parents also recorded their responses to the children's behavior, such as reinforcing nonhitting behavior and employing a time-out when one of the boys did hit. There are threats to the credibility of self-reporting. In this example, the parents kept well-organized records of their observations and reflected on whether they felt they were consistent in their measurements.

Quantitative observation ratings, both standardized and self-written instruments, are often administered in a single system evaluation or research design. A **single-system design** is an evaluation or research study in which the desired results are measured both before and after an intervention has been administered to a single system, which can be an individual, family, group, organization, or community. Thus, the fourth step was to have a baseline measure of the children's hitting and the parents' responses before the social worker discussed alternate ways for the parents to interact with the children. This study used an AB design, which consists of a baseline measure of target behaviors and then a measure of those same behaviors after the intervention has been delivered. *A* refers to the baseline period before intervention, and *B* refers to the intervention period. The intervention in this case was a ten-week parent-training course that supported the use of reinforcement for nonhitting behavior (e.g., verbal praise, weekly rewards such as trips to the park) and time-out for hitting behavior (e.g., two minutes at the kitchen table). There was a noticeable change in the boys' behavior during this intervention phase. Thus, the fifth step in the example was agreeing to the consistent and reliable implementation of the intervention and single-system design evaluation.

The charting of the children's noticeable change through this basic AB single-system design showed the parents that changes in their own behavior resulted in the desired changes in the boys' behavior. From an evaluation credibility standpoint (discussed later in this chapter), the single-system designs listed here could be considered to provide more valid evidence that, in fact, the social worker's intervention with the parents was a main influence in the change of desired behaviors:

- An **ABA design** consists of expecting the inappropriate behavior to return to baseline level when the intervention is withdrawn. The parents were encouraged to continue to chart their children's behavior after the intervention with the social worker ended. The expectation, however, was that the parents would continue to use the skills they learned in the intervention and be able to *maintain* the children's appropriate behavior at the desired B level or better. A refers to the baseline period before the intervention, B refers to the intervention period, and A refers to the period after the intervention ended.

- A **multiple-baseline design** consists of measuring the impact of the intervention across different behaviors, persons, or settings. The effectiveness of the intervention is demonstrated if the desired changes can be generalized to other conditions. In our example, the parents could chart other target behaviors, such as finishing chores or going to bed on time. In other settings, social service workers may want to measure the same intervention across different clients. In one of the case examples earlier in this text, two master's-level students conducted a multiple-baseline design using the Goal Attainment Scale with youth attending a drop-in center. The results demonstrated that setting goals in an informal manner was effective in helping the youth reach their goals.

For a more thorough discussion of quantitative approaches to observation and the use of single system design, see Bloom, Fischer, and Orme (2009). The single-system design is a common tool taught in undergraduate and graduate social service programs to meet the Council on Social Work Education's learning objective that students be able to evaluate their own practice.

Here are some final tips on the use of quantitative approaches to observation and of single-system design:

1. Do not underestimate clients' ability to record their own behavior and that of others. People respond to seeing changes in behavior graphically displayed in frequency tables and charts. Records of behavior are especially effective when attempting to change unhealthy habits, such as smoking and overeating.
2. Do not underestimate the change in perceptions that usually accompanies a change in behavior. In the parent-training example, during the fifth week the mother threw the charts on the table and said, "This stuff does *not* work," even though the charts were showing a positive change in behavior. When the social work intern explored this statement more, the mother disclosed that her friends and relatives continued to say that the only way to discipline children is

through physical force. Thus, the mother was trying to change behavior in a way that did not coincide with long-held attitudes. Many behavioral interventions often add a cognitive change component.

3. Some change will occur before the actual treatment or intervention stage. From a design credibility standpoint, that means that there may be some distortion between the baseline and the intervention stages. The point emphasized throughout this text is that the process of the evaluation is as important as the outcome. Thus, change can occur from the very beginning of the evaluation.

4. Train all persons to carry out the observation as consistently as possible. It takes a lot of time to specify the target behaviors in a way that is conducive to consistent recording. Again, the process of identifying target behaviors, intervention, and the procedures for recording baseline and intervention data can lead to desired changes.

Secondary Documents.

In quantitative approaches, documents are collected that answer predetermined questions. In evaluations for accreditation or auditing purposes, persons know ahead of time the criteria for reports that need to be submitted. The form that the reports are to take has been predetermined. In the study of family support interventions (FSIs), the evaluators collected and analyzed the requests for proposals (RFPs) filed by the participating agency with the state funding agency. Quantitatively, it was assumed that there would be some consistency in how the RFPs were written since all agencies were responding to the same, predetermined guidelines. The evaluators conducted a **content analysis** with a predetermined checklist of items expected to be contained in the RFPs.

Another major source for secondary documents from a quantitative approach is reports of data collected by other agencies that have some relevance to the current evaluation questions. The evaluation team helping key stakeholders develop a countywide, family violence prevention plan analyzed reports of family violence, including the following:

• National Incident-Based Reporting System cases of domestic violence reported to the county sheriff's office in a one-year period
• Annual reports of domestic violence from the countywide family violence shelter

- The number of founded cases of child abuse and neglect reported in the county
- The number of abuse reports for persons older than age sixty-five years in the county

These reports, studies of family violence reported in the literature, and new data collected by the evaluation team all became part of a report titled "Status of Family Violence." This report was the primary tool used to guide the strategic planning process.

Since evaluators have no control over how secondary data are collected, they cannot always guarantee the validity or reliability of the secondary documents. Persons should critically review the methods used to collect the data reported in secondary documents. Even if they agree that the data were collected reliably, they can still challenge the data's validity to the current evaluation question. In the family violence prevention planning evaluation, the elder abuse reports were primarily of victims in institutional settings. The numbers reported could be even higher when reports of elder abuse in the home are also included.

Two other examples of studies or evaluations where secondary data were analyzed quantitatively are the following:

- A study describing the relationship between deinstitutionalization of persons with mental illness to an increase of persons with mental illness being imprisoned. In this study, municipal public criminal records were analyzed using a closed-ended checklist for type of arrest, number of arrests, dates of arrest, and days in prison. These records were of persons diagnosed with a mental illness who were recently discharged from an inpatient mental health facility.
- A needs assessment to determine the funding priorities for the next five years of a local United Way agency. A quantitative content analysis was conducted to categorize the findings of these reports and count the target groups (e.g., youth, adults, older adults) most often identified in the reports.

DATA CREDIBILITY

The utility and relevance of findings and implications of those findings for any evaluation are determined by the rigors implemented to assure the credibility of the data. For explanatory studies, this means that a hypothesized causal relationship between an intervention (independent variable) and desired outcomes (dependent variables) can be attributed solely to the intervention. For evaluations using quantitative approaches, objectivity is the goal to be achieved. Objectivity means that evaluator bias and other biases (**extraneous variables**) to the data are controlled so as not to become alternative explanations for the desired outcomes. This is different from qualitative designs, in which evaluator bias is acknowledged and documented as part of the contextual description of the findings.

The larger, centralized, publicly funded evaluation examples used in this book lent themselves more easily to quantitative processes than did the smaller, localized, single-agency evaluation case examples. First, stakeholders wanted the report to contain brief, easy-to-understand statistical findings from quantitative data analysis. Second, because more than one intervention was being evaluated, collecting data from a sample of a larger population of participants was the most efficient selection approach. Third, implementing consistent data-collection approaches across all localized interventions using the same closed-ended questions produced comparative findings that helped the funder make planning and implementation decisions similarly across all programs. Fourth, one of the conceptual assumptions underlying quantitative data-collection processes is the goal to collect data as objectively as possible.

One very specific quantitative approach to reducing evaluator bias discussed earlier in this chapter is the implementation of a reliable, valid, standardized, closed-ended survey instrument with all evaluation participants. The assumption is that using the same, closed-ended instrument will reduce the influence of the evaluator's own views and values on the findings and interpretations.

Another way to control for evaluator bias is to train all persons collecting and analyzing data to do so in the same manner, thereby increasing inter- and intrarater reliability. Objectivity can be enhanced by following data-collection procedures already demonstrated in the literature to be effective. This includes choosing an instrument that is valid for the evaluation question and measures the concepts being studied.

A primary way in which credibility is achieved through quantitative approaches is to implement the appropriate evaluation design that controls the threats to internal and external validity (Campbell & Stanley,

1963; Cook & Campbell, 1979). **Internal validity** is the ability to attribute desired results to the evaluated intervention or program controlling for other factors that might be affecting changes. Controlling the testing conditions to rule out alternative explanations for findings is the best way to reduce threats to internal validity. In addition to implementing the measurements consistently, also try to reduce the amount of time between measurements to reduce attrition in sample size.

External validity is the ability to generalize evaluation results from the participants to the larger population. Selecting participants randomly and having a control group that receives no intervention is the most effective way to quantitatively increase the generalizability of the findings. Having a "no intervention" group is often not feasible or ethical. Thus, many quantitative studies have a comparison group in which participants receive some intervention but not the components of the intervention theorized to create the desired client outcomes. The assumption is that the findings will apply to the larger population because all members of that population had an equal chance of participating. Thus, the sample should be a fair representation of the population. Further, controls for skewed characteristics in the sample can be implemented during the statistical analysis.

The **classic experimental design** is the research design in which participants are randomly selected and assigned to intervention and control groups and pre- and post-intervention ordinal level and higher measures of results are given to both groups (see figure 11). Inferential statistical analysis determines whether the observed changes in clients receiving the intervention are statistically significant on the pre- and posttest measures relative to the comparison group. The classic experimental design produces the most control for threats to both types of validity.

As mentioned earlier, random selection of participants and random assignment to control groups are often not feasible, nor are they always ethical in an agency setting, since the procedure involves some people in need of an intervention possibly not receiving it. If an agency has a normal waiting period for clients, the waiting list can be used as the comparison group, since these clients are not currently receiving the intervention and will not be receiving it for some time. Persons receiving different forms of the same intervention can also serve as a comparison group, thus allowing all participants to receive some form of intervention. Finally,

```
R    O1    X    O2
R    O3         O4
```

R   = Random selection to the intervention or control group that
        receives no intervention
O1 = Pretest for persons receiving intervention
O2 = Posttest for persons receiving intervention
O3 = Pretest for control group not receiving intervention
O4 = Posttest for control group not receiving intervention

It is hypothesized that the difference in the posttest and pretest of participant outcomes (dependent variables) for those receiving intervention (independent variable) (O2 – O1) will be statistically significantly different from the difference of control group outcomes (dependent variable) in the posttest and pretest for those not receiving intervention (absence of independent variable) (O4 – O3).

Figure 11.
Classic experimental pre- and posttest design

individuals in the community who have similar demographic backgrounds but are not in need of and, therefore, did not receive the intervention can serve as a comparison group. This method was used for the evaluation of FSIs. It was expensive, however, because it involved purchasing telephone numbers from a research firm. In the next chapter, on descriptive evaluations, different versions of an experimental design, called quasi-experimental designs, are discussed.

A single-system design is also a quantitative research design that can be implemented to test hypothesized relationships between intervention and participant outcomes. Single-system design was discussed previously in the section on observation and measures client outcomes before and after an intervention is administered. See Bloom, Fischer, and Orme (2009) for a discussion of single-system designs and the types of standardized instruments that may be used for single-system designs. Measuring changes in multiple outcomes or across multiple persons or across multiple settings is the way single-system designs strengthen the generalizability of the results. If the same outcomes are achieved across these multiple conditions, then one can attribute the change to the intervention.

The list of items to consider when ensuring the credibility of quantitative, explanatory evaluations is found in checklist 25.

Checklist 25. Procedures to Increase Credibility of Quantitative
                  Approaches to Data Collection

Check the quantitative data-collection approaches to assure credibility
of the data that you followed in a current evaluation at your agency or
practicum setting.

___   1. Received approval from an institutional review board that
          ethical considerations are addressed.

___   2. Participants are selected randomly to an intervention group
          and a no-intervention group.

___   3. Outcomes are measured using a standardized instrument with
          high validity and reliability.

___   4. If different persons administer the data collection, there is
          high reliability between how those persons administer the data
          collection.

___   5. A predetermined, agreed-on response rate of participation is
          reached.

___   6. There is high interrater reliability for the administration of
          quantitative observation instruments.

___   7. There is high interrater reliability for the administration of
          content analysis of secondary documents.

___   8. Measurement of extraneous variables is included to assess
          alternative explanations of the outcomes.

___   9. Triangulated at least three different data-collection methods.

___   10. Outcomes are measured as ordinal-, interval-, or ratio-level
          variables.

___   11. Appropriate inferential statistical analysis was completed to test
          the hypothesis.

___   12. Kept a codebook of variables and values of data-collection tools.

QUANTITATIVE DATA ANALYSIS

The final way to reach objectivity in an explanatory evaluation is through statistical analysis of the quantitative data. The quantitative approach to data analysis can be applied to data collected and recorded via all three data-collection methods: (1) asking questions, (2) making observations, and (3) collecting secondary data. The goal of quantitative data analysis is to reduce the large amounts of data to manageable descriptive and inferential statistical analyses that credibly describe the participants and settings and, in explanatory evaluations, test causal relationships between the intervention and outcomes of the participants.

The discussion in this section covers the range from descriptive to inferential or causal analysis. In the next chapter, examples are given of using descriptive statistical analysis for descriptive evaluations.

Descriptive Statistical Analysis.

Responses to data collected quantitatively must be coded and tabulated. Easy-to-use software has made data coding, entry, and tabulation much more user-friendly than ever before. It allows social service workers to manage large amounts of data more reliably than when manually tabulating results and analyses. The most common statistical software taught in social work courses and used in social service agencies is SPSS. The most recent versions of SPSS are compatible with most personal computers. A good source for learning how to master SPSS is Babbie, Halley, and Zaino (2012).

Also, many academic settings are beginning to teach students to enter and analyze data using more common software found in agency settings, such as Excel. The reason for this transition is that many agencies do not have SPSS, and thus students do not always know how to generalize their quantitative software skills to another quantitative tool.

The first step to quantitative computer software analysis is to develop a codebook for data entry. The codebook will identify the numerical values that you assign to each variable entered for analysis. Each question or item on a survey represents a variable. The answers to each question represent different values for that variable. One purpose of entering the values into a computer software program is to describe the occurrence of different values across respondents. These descriptive statistics report and graph the frequency, percentages, and distributions of responses. Another purpose is to describe the relationship between values of one variable and values of other variables. These inferential statistics allow the social service worker to test whether the hypothesized relationship between independent and dependent variables occurred.

Levels of measurement are the variables used for statistical analysis grouped by the ability to make inferences from the data. The levels are listed here in terms of the strength of the inferences they allow you to make, from weakest to strongest: nominal, ordinal, interval, and ratio. The variable gender will have two possible values: male or female. It does not matter which is labeled 1 and which 2, since these values are nominal. **Nominal** values are simply numbers used to name a value. The assignment of one value rather than another implies no rank ordering.

Ordinal values are numbers that assign more value to some responses than to others. These values can be placed in a meaningful order. In the focus groups with workers and client advocates in a mental health setting, the respondents were instructed to rank order their top five competencies from the list of twenty-six competencies shown in case example 22. The highest numerical values were given to those competencies listed as first, the second-highest values to those listed as second, and so on. All the values were added to determine the top five competencies.

Interval values go a step beyond ordinal values by rank ordering along equal intervals. Age is an interval variable because it is measured the same way by everyone, in terms of years. The same can be said of income, which is measured in total dollar amounts. Age and income become ordinal variables if they are given in terms of categories, such as (a) age twenty-five to twenty-nine, (b) age thirty to thirty-four, and (c) age thirty-five to thirty-nine, or (a) $25,000–$29,999, (b) $30,000–$34,999, and (c) $35,000–$39,999. In terms of the ordinal variable examples, one can simply say that persons choosing c were older or richer than persons marking b or a. In terms of the interval variable examples, however, one can report how much older and how much richer respondents are. Age and income are also examples of the highest level of measurement, **ratio** values, because there is an absolute zero point. This means that 0 connotes total absence of the variable: not born or no money.

The higher the level of measurement, the more one is able to move from descriptive to inferential statistical analysis. In this age of accountability, there is much pressure from stakeholders to show (by answering descriptive evaluation questions) or even prove (by answering explanatory evaluation questions) that the evaluated intervention resulted in the desired outcomes. Thus, in quantitative approaches to answering evaluation questions, it is important to construct instruments that have variables and values at ordinal, interval, or ratio levels.

It is also important to construct instruments whose variables are all conceptual and at the same level of measurement. It is common to arrange responses to a question along a Likert scale, on which the values go from high to low or low to high. There is, however, disagreement as to whether Likert-type variables should be treated as ordinal, interval, or ratio. Look at the values for the knowledge and benefit scales of the CAT-MH found in case example 22. Would you say that these values are ordinal, interval, or ratio? The authors presented the results as ordinal—as descriptive statistics of a mean or average for each competency—allowing the reader to see the ranking from highest to lowest (Clasen et al., 2003, p. 14). "The lowest mean was 3.62, ranking between important (value of 3) and very important (value of 4). For most items means were over 4.00 (out of a possible 5.00 for extremely important)" (Clasen et al., 2003, p. 13). The authors were interested not in how much higher competencies were rated (which would be interval level) but simply in the fact that some competencies were rated higher than others. Later, they acknowledged that there were differences in the two subscales because the benefit subscale had a "don't know" option and the knowledge subscale did not. "At the present, don't know represents the center option" (Clasen et al., 2003, p. 13). A similar center option was not available for the knowledge subscale. Thus, there was not an absolute 0 to allow the variable to be treated as ratio-level data.

The descriptive statistics most commonly reported in evaluations are frequencies, percentages, measures of central tendency, and measures of variability. **Frequencies** are the number of times the value for a variable occurred. Frequencies alone can be misleading because the statistic does not report how many times the value *could* have occurred. For example, a school can report the number of students who passed proficiency exams, but that number alone is meaningless unless it is also reported how many students took proficiency exams. Similarly, reporting how many people used a service over the past year tells us nothing about how many people could potentially have used the service. **Percentages** are the number of times the value was selected divided by the number of participants responding to the variable measured. It is best to provide frequency and percentage for each value reported.

Measures of central tendency are statistics that illustrate how values are distributed among respondents. The **mean** or average is computed by dividing the sum of variable response by the total number of respondents. The **median** is the value that is midpoint. There are an equal number of values above and below the median. Means and medians cannot be calculated for nominal data because the numbers only categorize the variable. One numerical value is no higher than another. The **mode** is the value that occurs the most often. The mean is a deceptive measure if the values are highly skewed toward one end. In such cases, it is best to use the median or to report all three measures of central tendency.

Measures of variability are statistics that illustrate how spread out are the values. They are used for interval- and ratio-level variables. The **range** lists values from lowest to highest and indicates the distance between those values. Ranges are usually reported for age and income. The **variance** (the squared difference of all scores from the mean) and the **standard deviation** (the square root of the variance) illustrate how much the values are spread out from the mean. The higher the standard deviation, the greater is the variation in values. As we saw earlier, values are, according to probability theory, always distributed along a bell-shaped curve, with 95 percent falling within two standard deviations of the mean. Results with a standard deviation higher than 3 have highly spread-out values.

So far, the discussion has covered statistics that describe one variable at a time, called **univariate analysis**. What if you want to analyze two or more variables at a time—for example, whether gender or worker position (e.g., mental health aide, social worker, psychologist) was related to score on the CAT-MH? One **bivariate analysis**, cross-tabulations or contingency tables, can be calculated with SPSS and other statistical software programs. **Cross-tabulations** are conducted with the two or more variables and display the frequency and percentages of responses in each cell. Using gender and response for each competency on the CAT-MH, the ten cells in a cross-tabulation for the knowledge subscale for each competency would be (a) men who responded 1, 2, 3, 4, and 5 and (b) women who responded 1, 2, 3, 4, and 5. The table and percentages provide a visual comparison of scores but do not indicate whether those differences are statistically significant. Cross-tabulations can be used with any level of measurement, but other analyses are more appropriate when testing relations among ordinal, interval, or ratio variables.

Another descriptive statistic used with interval and ratio levels of measurement is correlations. **Correlations** show how values on one variable change in relation to values on a second variable. That is, they show the direction (positive or negative) and strength (ranging from 0 to 1, with 1 being a perfect correlation) of the relation. Scattergrams visually display the correlation between variables. Scattergrams and correlations are useful descriptive statistics in single-system designs. In the parent-training intervention, there was a positive correlation when an increase in the parents' use of reinforcement was related to an increase in the children's appropriate play. There was a negative correlation when an increase in the parents' use of reinforcement was related to a decrease in the children's inappropriate hitting.

Inferential Statistical Analysis.

There is much pressure today from some stakeholders, especially funders, to demonstrate a causal relationship between the intervention or program and desired changes or outcomes in targeted client systems. For example, stakeholders wanted to describe or explain a relationship between the family support interventions (FSIs) and an improvement in family functioning and school performance outcomes.

Quantitative approaches to data collection, data analysis, and controls for credibility are all necessary to explain that interventions are responsible for the measured outcomes. The following four conditions are minimally necessary to test explanatory evaluation hypotheses:

1. The hypothesized relationships must be grounded in theories and interventions that have been tested in other settings and reported in the literature.
2. Participants must be selected randomly so that the measured outcomes can be compared to a normal, naturally occurring distribution.
3. Reliable and valid instruments must be used to rule out error as a possible explanation for the results.
4. Outcomes must be measured at the interval and ratio levels to allow for statistical analyses that test the relationship between values.

Once these conditions are in place, then one must accurately select the appropriate inferential statistical test, basing the selection process on the following four criteria.

1. Match the statistical test with **nondirectional hypotheses** (e.g., there is a relationship between FSIs and family functioning) or **unidirectional hypotheses** (e.g., FSIs increase family health) as appropriate. Inferential statistical analyses are calculated to reject the **null hypothesis**, which is the statement that the relationships between variables do not exist.

2. Match the statistical analysis to the appropriate level of measurement: nominal, ordinal, interval, or ratio.

Chi-square can be used to test the null hypothesis between variables measured at all levels, but other tests may be more appropriate for non-nominal data. Chi-square is often used in social service evaluations for which a comparison-group sample is not available and the nominal-level variables available for analysis all come from one sample.

The **t-test** tests whether to reject the null hypothesis by comparing the means of two samples (e.g., participants receiving intervention and those in a comparison group). The measure of desired results (i.e., the dependent variable) must be at least at the ordinal level and the intervention (i.e., the independent variable) at the nominal level.

Analysis of variance (ANOVA) tests whether to reject the null hypothesis by comparing the means of more than two samples. The levels of measurement are the same as with t-tests.

Regression analysis tests the strength of change predicted to occur as a result of the intervention. The desired results and the intervention must be at the interval level or higher. The participants must be selected or assigned to the samples randomly.

3. When conducting statistical analyses to test the predictive, explanatory evaluation question, select the level of statistical significance before conducting the analysis. **Statistical significance** is the existence of a relationship between the intervention and results outside an acceptable level for chance. The .05 level is most commonly used and implies that the evaluator will accept that five times out of one hundred the results were

due to chance rather than the intervention. Statistical significance is relevant only if the participants were selected or assigned to intervention or comparison groups randomly. These conditions are not often feasible for social service evaluations (Potocky-Tripodi & Tripodi, 2003).

4. When computing the statistical significance of differences between samples, conduct a power analysis. **Statistical power** "is the ability of a statistical test to correctly reject the null hypothesis (i.e., the probability of not making a Type II error). It is the function of three parameters: the effect size, the sample size, and the p value (which is the probability of making a Type I error)" (Potocky-Tripodi & Tripodi, 2003, p. 140). A **type I error** occurs when the null hypothesis is rejected and, thus, an erroneous claim is made that there was a relationship between intervention and change. A **type II error** occurs when the null hypothesis is not rejected, and a true relationship between intervention and change is not identified.

The p-value used in the power analysis is directly related to sample size. "Thus it is essential for researchers to understand this fundamental truth: with small sample sizes, even very large effects (i.e., strong relationships) will not be statistically significant; conversely, with large sample sizes, even very small effect sizes (i.e., weak relationships) will be statistically significant" (Potocky-Tripodi & Tripodi, 2003, p. 140).

As much as one may want to utilize what stakeholders consider the more important or powerful statistical analyses, a social service or education evaluation must use the analyses that are appropriate for the evaluation questions asked, the method of participant selection followed, and the level of measurement of the data collected. For an example of reporting the quantitative statistical analyses used and the limitations of those analyses, see case example 23.

Case Example 23. Reporting of Statistical Analysis in the Final Evaluation
Report

The excerpt here is taken from the final evaluation report of the family support interventions (FSIs) evaluation.

Frequencies and cross-tabulations were calculated for most of the questions asked in the telephone survey. Cross-tabulations were conducted so the frequencies could be broken down by group (i.e., FSI Intervention, time 1) and dependent variable (i.e., use of social services). For instance, a cross-tabulation was run so information about participants of the FSI intervention group in time 1 would display along with their responses for use of social services.

The mean was calculated for several unique variables and one aggregated variable (the FAD). To calculate the mean FAD score, the sum of the twelve FAD, general-functioning questions was calculated. The sum was divided by the number of questions answered. If 40 percent or fewer of the questions were answered by a respondent, the entire FAD score for that respondent was eliminated. Overall, a mean was calculated based on the mean score for each participant. Different statistical analyses were calculated to present the findings appropriately. Over time, when discussing the respondents of the same group (FSI time 1 and FSI time 3), the data are presented descriptively. Statistical analysis is not appropriate to compare all of the respondents in time 1 and all of the respondents in time 3 because there is not an equal comparison (i.e., not all of the people that responded in time 1 responded in time 3). However, when comparing two separate groups, for instance FSI intervention and FSI comparison for the same time, two statistical tests were conducted. When comparing the percentages of two different groups, the Pearson chi-square was conducted, and when comparing the means, the independent samples t-test was conducted. It should be noted that since the FSI intervention sample used in the telephone survey was a convenience sample, these statistics should only be used to generalize to all FSIs with caution.

MAJOR POINTS

In evaluations that rely solely on quantitative approaches to test explanatory questions, the evaluator's goal is to test the causal relationship or hypothesis between the evaluated intervention or program and desired results. Participants are randomly selected to receive intervention or to not receive the intervention in order to attribute any measured change in participant outcomes to the intervention. Data can be collected by asking closed-ended questions, conducting observations with closed-ended categories, and conducting a closed-ended contextual analysis of secondary data. Data are reduced to statistics and analyzed to determine whether there is a statistically significant difference in the outcomes for those receiving the intervention (treatment group) compared to those not receiving the intervention (control group). Credibility of the data is reached through the following procedures: implementation of the classic experimental pre- and posttest design or of a single-system design, random selection to intervention, implementing standardized instruments with proven validity and reliability, and following research protocol that reduces internal and external threats to validity.

CRITICAL-THINKING QUESTIONS

1. From the following evaluation questions, identify the independent and dependent variables:
   a. The implementation of brown bag discussions with teachers about how to identify mental health concerns for students will result in more appropriate referrals from teachers for students to receive mental health services.
   b. There will be less office referrals for student conduct after the Positive Behavior Intervention System (PBIS) is implemented.
   c. There will be a reduction of emergency room visits to the county hospital after a federally qualified health clinic is started in the county.
   d. Families and Schools Together (FAST) improves family functioning.
2. Take one of the examples above and operationalize how the dependent variable can be measured. Identify a standardized instrument with proven validity and reliability that can be used to measure the dependent variable.
3. What are the pros and cons of implementing a classic experimental design to evaluate social service or education programs?
4. Do you agree with the author's assertion that single-system designs, even when measuring the outcomes of only one participant, is a quantitative research design that can be used to test explanatory hypotheses? Why?
5. Take one of the hypotheses from question 1. How would you develop a research protocol that reduces the threats to internal and external validity?
6. Does following the procedures discussed in this chapter come easily to you? Why?

DOCUMENTATION TASKS

Answer the following questions for explanatory questions being asked in this evaluation:

Are the evaluation conditions appropriate for explanatory questions?

How are the participants randomly selected?

How are data quantitatively collected?

___ Individual interviews

___ Focus groups

___ Written surveys

___ Observation

___ Secondary documents

How are the data quantitatively analyzed?

___ Outcomes were measured at the ordinal, interval, or ratio levels

___ Codebook of variables and values is kept

___ Inferential statistics demonstrating a causal relationship between intervention and outcomes were computed

How is the credibility of the data quantitatively assured?

___ Experimental group design

___ Random selection to intervention and comparison group

___ Increasing reliability

___ Consistency of data-collection methods

___ Using standardized instruments with high reliability

___ Controlling for threats to validity

___ Measurement of extraneous variables

___ Using standardized instruments with high validity

___ Following an experimental group design

Mixed-Methods Research Designs: Descriptive Evaluations

11

EVALUATION DECISION-MAKING QUESTIONS

Are the evaluation conditions appropriate for descriptive questions?
Are the participants purposively or randomly selected?
Are the data qualitatively or quantitatively collected?
Are the data qualitatively or quantitatively analyzed?
Is the credibility of the data qualitatively or quantitatively assured?

EVALUATION CONDITIONS APPROPRIATE FOR
MIXED-METHODS RESEARCH DESIGNS

Descriptive evaluation questions pose a relationship between intervention and outcomes but do not pose a hypothesized, causal relationship between intervention and outcomes, as explanatory questions do. A descriptive question is also different from an exploratory question, which assumes no relationship between content and themes that emerge during the data-collection process.

Descriptive evaluation questions can be answered through qualitative or quantitative data-collection approaches. Some descriptive questions call for open-ended, qualitative data, such as asking a participant, "What do you like about the services at this agency?" Some descriptive questions call for closed-ended, quantitative data, such as "On a scale from 1–4, with 1 being 'least favorable' and 4 being 'most favorable,' how would you rate the services at this agency?"

Only one data-collection approach was discussed in each of the previous chapters. Truly exploratory evaluations use only qualitative approaches in order to not impose predetermined hypotheses of the relationship between data. Truly explanatory evaluations use only quantitative approaches in order to test the hypothesized relationship between intervention and outcomes.

Descriptive evaluations are implemented more often than exploratory evaluations for many reasons:

1. Exploratory evaluations are very time consuming. Much time is needed to conduct open-ended interviews, transcribe the interviews, ensure credibility of data, and complete a theme analysis.
2. Exploratory evaluations may appear to not have a clear focus. The emerging themes may or may not be related to the information that stakeholders are seeking. Stakeholders must be content to allow themes to emerge, even if those themes are not, in their view, relevant. Exploratory data collection requires the evaluator to constantly put assumptions in check in order to be true to the emerging themes. This skill requires much practice and discipline.
3. Exploratory evaluations may be empowering to the participants. Persons can become empowered by having their voices and story heard. Some stakeholders may not be interested in the evaluation being empowering for the participants.

Descriptive evaluations provide a clear focus and can be conducted efficiently with the available resources. Often, stakeholders have a clear evaluation question in mind. For example, "Are consumers satisfied with this service? How is a referral between agencies completed? How are clients made aware that they are eligible for this service?" Data-collection procedures described in the previous two chapters can be implemented quickly and with limited resources to answer the foregoing questions, qualitatively and quantitatively. Descriptive evaluations can still be empowering for participants because their input is solicited, but their input is often restricted to the foci decided by the evaluators.

Descriptive evaluations are implemented more often than explanatory evaluations for the following reasons:

1. It is not always feasible to implement an experimental design, which is required to test explanatory, hypothesized causal relationships between interventions and client outcomes. Agencies usually do not always have the resources to collect data from large sample sizes, to randomly select persons to intervention and non-intervention groups, or to purchase standardized instruments, nor do they have the staff or resources to hire someone to conduct the inferential statistical analysis of the results. Agencies implement quasi-experimental designs, which may have nonrandom samples, no comparison groups, and no pre- or post-measure of outcomes. These quasi-experimental designs prevent the evaluator from testing a causal relationship between intervention and outcomes.
2. It is not ethical to have a non-intervention group, which is required for explanatory studies. Agencies can use a wait-list group as the comparison group since the clients do not receive services while on the wait list. Agencies can use a comparison group that still provides the client with an intervention different than the tested intervention.

Most evaluations tend to be descriptive for the reasons listed previously. Descriptive evaluations also tend to be published at least as comparably as exploratory and explanatory evaluations or studies. As an example, read any systematic review of an intervention that is published in the Campbell Collaboration library of evidence-based interventions (http://www.campbellcollaboration.com). All of the systematic reviews describe the author's selection process of empirical research considered for the review. Most of the systematic reviews require that the intervention was tested using a random controlled trial (RCT) methodology, in which participants were randomly selected to the intervention or non-intervention group. The authors of systematic reviews list all of the relevant studies or evaluations they located that tested the impact of the tested intervention. The authors then state how many of those articles use an RCT, usually a very low percentage.

For example, Wilson, Lipsey, Tanner-Smith, Huang, and Steinka-Fry (2011) completed a systematic review of school dropout prevention and intervention programs. Their selection criteria included "studies must have used experimental or quasi-experimental research designs, including random assignment, non-random assignment with matching, or non-random assignment with statistical controls or sufficient information to permit calculation of pre-treatment effect size group equivalence" (p. 8). "The literature search yielded a total of 23,677 reports, 2,794 which were deemed potentially relevant and retrieved for eligibility determination. Of those, 548 reports describing 167 different studies were included in the final review" (p. 8).

The point is that all three types of evaluation questions provide valuable information for program improvement and can contribute significant findings to the research literature related to the evaluated intervention. Evaluations following all three types of research questions can be implemented using empirical and rigorous research methods and contribute to evidence-based knowledge. There is a professional preference to utilize only evidence-based interventions that have proved effective through the most experimental conditions possible. At the same time, most of those evaluations that practitioners use are descriptive in nature. Exceptions are those evaluations that may have the funding and connections to other evaluation resources to implement an experimental design.

There are three different descriptive evaluation scenarios: (1) qualitative descriptive evaluation questions, (2) quantitative descriptive evaluation questions, and (3) descriptive evaluations answered by qualitative and quantitative methods. There will not be an in-depth discussion of the methodologies in this chapter, since most of the data-collection methods were discussed in chapters 9 and 10. Rather, case examples are used here to show how already-discussed methods have been used to answer a descriptive rather than exploratory or explanatory question.

QUALITATIVE DESCRIPTIVE RESEARCH DESIGNS

The major difference between qualitative exploratory evaluations and qualitative descriptive evaluations is that in the former there are no pre-determined variables, whereas in the latter, there may be an identified intervention (independent variable) and general ideas about possible participant change (dependent variable). See if you can recognize which of these questions is exploratory and which is descriptive:

- What is it like to be a participant in the grief group?
- What is it like since your sister died?

Both general questions are open ended and thus qualitative, but one focuses on a specific intervention (descriptive question) and the other has no parameters on what the person may talk about (exploratory question).

Having some parameters to a qualitative descriptive evaluation keeps the evaluation focused on the matters deemed important by the key stakeholders. For example, in the open-ended focus-group questions about direct-care mental health worker competencies, the key stakeholders wanted representation from the following constituents: mental health workers, clients, client advocates, the union (which regulated training and enforcement of competencies), and supervisors. An exploratory design may have conducted focus groups with any one of those groups and would not necessarily compare the results between groups. The descriptive mental health competency evaluation purposively wanted to compare the results among those key constituents.

Another difference between qualitative exploratory and qualitative descriptive evaluations is how the data are analyzed. In a descriptive evaluation, the results are often categorized by the question asked. The question itself becomes the category, such as, "What are the outreach methods you have used to inform families that they are eligible for the Children's Health Insurance Program (CHIP)?" Common themes then emerge from the answers to that specific question. In a truly exploratory evaluation, the questions are broader, and themes may actually overlap from responses to different questions. An exploratory evaluation is more conversational and thus does not lend itself to categories connected to a specific question.

QUANTITATIVE DESCRIPTIVE RESEARCH DESIGNS

The major difference between quantitative descriptive evaluations and quantitative explanatory evaluations is that the former tests a hypothesized, causal relationship between the intervention (independent variable) and participant outcomes (dependent variables). The latter poses a possible relationship between intervention and participant outcomes but does not attempt to test whether the intervention caused the participant outcome.

The quantitative descriptive research designs, thus, may be missing one or more of the components of the classic experimental design and are appropriated called **quasi-experimental designs**. Some of the most common quasi-experimental designs are now discussed.

Posttest-Only, Comparison-Group Design.

In the posttest-only, comparison-group design, there is an intervention and a comparison group but no pretest measures (see figure 12). A comparison group is different from a control group in that the participants still receive some intervention, but the comparison-group intervention does not contain the components that are theoretically related to changes in participant outcomes. For example, an evaluated intervention may be specific cognitive behavior techniques to stop smoking, such as reinforcement, aversive stimuli, relaxation, desensitization, and imagining smoke-free behavior. Rather than denying some randomly selected participants any intervention at all, a comparison treatment may be to talk to a coun-

R   X   O1
R   X2   O2

R   = Random selection to the intervention or comparison group, which receives a different intervention
X   = Evaluated intervention or program
X2 = Comparison group
O1 = Posttest for persons receiving intervention
O2 = Posttest for comparison group, which receives a different intervention

A statistically significant difference between O1 and O2 may indicate a relationship between the evaluated intervention and participant outcomes.

Figure 12.
Posttest-only, comparison-group design

selor about the stress to stop smoking. Thus, all participants receive some intervention, but the effective components of the evaluated intervention are not delivered to the comparison group. Thus, any measured change in smoking behavior that is significantly different for those in the cognitive behavioral intervention than those in the comparison group may be related to the intervention.

Without **baseline** data, that is, a measure before the client receives intervention, there is no way to know how much, if any, the participants changed. In the family support intervention (FSI) evaluation, there was no baseline measure on the Family Assessment Device (FAD). Many of the participants may have already been high on the scale measuring family functioning before the first telephone survey, thus leaving no room for improvement. Random selection to intervention and comparison groups increases the controls for threats to external validity in this design.

Pretest and Posttest, No-Comparison-Group Design.

Without comparison groups, the generalizability of results beyond the participants is reduced (see figure 13). But having a pre- and posttest measure helps control for alternate explanations for reported changes in the clients. There are some statistical analyses that can still test the relationship between intervention and client change.

Time-Series Design.

In time-series designs, the measures are given multiple times, preferably several times before and several times after the intervention is implemented

O1   X   O2

X = Evaluated intervention or program
O1 = Pretest for persons receiving intervention
O2 = Posttest for persons receiving intervention

A statistically significant difference between O1 and O2 may indicate a relationship between the evaluated intervention and participant outcomes.

Figure 13.
Pretest and posttest, no-comparison-group design

O1   O2   X   O3   O4

X = Evaluated intervention or program
O1 = Pretest for persons receiving intervention
O2 = Additional pretest for persons receiving intervention
O3 = Posttest for persons receiving intervention
O4 = Additional posttest for persons receiving intervention

A statistically significant difference between O2, O3, and O4 and no significant change between O1 and O2 may indicate a relationship between the evaluated intervention and participant outcomes.

Figure 14.
Time-series design

(see figure 14). Having multiple measures should control for threats to internal validity related to administration of the instrument. Drastic changes in pre-intervention measures may be due to factors unrelated to the intervention. Measures of desired change after the intervention demonstrate maintenance of the desired outcome. Time-series designs can be used with or without comparison groups.

Posttest-Only, No-Comparison-Group Design.

The posttest-only, no-comparison-group design has the least control for threats to validity. A posttest measure is given after the intervention (see figure 15). Without baseline data and a comparison group, it is very difficult to attribute client change solely to the intervention.

X   O1

X = Evaluated intervention or program
O1 = Posttest for persons receiving intervention

Desired changes in participant outcomes may be related to the intervention but not very convincingly without a pretest and comparison group.

Figure 15.
Posttest-only, no-comparison-group design

MIXED-METHODS DESCRIPTIVE RESEARCH DESIGNS

The evaluation of Family Support Interventions (FSI) used a qualitative and quantitative design. For example, see case example 24. The quantitative design was a quasi-experimental, time-series, comparison-group design. Random samples of FSI clients across the state were asked to participate in the quantitative survey measuring general family functioning at three different times over a two-year period. At the same time, a purposive sample of staff and clients from each FSI participated in an open-ended focus group with questions about the participants' view of what makes their FSI successful. The logic of the combined designs was twofold: (1) a quasi-experimental design asking clients across all FSIs to complete the general family functioning scale was warranted because it was assumed all FSIs had as a goal to improve family functioning, and (2) the qualitative design to purposively recruit stakeholders at each of the FSIs would have the best data of what, besides improved family functioning, constituted success of their interventions.

Case Example 24. Mixed-Methods Research Design for
Descriptive Questions

This is the mixed-methods research design for the evaluation of thirty-eight, statewide family support interventions (FSIs).

Quantitative descriptive question: Are the FSIs related to a positive change in family functioning as measured on the Family Assessment Device (FAD)?

Quantitative descriptive design: Time-series comparison-group design

R	X	O1	O2	O3
R		O4	O5	O6

Data analysis: A statistically significant difference between O1, O2, and O3 compared to any difference between O4, O5, and O6 may indicate a relationship between the evaluated intervention and participant outcomes.

Credibility: Threats to validity and reliability were controlled by having a randomly selected control group, administering the same instrument in the same manner to FSI clients and members of the control group, training the team conducting the survey to be objective and consistent, and implementing the instrument at three different times.

Qualitative descriptive question: What makes an FSI successful?

Purposive participant selection: Direct-care staff, administrators, community partners, and clients

Open-ended focus groups: What makes the FSI successful? How do you know when the FSI is successful? What secondary documents are evidence that the FSI is successful? How do you measure the success of the FSI?

Data analysis: Theme analysis—success grouped according to system level change: individual, family, agency, and community.

Credibility: Member checking, peer debriefing, and theme redundancy

The findings from the focus groups showed that there were differences of success across the FSIs. The findings from the quantitative survey did not demonstrate that the FSIs improved general family functioning compared to persons who did not receive intervention from the FSIs. One conclusion was that family functioning may not have been an intended outcome of all FSIs.

There were limitations to the mixed research design in case example 24. Some of the quantitative data were skewed because of small response rates from some FSIs, client characteristics across FSIs were not always similar, there was no pre-intervention distribution of the survey to measure baseline before the intervention, and the FAD may not have been the most valid instrument for measuring success of FSIs. Another limitation was that participants in the qualitative focus groups were empowered to tell their narratives of success, but funders did not always support those narratives.

In retrospect, it may have been better to collect data qualitatively during the first year of the grant and then implement a quantitative survey that was the most valid on the basis of the findings from the focus groups. The mixed sampling method was proposed instead because of the pressure to have quantitative results in the first year.

PARTICIPANTS SELECTION: PURPOSIVE OR RANDOM

Qualitative Descriptive Evaluations.

Participants are chosen purposively, that is nonrandomly, for qualitative descriptive evaluations. Qualitatively, persons are chosen as they meet the contextual characteristics of the desired sample. An example is allowing staff to choose a person to be interviewed who fits each of the following categories: direct-line staff, supervisory staff, upper administration, client, and community partner. This purposive sampling method was used in many of the examples in this book where the intervention was implemented at multiple sites. Why certain people were selected was by itself revealing qualitative data. The goal for this type of purposive selection is to understand the context behind the participants' responses to the data collection.

An advantage of the qualitative purposive sampling method is that the stakeholders can influence the selection process. The persons whom they choose to participate in the evaluation may provide more relevant meaning to the data than persons randomly chosen who may not be as familiar with the program. For example, a client who had positive outcomes may be able to give a rich description of the intervention processes that helped affect those outcomes. At the same time, I encourage stakeholders to include consumers who had negative experiences with the intervention. Presenting only favorable data or collecting data only from persons who had positive experiences will lead readers of the evaluation to question the credibility of the results.

Disadvantages of qualitative purposive sampling are the following:

- The selection biases may present skewed results.
- The contextual characteristics of participants across multiple sites (e.g., rural versus urban sites) may be very different and thus affect the ability to compare results across settings.
- Qualitative purposive sampling sizes are usually small because collecting open-ended data is often more time consuming than using closed-ended quantitative measures. Small sample sizes limit the generalizability of the findings to other populations.

Quantitative Descriptive Evaluations.

Quantitative, purposive participant selection is often a result of not being able to randomly assign persons to an intervention and non-intervention group. In some of the examples in this book, the entire population was solicited for participation, and there were no participants who did not receive the intervention. The findings could be generalized only to the sample of participants. Without a control or comparison group, there is no way to test whether the results would have occurred without the intervention. Not having a random sample limits the quantitative analysis to descriptive statistics and invalidates the opportunity to conduct inferential statistics for a causal relationship.

Mixed-Methods Descriptive Evaluations.

In some descriptive evaluations, qualitative *and* quantitative purposive selection may be desired. An example is the mental health competencies evaluation. All workers in the seven behavioral health centers across the state were asked to complete the quantitative instrument measuring one's prioritization of which competencies all mental health workers should master. There was no comparison or control group. After descriptive data of the findings were analyzed, a purposive sample of key stakeholders was selected by individual behavioral health centers to participate in a focus group. Each behavioral health center participating in the focus group was to select one person who represented the following categories: direct-line mental health workers, supervisors, administrators, union representatives, and client advocates. Each participant provided his or her feedback to the results of the quantitative survey.

There were advantages and disadvantages to the purposive selection process used in the mental health competency evaluation. An advantage was that the findings were triangulated by collecting data both from a survey and from a focus group. Thus, some of the same mental health competencies were selected through both data-collection methods. A disadvantage is that the results could be biased by both participant selection processes. A small response rate from some groups of persons (e.g., social workers) or some behavioral health centers may skew the results. The persons selected for the focus groups may assume more power in trying to prioritize the competencies, since they could provide more open-ended data than was asked in the surveys.

DATA COLLECTION, DATA ANALYSIS, AND DATA CREDIBILITY: QUALITATIVE OR QUANTITATIVE

Qualitative Descriptive Evaluations.

The qualitative implementation of data-collection methods (asking questions, observing, and analyzing secondary data) has been discussed in detail in chapter 9. Two examples are given here of applying qualitative methods to answer descriptive questions. Case example 25 is an example of an individual, qualitative descriptive interview guide. Case example 26 is an example of a focus-group, qualitative descriptive interview guide. Both examples are qualitative because the questions are open ended. The examples are both descriptive because there is a clear focus related to the intervention being evaluated.

Case Example 25. Qualitative Interview Guide to Answer a Descriptive
Evaluation Question

This interview guide was used to answer the descriptive question "How do consumers experience strengths-based case management (SBCM)?"

Interview at the Rehabilitation Unit after the SBCM Intake Interview

1. What was it like to meet the worker from SBCM?
2. What was the purpose of the meeting with the SBCM caseworker?
3. What other things did the two of you discuss?
4. Please describe the meeting from beginning to end.
5. Is there anything else you would like to tell me about the reasons you are in the rehabilitation program?
6. Is there anything else you would like to tell me?
7. Do you have any questions for me?

Interview at One Month and Three Months after Discharge from the Rehabilitation Unit

1. Have you met the case manager at the _____ SBCM site?
2. What was the first meeting like?
3. What was the purpose of that first meeting?
4. Please describe the meeting from beginning to end.
5. What do you like about the meeting at the _____ site?
6. How are the meetings with the workers at SBCM different from meetings with other workers you have had?

7. Is there anything you would like to change about the meetings with the caseworker?
8. Is there anything else you would like to tell me about the reasons you are in case management?
9. Is there anything else you would like to tell me?
10. Do you have any questions for me?

Case Example 26. Qualitative Focus-Group Interview Guide to Answer a Descriptive Evaluation Question

Consumer Focus-Group Questions

Introduction (five minutes)

The following is an informal checklist of items to cover before starting the focus groups. Cover the content in the words that work best for you.

Introductions

___ My name is _____. I'll be asking the questions today.
___ My name is _____. I'll be taking notes today.

Details about the Consent Form

___ This focus-group discussion is part of a two-year study _____ evaluating the outreach efforts of counties to enroll children who are eligible for the Medicaid expansion program commonly called Healthy Start or CHIP.
___ This focus group will be taped. Please talk slowly and clearly so my colleague can take good notes.
___ Your participation is voluntary and confidential. Also, please respect the confidentiality of the other persons in the room. Do not repeat their comments to anyone else outside of this room. Please take time to read the consent to participate form before we go any further.
___ At the end of this interview, you will receive a $15 gift certificate to _____ grocery.
___ The entire focus group will last no longer than one hour.
___ Do you have any questions?
___ If not, please sign the consent form if you agree to participate in this focus group. If you do not agree with the form, you do not have to participate in this focus group.

Format of the Focus Group

___ I will read one question at a time. Each person will have the chance to answer the question. Please, only one person respond at a time. I may need to limit how much time we give to each question.

___ I understand it may be difficult to hold your responses, but I need to structure the responses so that I can record them accurately. We have provided you with paper and pencils to write down your thoughts while waiting to respond so that you don't forget the important points you want to say.

___ If there is something you did not have a chance to say, we will have a few minutes at the end of the focus group to go over your responses.

___ Any questions before I go on?

Consumer Focus-Group Questions

The interviewer will ask each question with one person at a time. (Allot fifteen minutes.)

1. How did you first find out about the health insurance program for your children called Healthy Start or CHIP? For example, did you hear about Healthy Start from a caseworker? Health advocate? Hospital staff? Friends or family? Advertisements? How did you apply for Healthy Start (or CHIP)? What persons helped you apply for Healthy Start (or CHIP)? Was your child accepted into the program? If no, why not? Is your child still in the program? If no, why not?

2. What or who helped you the most to enroll your child(ren) in Healthy Start? (Allot five minutes.)

3. What were the obstacles to enrolling your child(ren) in Healthy Start? (Allot five minutes.)

4. Are you aware of specific outreach efforts in your area to enroll minority groups in Healthy Start? (Allot five minutes.) (If yes, the interviewer lists the strategies and the target minority group on the flip chart.)

5. Were there any posters, billboards, or flyers you saw describing Healthy Start? (Allot ten minutes.) If yes, what and where were they? Did these flyers influence you to call Healthy Start? Were there any commercials you heard describing Healthy Start? If yes, what and where were they? Did these commercials influence you to call Healthy Start? Were there any _____ (other efforts in the plan that have not yet been discussed)?

If yes, what and where were they? Did these efforts influence you to call Healthy Start?

6. Were you part of an evaluation of _____? (Allot five minutes.) If yes, please explain.

7. That covers all of my questions. Do you have anything else to add about Healthy Start or CHIP and your outreach strategies? (Allot five minutes for questions 7 and 8.)

8. Do you have any questions for me?

Thank you for your participation!

The procedures for arriving at common themes can be the same for qualitative exploratory and qualitative descriptive questions except that descriptive evaluations may have predetermined categories for which to group the open-ended data. Earlier in this chapter, there was a discussion that qualitative descriptive interview data are often grouped by the evaluation question. Such a theme analysis was conducted for the results of the interviews in case examples 25 and 26.

The procedures for arriving at the credibility of the data can be the same for qualitative exploratory and qualitative descriptive questions. The biggest differences I have seen in ensuring data credibility of qualitative data has been more an issue of feasibility, stakeholder preference, and falling short on some areas of evaluation rigor than an issue of whether the question was exploratory or descriptive. For example, compromise of the following credibility checks may weaken the findings of data from the viewpoint of the participants:

- Not conducting a reliability check of the transcription of taped interview data.
  Resolution: Have more than one person type the transcription of random sections of the interview. Compare the results until an agreed upon percentage of agreement is reached.
- Not conducting a thorough member check.
  Resolution: Agree on the member check procedure before any interview is conducted. Will you give the participants the full transcript? A summary of the transcript? A summary of the themes? You need justification for your choice.

- Not conducting a thorough theme analysis.
  Resolution: Have more than one person conduct a theme analysis of the same data. Discuss why each person came up with his or her codes. Document the final codes and categories on the basis of the discussion.
- Not conducting a thorough literature review of related data.
  Resolution: Discuss the findings of the evaluation with an expert in the focus of your participants or the intervention. Ask these peers for references that may be pertinent to the emerging themes of the evaluation.
- Not carrying out rigorous evaluation methods.
  Resolution: Keep a procedural and reflective journal. Be so thorough that an audit of your journals documents the reasoning behind the evaluation decisions made.

Quantitative Descriptive Evaluations.

The quantitative implementation of data-collection methods (asking questions, observing, and analyzing secondary data) has been discussed in detail in chapter 10. There really is no variation in how the data are collected quantitatively for a descriptive or explanatory evaluation. More threats to the validity of the administration of the research design and the research protocol though will reduce the strength of demonstrating a causal relationship between the intervention and measured outcomes. Similarly, more threats to the validity of a needs assessment will reduce the strength of the results and thus the justification to meet the needs identified in the evaluation.

The example of a needs assessment illustrates how the threats to validity can affect the strength of the results. The overall descriptive question was "Is there a need in this county for a federally qualified health clinic?" The evaluation was conducted as part of a federally funded grant and used graduate students who were taking a program evaluation course. This service-learning project allowed the students to master evaluation and research design, data collection, and analysis, and it met the needs of the community partner that was overseeing the evaluation. The quantitative interview questionnaire used in this needs assessment appears in case example 27.

Case Example 27. Quantitative Needs Assessment Interview Questionnaire

Medical Needs Questionnaire*

Team ID _____   Street Address _____

Date ___/___/_____   Begin time_____   End time_____

Hi, I'm a student with Wright State University doing research about locating a health clinic nearby this area. (*Read if needed.*) Our research is supported by the U.S. Department of Health and Human Services. Houses in your neighborhood have been randomly selected for this survey.

I need to speak with an adult who lives in this household. Are you 18 years of age or older and able to answer questions about health issues in your household?

It will take 10 minutes. We won't ask your name or identify you in any way and you can skip any questions you aren't ok answering.

Check appropriate gender: ❏ Male   ❏ Female

1. Is there one place that you usually go to when you are sick or need advice about your health?
   ❏ Yes   ❏ Don't know
   ❏ No   ❏ Refused

2. What kind of place do you go to most often? Is it a clinic, a doctor's office, an urgent care, a hospital emergency room, or some other place?
   ❏ Clinic
   ❏ Doctor's office
   ❏ Urgent care
   ❏ Emergency room
   ❏ Other (specify) _____

3. Would you and your household use a health center if it were nearby and it used a sliding-fee payment scale based on your income?
   ❏ Yes   ❏ Don't know
   ❏ No   ❏ Refused

   a. How many people in your household, including you, would use it?
      _____ (*Write a number.*)

4. *Not* including overnight hospital stays, visits to the hospital emergency room, home visits, or telephone calls, about how long has it been since you last saw a doctor or health care professional about your health (such as routine checkup, physical—*not including dentist visits*)?

 ❐ Never   ❐ Don't know
 ❐ Number of days _____ ❐ Refused
 ❐ Number of weeks _____
 ❐ Number of months _____
 ❐ Number of years _____

 a. And about how long has it been since anyone else in your household has been to a doctor or health-care professional about their health (such as routine checkup, physical—*not including dentist visits*)?

  ❐ Never   ❐ Don't know
  ❐ Number of days _____ ❐ Refused
  ❐ Number of weeks _____
  ❐ Number of months _____
  ❐ Number of years _____

5. During the past 12 months, did you go to the emergency room because you could not get a needed appointment to see a health-care provider?

 ❐ Yes ❐ Don't know
 ❐ No   ❐ Refused

 a. Has anyone else in your household gone to the ER because they could not get a needed appointment?

  ❐ Yes ❐ Don't know
  ❐ No   ❐ Refused

6. Was there a time in the past 12 months when you needed to see a doctor but could not because of cost?

 ❐ Yes ❐ Don't know
 ❐ No   ❐ Refused

 a. Was there a time in the past 12 months when someone else in your household needed to see a doctor but could not because of cost?

  ❐ Yes ❐ Don't know
  ❐ No   ❐ Refused

7. In the past 12 months, have you not filled a prescription because of the cost?

    ❐ Yes   ❐ Don't know

    ❐ No   ❐ Refused

  a. Has anyone else in your household not filled a prescription because of the cost?

    ❐ Yes   ❐ Don't know

    ❐ No   ❐ Refused

8. What reasons, **other than cost**, keep you or someone in your household from seeing a doctor or getting prescriptions filled? (*Pause, then read the list, and check all that apply.*)

    ❐ No transportation

    ❐ No insurance

    ❐ Doctor's office won't take my kind of insurance

    ❐ Doctor's office is too far away

    ❐ Drug store is too far away

    ❐ Doctor's office doesn't speak my language

    ❐ Long wait times

    ❐ Need for evening appointments

    ❐ Need for weekend appointments

    ❐ Other (*specify*)

    _____

    _____

9. From the time you leave home, on average, about how long does it take to get to your main source of routine medical care? (*Record the answer in minutes.*)

    _____ minutes

10. Has a doctor, nurse, or other health professional ever told you that you had any of the following? (*Pause, then read the list, and check all that apply in left-hand column.*) Then ask, how about for anyone else in your household? (*Pause, then read the list, and check all that apply in right-hand column.*)

You	**Anyone else in your household**
❐ High blood pressure	❐ High blood pressure
❐ High cholesterol	❐ High cholesterol
❐ Diabetes	❐ Diabetes
❐ Angina (periodic chest pain) or coronary heart disease	❐ Angina (periodic chest pain) or coronary heart disease
❐ Sickle cell	❐ Sickle cell
❐ Asthma	❐ Asthma
❐ Cancer	❐ Cancer

11. What types of health services are you interested in having in a health clinic if one could be located nearby? (*Pause, then read the list, and check all that apply.*)
    - ❏ Comprehensive primary health care (adults, pediatric, acute and chronic disease)
    - ❏ Behavioral health (e.g., mental health or substance abuse therapy or counseling)
    - ❏ Prenatal and perinatal (e.g., care before, during, and after pregnancy)
    - ❏ Health screenings (e.g., cancer, cholesterol, lead poisoning, vision, hearing)
    - ❏ Diagnostic laboratory (e.g., blood tests, X-rays, other testing)
    - ❏ Voluntary family planning
    - ❏ Preventive dental (e.g., teeth cleanings, dental assessments)
    - ❏ Pharmacy

12. Are you interested in any additional services? (*Pause, then read the list, and check all that apply.*)
    - ❏ Transportation for appointments
    - ❏ Outreach (e.g., assistance in signing up for health benefits)
    - ❏ Patient education
    - ❏ Environmental health risk reduction
    - ❏ Translation services

    (*If checked, then say*) Help me understand better. Do you need:
    - ❏ Sign-language interpreter
    - ❏ Foreign-language interpreter

    For which languages? _____
    - ❏ Other (specify) _____

Final Questions

13. What is your age? _____

14. Which one or more of the following would you say is your race? (*Check all that apply.*)
    - ❏ White
    - ❏ Black or African American
    - ❏ Asian
    - ❏ Native American, American Indian, or Alaskan Native
    - ❏ Hispanic or Latino
    - ❏ Other (specify) _____
    - ❏ Don't know
    - ❏ Refused

15. Are you currently employed for wages, self-employed, or not employed for wages? (*Read the additional options below the choice that is selected—check **all** that apply.*)
    - ❒ Employed for wages
    - ❒ A student
    - ❒ Retired
    - ❒ Self-employed
    - ❒ Receive wages
    - ❒ Don't receive wages
    - ❒ A student
    - ❒ A homemaker
    - ❒ Retired
    - ❒ Not employed for wages
    - ❒ Out of work more than one year
    - ❒ Out of work less than one year
    - ❒ Unable to work
    - ❒ A student
    - ❒ A homemaker
    - ❒ Retired

16. How many children (younger than age 18) live in your household?   _____
    How many of the children have health insurance?   _____

17. How many adult *women* (18+ years) live in your household?   _____
    How many adult women have health insurance?   _____

18. How many adult *men* (18+ years) live in your household?   _____
    How many adult men have health insurance?   _____

    Total members in household (add from numbers recorded on right above)

    _____

19. What is your household income? (*Present color codes for income ranges by household size at three poverty thresholds. Request that the person point out the color in which the household income falls.*) FPL stands for federal poverty level. The color codes distinguish where one may fall on the FPL.
    - ❒ <100% FPL (blue)
    - ❒ 100–200% FPL (purple)
    - ❒ >200% FPL (green)
    - ❒ Don't know
    - ❒ Refused

20. Have any of the following happened because you had to pay medical bills? (*Check all that apply.*)
    - ❏ Unable to pay for basic necessities such as food, heat, or rent
    - ❏ Used up all or most of your savings
    - ❏ Had large credit-card debt or had to take a loan or debt against your home or had to take a loan of any kind
    - ❏ Had to declare bankruptcy

21. What is the highest grade or year of school you completed? (*Check one box.*)
    - ❏ Never attended school or only attended kindergarten
    - ❏ Grades 1–8 (elementary school)
    - ❏ Grades 9–11 (some high school)
    - ❏ Grade 12 or GED (high school graduate)
    - ❏ College 1–3 years (some college or technical school)
    - ❏ College 4 years or more (college graduate)

    Those are all of the questions that we have for you today. We really appreciate you taking the time to speak with us. Do you have any questions for us?
    (*Pass out the yellow information card before you leave.*)

*Reprinted with permission by Talbert House, Cincinnati, Ohio and Wright State University.

The following steps were taken to reduce threats to validity:

- Students pilot tested earlier versions of the questionnaire. The questionnaire in case example 27 is actually the third, revised version.
- Questions for the questionnaire were taken from standardized instruments used in other needs assessments relevant to the current study.
- Students were trained on two different occasions on how to conduct the door-to-door interview consistently and reliably.
- Students were assigned in pairs to conduct the surveys so as to reach reliability and completeness of the data.
- Trained evaluators oversaw the training and the actual data collection.
- Participants were selected using a stratified random selection process. The participants were selected because they lived in one of the two cities with the lowest median family income for the county. Neighborhoods within those two cities were randomly selected by zip code. The sample included home owners and renters.
- Students collected data on two occasions and were much more confident and efficient during the second set of interviews.

Even with these precautions and attention to methodological rigor, the following threats to validity still occurred:

- During the first date of interviewing, there was a very low response rate. Many residents chose not to answer the survey. The most important question was question 3, "Would you and your household use a health center if it were nearby and it used a sliding-fee payment schedule based on your income?" It was decided for the second day of interviewing to at least ask question 3 if the person did not want to take the entire interview. This change in procedure resulted in a higher response rate. But one team's completed surveys were primarily only a response to question 3, whereas all of the other teams had more completes of the entire survey. Such a variation made the evaluators question whether the one team was conducting the interviews in a manner consistent with the other teams.
- Even with the training and overseeing of the surveys, there may have been variation in how some teams asked the questions. The fact that the survey was quantitative and had only closed-ended responses did help keep all of the survey answers consistent.
- The surveys were conducted during the winter and inclement weather, which may have resulted in low response rates.

These possible threats to the validity of the data were documented and will be noted in the final report. Nevertheless, nearly three hundred of the anticipated four hundred interviews were conducted, and important data for the needs assessment were collected and analyzed.

Mixed-Methods Descriptive Evaluations.

Examples of mixed-methods descriptive evaluations were given and discussed under the beginning section of this chapter. Case example 28 shows an example of reporting the results from mixed-methods designs.

Case Example 28. Reporting of Qualitative and Quantitative Data Analysis in the Final Evaluation Report

The results of the focus groups with stakeholders from ten Ohio counties about their successful outreach efforts to enroll eligible children in CHIP were reported both qualitatively and quantitatively.

Qualitative Reporting of Qualitative Focus-Group Data

In the final report, direct quotes from direct-care staff, administrators, and consumers that exemplified the successful strategies listed above were provided. The following are some excerpts from direct-care staff related to the successful strategy of agency collaboration:

> We work with Head Start a lot. They go do a home visit and they enroll a child there. They'll find out this family doesn't have medical insurance and they'll ask the parents first if we can give CHIP outreach your name and address to contact you. And we work with doctors. They give us referrals. The doctors say, "They're having trouble getting medical insurance." We'll go chase the clients down and help them fill out the application. . . . They don't even have to come to Human Services.

> We entered into a contract with neighborhood agencies, because we felt that would be a good way to get applications with the community. Not everybody would want to come into our agency to apply or to mail in the application. We felt that, if they were centered in the community they could work with that community. The contract stipulated they would only be paid for the application if it was an application we were able to approve.

> I work at the Health Department and have called people at Human Services and asked them about what I need to get this person to be eligible either for their pregnancy or their child to go through services here. Maybe I even work with somebody receiving Women Infants and Children (WIC) benefits.

> The parents did not want to come into our agency. For whatever reason, maybe transportation because I was far from school. So the school said, and I agreed with them wholeheartedly because it was their neighborhood, if the parent comes to school, we will fax the completed application to you.

> And I think one other thing that's helping that all of us sitting in this room today are doing is we use the same family assessment. Wherever they go first. Whether it's Head Start or the Health Department or Human Services. One of the questions on there is "Do you have insurance?" This triggers the person that's doing the assessment [to make the referral]. (Meyer, Yung, Ranbom, Cauley, Brun, & Fuller, 2001, pp. 125–126).

Quantitative Reporting of Qualitative Focus-Group Data

The following is a list of the most common outreach strategies across the ten counties as discussed in the direct-care staff focus groups. The numbers in parentheses refer to the number of the ten counties in which the strategy was mentioned:

- Print and broadcast media (10)
- Providing direct assistance to help persons fill out the application (10)
- Collaborating with other referral agencies to inform potential clients about CHIP (10)
- Distributing promotional items at a public fair (7)
- Word-of-mouth referrals (7)
- Providing workshops, presentations, or meetings with other agencies about CHIP (5)
- Home visits (2)

The most successful outreach activities were the following:

- Direct assistance to help potential clients fill out the application (7)
- Collaboration with agencies (6)
- Broadcast media, including broadcasts from adjoining counties (3)

The least successful outreach activities were the following:

- Print resources, specifically a mass mailing or mass distribution of brochures at a fair (3)
- Broadcast media (3) (Meyer et al., 2001, pp. 121–122)

MAJOR POINTS

Descriptive evaluations attempt to demonstrate a relationship between an intervention and desired outcomes or to describe the needs based on a needs assessment. A descriptive evaluation is different from an exploratory evaluation in that a descriptive evaluation has a predetermined focus on an intervention or population. A descriptive evaluation is different from an explanatory evaluation in that a descriptive evaluation can only identify a possible relationship between the intervention and client change rather than being able to test whether the intervention caused the client change. Even though an empowering, exploratory evaluation or a theoretical explanatory evaluation may be more desirable for some stakeholders, descriptive evaluations are more common because of feasibility, some stakeholders' requests, and persons' familiarity with rigorous evaluation methods. In this chapter, qualitative and descriptive as well as quantitative and descriptive designs were discussed. Examples of qualitative interview guides and a quantitative needs assessment questionnaire were discussed. The chapter ended with an example of the results reported for a mixed-methods descriptive evaluation.

CRITICAL-THINKING QUESTIONS

1. Read each of the evaluation questions or statements below and state whether the question or statement is exploratory, descriptive, or explanatory.
   a. What are the main outreach activities you performed to inform potential families that they were eligible for the Children's Health Insurance Program (CHIP)?
   b. There is a relationship between being a participant of the family support intervention (FSI) and improving family functioning.
   c. What is it like to be a survivor of cancer?
   d. Would you go to a health clinic if it was built nearby and was affordable?
   e. The suicide prevention presentation at the local high schools resulted in an increase of referrals for depression and a decrease in suicides.
2. Read an evidence-based study related to an evaluation you are planning or a study of an intervention of interest to you. What type of research or evaluation questions do the authors state are being posed: exploratory, descriptive, or explanatory? On the basis of the discussions throughout this book and especially in this chapter, do you agree with the author's claim to that type of question being posed? Why?
3. Should there be more exploratory evaluations conducted? Why?
4. Should there be more explanatory evaluations conducted? Why?
5. Are descriptive evaluations worth the effort if there is less control for the credibility of the data compared to explanatory evaluations? Why?
6. It was stated that a comparison group of an intervention that has not proved to be effective is more ethical than no intervention at all for a control group. Do you agree that it is OK to provide the comparison group an inferior intervention? Why?
7. Were there some terms used in this chapter that you do not agree with? Why?

DOCUMENTATION TASKS

Complete the questions below for every descriptive evaluation question being asked.

What is the overall research design?
___ Qualitative
___ Quasi-experimental
___ Single systems
How are participants selected?
___ Purposively
___ Randomly
Which data-collection method is being used? Attach data-collection tools.
___ Open-ended individual interviews
___ Open-ended focus groups
___ Open-ended written surveys
___ Open-ended observation
___ Open-ended analysis of secondary documents
___ Closed-ended individual interviews
___ Closed-ended focus groups
___ Closed-ended written surveys
___ Closed-ended observation
___ Closed-ended analysis of secondary documents
How are the data being analyzed?
___ Theme analysis
___ Statistical analysis
How is the credibility of the data-collection methods ensured?
___ Member checking
___ Peer debriefing
___ Evaluation audit
___ Triangulation
___ Reducing threats to validity
___ Increasing reliability
___ Other _____
    _____
    _____

DOCUMENTING EVALUATION DECISIONS: COMING FULL CIRCLE

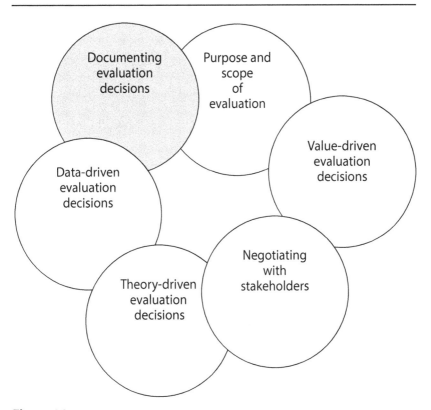

Figure 16.
Interactive model of evaluation: Documenting evaluation decisions

Ongoing Evaluation Reports

12

EVALUATION DECISION-MAKING QUESTIONS

Have you documented the important decisions agreed on by stakeholders concerning the following items?

___ Scope and purpose of the evaluation

___ Persons who are serving on the evaluation advisory committee

___ Evaluation plan

___ Evaluator contract for services

___ Evaluation questions

___ Logic model guiding evaluation decisions

___ Review of evidence-based practice guiding evaluation decisions

___ Data-collection methods

    ___ Participant selection

    ___ Evaluation design

    ___ Qualitative data-collection methods

    ___ Quantitative data-collection methods

    ___ Methods to ensure credibility

    ___ Methods for data analysis

___ Timeline for completion of evaluation tasks

___ Timeline for submission of reports

When writing the final report, who is the audience?

___ Consumers

___ Staff

___ Academic

___ Funders

What is the expected format of the final report?

DOCUMENTING DECISIONS THROUGHOUT THE EVALUATION CYCLE

The material in this book—especially the case examples, illustrations, and checklists—is meant to help the reader make evaluation decisions from the origination of the evaluation question to the final data analysis, decisions related to the following:

- *Clarifying the purpose and scope of the evaluation (chapters 1 and 2)*
- *Negotiating with key stakeholders about the values and ethics that drive evaluation decisions (chapters 3, 4, and 5)*
- *Identifying relevant theories that drive evaluation decisions through a logic model and literature review (chapters 6 and 7)*
- *Choosing the best approaches to data collection that drive evaluation decisions (chapters 8, 9, 10, and 11)*

The evaluation decision-making questions and documentation tasks in each chapter are meant to help the reader document these decisions as the decisions are made throughout an evaluation. It is important to document evaluation decisions as they are made. Evaluations often consume one or more years. People may forget at the end of an evaluation of the decisions they agreed to months and years earlier. Document evaluation decisions as if someone might conduct an audit of the entire evaluation process. Such thorough and comprehensive documentation will provide evidence and support of the decisions made along the way.

This chapter can help the reader document the connections among all the previous evaluation decisions made. Documentation is a necessary part of the accountability that social service workers owe key stakeholders because it records the original evaluation plan and any changes made to that plan. Documentation demonstrates to stakeholders how the findings, interpretations, and conclusions contained in the final report were related to the evaluation questions. It demonstrates how important values and theories were considered during the course of answering the evaluation questions. With this chapter we come full circle. Documentation should occur at every step of the evaluation, not just at the end.

Remember the list of potential reports summarized in checklist 3 that should be part of the stakeholder agreement? Only one of those documents was the final evaluation report. All the others are produced at different stages of the evaluation, beginning with the evaluation plan written in response to the request for proposals (RFP) to receive funding for an intervention.

This chapter serves as a review of the previous material by demonstrating how documentation conveys the evaluation decisions agreed on by key stakeholders. Evaluation reports are necessary to show how conclusions are based on the evaluation decisions addressed in the procedural journal activities at the end of each chapter. All those decisions are combined and summarized in the appendix.

The evaluation decisions discussed throughout this book happen along a plan-implement-evaluate-change continuum discussed in chapter 6 and diagrammed in figure 8: (1) evaluation decisions are planned, (2) evaluation procedures are implemented, (3) the implementation of evaluation decisions is itself evaluated, and (4) the evaluation itself undergoes change. This cycle is repeated until the previously agreed-on ending of the evaluation period. There needs to be an ending point to determine whether the goals of the evaluation were met and the evaluation questions were answered. Most evaluations are funded by internal and external sources that have deadlines. Social service workers can always apply for more funding and support to conduct additional evaluations to further promote the changes and knowledge gained from the previous evaluation and to address the limitations of prior evaluation decisions.

DOCUMENTING THE EVALUATION PLAN

Ideally, the development of a new evaluation plan follows this sequence:

1. Social service workers identify a concern among clients that needs intervention (e.g., eligible children are not being enrolled in the Children's Health Insurance Program, or CHIP).
2. They review the academic and professional literature to learn about interventions and evaluations that have addressed these concerns.
3. They develop simultaneously the most appropriate implementation and evaluation plans on the basis of the review of the literature and discussion with supportive stakeholders.

4. Then, they submit a response to a request for proposals (RFP) created from the information learned in the first three steps.

More common, however are the following scenarios.

1. *Social service workers submit an RFP to receive funding to implement an intervention.* They include a general evaluation plan, as required by the funder. An outside person may even be named to conduct the evaluation, but the evaluation is not yet fully developed. The primary focus is on describing the intervention. The evaluation will be further planned and developed if the RFP is accepted. The evaluation is an afterthought, not a plan integrated into the intervention.

Take the evaluation seriously. Take the time to get feedback from the proposed evaluator. His or her attention to the evaluation plan can improve the presentation of the need for the intervention. The best evaluation plans are those developed alongside intervention plans, and vice versa. Both evaluation and implementation plans should be based on a thorough review of the evaluation and research literature related to the proposed intervention and desired client changes. Be able to answer the question "How do you know this intervention will work?" One credible answer to that question requires a review of the literature, a clarification of the logic model behind the proposed intervention, and a clear plan to measure those desired results. Another credible answer is to develop an evaluation to explore client experiences related to the studied concern. Propose a feasible plan within the funding available and the timeline stated in the RFP.

2. *An evaluation team responds to an RFP to evaluate an intervention, a program, or multiple programs.* The RFP is often announced by the program's funding source. The evaluators propose a plan based on their review of the literature related to the interventions and client systems and on their own experiences with similar programs and populations. The evaluators may propose an evaluation plan based on the theories, literature, and logic models stated in the RFP, which are in turn based on the conditions of the agency contracts. The assumption of an evaluation plan in this case is that the programs are implemented according to the terms of the grant contracts the agency workers signed with the funding source.

Take the evaluation seriously. If you are in an agency that is asked to participate in this type of externally driven evaluation, become active in the planning, implementation, and review of the evaluation. Clarify the purpose of the evaluation and how the results will affect future funding. Clarify any changes the agency has made to the original proposal to the RFP, and get documented approval of any changes made to the intervention and evaluation plans in the contract. Learn from the evaluation, and take the initiative to plan future internally driven evaluations.

3. *A student develops an evaluation activity or an entire evaluation plan for a class assignment, thesis, or dissertation.* The student is conducting the evaluation activities for academic purposes. She gets permission to conduct the activity but does not really see her activities as leading to agency planning and program decisions.

Take the evaluation activity seriously. Evaluating one's own practice is a learning outcome expected under the Council on Social Work Education's (2012) Education Policy and Accreditation Standards and also an ethical practice mandated in the National Association of Social Workers' *Code of Ethics* (NASW, 2008). Integrate the student's learning process with that of agency improvement. How can the agency best utilize her application of evaluation skills? What data-collection tasks and overall evaluation plans can she assist the agency in conducting?

4. *An individual social service worker wants to evaluate an intervention with one or more clients.* The evaluation plan is not connected to a funding source. The worker wants to truly understand whether and how his intervention is helping clients. He may want to explore the experiences of different client systems.

Take the evaluation seriously. Give the worker time to develop the evaluation plan. Reinforce his efforts to evaluate practice. Encourage single-system design evaluations to help workers evaluate intervention with one client at a time. Build the agency's capacity to encourage more employees to conduct evaluations. Have evaluation support groups. Have literature review and reading groups. Financially reward evaluation planning.

The planning period starts with the RFP, a class assignment, or some other motivating event and continues until the evaluation activities are implemented. Ideally, data-collection activities do not begin until all stakeholders approve the plan. For one thing, a review process must occur to ensure that the data will be collected ethically. Also, data collection grounded in a solid plan allows others to see the credibility of the results reported. Sometimes, data are collected to guide the evaluation plan. In the example of the grant to develop a family violence plan, surveys were conducted with service providers to learn about the prevention activities already offered. This data-collection strategy still needed to be approved by the grant advisory group.

Documents created in the evaluation planning stage can become blueprints guiding and organizing future evaluation decisions. The RFP, the proposal submitted in response to the RFP, and the approved contract may contain the following:

1. *A literature review*: The successful interventions and evaluation procedures identified in that literature can be the jumping-off point for the replication of those procedures.
2. *A logic model*: Keep persons accountable to their stated or implied goals, activities, and expected results until they have documented reasons for changing them.
3. *The values*: If you have decided that clients will serve as advisers to the evaluation, make sure that they participate and feel welcome to give feedback. Ensure that the plan is informed by the SCREAM values discussed in chapter 3. If you are going to evaluate whether the intervention was delivered in a culturally competent manner, make this clear at the beginning.
4. *The timeline*: Establish deadlines for making planning, implementation, and evaluation decisions. Keep people to the timelines they agreed to in the evaluation stakeholder plan.
5. *The resources and contracted personnel*: The SCREAM value of resources is meant to remind social service workers to conduct evaluations that are within the agency's means. The evaluation stakeholder plan discussed in chapter 5 can serve as the contract specifying the tasks of each person responsible for the evaluation.

For an example of the original plan for the evaluation of family support interventions (FSIs), see case example 29.

Case Example 29. Documenting an Evaluation Plan

Scope of the Evaluation

The purpose of this externally driven evaluation was to evaluate the implementation of thirty-eight family support interventions (FSIs) employed
across the state. The key stakeholders were funders at the state level representing two different funding bodies, the Department of Education and the
Department of Jobs and Family Services. Local directors of the FSIs became
aware of the evaluation after the state contracted with the evaluation team.
The two-year, $250,000 evaluation was awarded through a competitive
request for proposals (RFP) to a team of university evaluators and
researchers. This data-collection team consisted of university social work
faculty from seven different universities across the state who conducted site
visits to all thirty-eight programs. Another evaluation team conducted the
participant telephone survey from one location. An evaluation advisory
board of state funders, local FSI stakeholders, and primary evaluators was
formed. FSI staff, community members, and consumers were represented
on the advisory board. All stakeholders agreed that the evaluation was
being conducted to describe the current implementation of FSIs and guide
future implementation decisions.

There were two general evaluation questions (one descriptive, the
other explanatory) that followed the evaluators' plan documented in the
RFP. The descriptive question was "How do different stakeholders (administrators, direct-care staff, community representatives, and consumers) perceive success of the programs?" The explanatory hypothesis posed was
"Consumers of the FSIs will significantly improve family functioning over an
eighteen-month period compared to persons with similar demographics
who did not receive the services of the programs."

The seven goals of the evaluation logic model below were written into
the RFP and approved by the stakeholders. There were specific objectives,
strategies, and timelines listed under each goal:

Goal 1. Provide a collaborative evaluation by organizing an interdisciplinary, cross-regional team of evaluators.
Goal 2. Coordinate all evaluation activities in consultation with the
state funders, FSI program directors, and parent consumers.
Goal 3. Assess current program results by providing qualitative
data from FSIs.

Goal 4. Analyze the qualitative data by identifying the results that the FSIs collect. These results will be organized according to the four systems: individuals, families, agencies, and communities.

Goal 5. Assess FSI participants' general family functioning by collecting quantitative survey data from consumers of services.

Goal 6. Develop an evaluation tool grounded in the qualitative data collection.

Goal 7. Disseminate the findings.

Adherence to SCREAM Values

The following SCREAM values were stated in the evaluation RFP:

- *Strengths* of client systems will be captured through open-ended interviews with FSI stakeholders and the use of a standardized instrument that measures family functioning.
- *Culturally competent* evaluation practices will be followed by conducting interviews with client systems from different backgrounds and including a comparison group that represents the demographics of the participants.
- *Resources* will be provided from the state funders for the evaluators to complete the agreed-on tasks. The main resource requested from the FSIs will be to provide time for local stakeholders to participate in the site visits and provide documentation requested from the evaluators.
- *Ethical* guidelines for assuring confidentiality and voluntary participation were approved by the institutional review board of the evaluators' university.
- The contractual *agreement* for the evaluation is between the funders, representing the state, and the university, as represented by the principal investigators. The evaluators and funders will explain the purpose and procedures of the evaluation to the evaluated program directors through written communication and meetings led by the evaluators and funders.
- *Multiple* systems will be represented by including consumers, direct-care staff, administrators, community representatives, and funders in the site interviews. The site interview guides will ask how FSIs measure changes in children, families, agencies, and communities.

Logic Model and Evidence-Based Practice Guiding Evaluation Decisions

The practice logic model written in the evaluation RFP for all FSIs was that healthy families be a short-term result for all programs. The primary desired long-term result for some community-based FSIs was the prevention of child abuse and neglect. The primary desired long-term result for the school-based FSIs was school readiness. There was variation in how local stakeholders perceived the program's theory for reaching the short- and long-term results. The literature review guiding the evaluation plan was based on theoretical and descriptive studies of community-based family support programs and evidence-based research and led to the evaluators implementing the Family Assessment Device to measure family functioning, the concept most appropriate to all FSIs.

Original Data-Collection Approaches Guiding Evaluation Decisions

The descriptive evaluation question will be answered through qualitative focus groups conducted with key stakeholders at each of the thirty-eight FSIs. The narrative responses to the interviews, observation notes, and secondary documents gathered will be organized according to changes in child, family, agency, and community. The explanatory evaluation question will be answered through a quantitative telephone survey conducted at three different times over eighteen months with FSI consumers and a comparison group. The survey will contain the twelve-item general functioning scale of the standardized Family Assessment Device.

EVALUATION PROGRESS REPORT

Evaluators, just like practitioners and planners, are expected to write formal progress reports. In many cases, these reports are expected every three to six months. They summarize the evaluation activities and preliminary findings. Following is one way to organize evaluation progress reports and the eventual final report.

Background Information.

In the background information section, state the circumstance that gave rise to the current evaluation, such as the evaluator's response to an RFP. Summarize the answers to these questions:

- Who authorized the evaluation and for what purposes?
- How will the evaluation be used to make program or implementation decisions?
- Who was hired to conduct the evaluation, and why were those persons selected?
- Who are the key stakeholders overseeing the evaluation?

- What is the timeline of the evaluation, and how is it connected to the planning and practice timelines?
- What are the values, theories, and data-collection expectations prior to beginning the evaluation?

Evaluation Purpose.

In the evaluation purpose section, state the evaluation questions as you see them given your interpretation of the background information. Phrase each set of questions in one of three ways:

1. The exploratory evaluation questions are . . .
2. The descriptive evaluation questions are . . .
3. The explanatory hypotheses are . . .

These three distinctions help clarify to the stakeholders the focus of each type of question. Go back to the discussions in earlier chapters to review the important relationship between type of question, theory (e.g., theory building, theory testing), and approaches (e.g., qualitative, quantitative) to data collection.

Evaluation Plan.

In the evaluation plan section, describe all aspects of the evaluation according to the decisions outlined at the end of each chapter and sum-marized in the appendix. Include the statement of values and the place of theory as these influenced the data-collection tasks. Specify who agreed to complete each data-collection task and within what timeline. For an example of a stakeholder agreement, see case example 30.

Case Example 30. Developing the Evaluation Stakeholder Agreement

The decisions that must be made in developing an evaluation stakeholder plan are applied here to the Children's Health Insurance Program (CHIP) outreach evaluation.

The authorizing stakeholders were the following: A review team from the state Department of Jobs and Family Services (DJFS) awarded an evaluation grant based on a competitive RFP process.

They agreed to complete the following tasks within the time frame stated: A representative from DJFS was assigned to the evaluation team. He met with the team to clarify the scope of the evaluation. He corresponded with the team through telephone conference calls monthly during the first six months of the evaluation.

They agreed to provide the following resources: The DJFS representative facilitated an information meeting with directors of county programs to receive local support for the evaluation team's county site visits. He sent a letter to the ten participating county agencies authorizing the activities of the evaluation team. He also collected the CHIP enrollment data that were analyzed by the evaluation team.

The evaluation advisory board consisted of the following: The DJFS representative communicated with two members of the evaluation team the expectations of the DJFS members who approved the evaluation grant. The DJFS representative reported to other stakeholders at the state agency.

They agreed to complete the following tasks within the time frame stated: All tasks of the advisory team were communicated and conducted by the DJFS representative.

They agreed to provide the following resources: All resources requested by the evaluation team were delivered by the DJFS representative.

The members of the evaluation team were the following: Seven faculty and staff who represented the following disciplines: social work, psychology, and community health.

They agreed to complete the following tasks within the time frame stated: (1) Conduct a quantitative analysis of CHIP enrollment data over a specified time period to determine the ten most successful counties across the state in enrolling eligible children. Two members of the evaluation team were primarily responsible for this task. The analysis was conducted in the first six months of the two-year evaluation period. (2) Develop the plan for conducting qualitative site interviews with key stakeholders in the ten most successful counties determined in task 1. Two members of the evaluation team developed the site visit plan. The site visit plan was completed by the end of the first six months. Site visits were actually conducted between the ninth and the twelfth months of the grant. The site visit information was analyzed and reported within the first six months of the second year of the grant. (3) Provide an annotated bibliography of research and evaluations nationwide related to CHIP enrollment. One faculty member and two of her students conducted the literature search to create the bibliography. The bibliography was completed within the first year of the grant and updated for the final report.

They agreed to provide the following resources: (1) Purchase the software to analyze the quantitative data. Analyze and report the data to the DJFS representative. (2) Purchase the equipment needed for the site interviews: tape recorders, special microphones to record up to ten focus-group participants, laptop computers to record the sessions, software to analyze the qualitative interviews, and poster board to facilitate the focus groups. Purchase grocery store vouchers for each consumer who participated in individual or group site interviews. Cover travel expenses, including overnight lodging for some of the site interviews. (3) Have access to library resources, that is, websites and academic research on the topic.

They agreed to provide the following products from the evaluation: Submit six-month progress reports. Submit a final report, including an executive summary. The final report included the procedures followed to carry out the three contracted tasks. The appendixes of the report included the procedures and findings of the three tasks.

Evaluation Progress.

In this section, describe progress toward achieving the tasks outlined in the evaluation design. Describe changes to any aspect of the evaluation, and note which stakeholders approved the changes. Facilitate the public dissemination of a progress report. For a summary of the midpoint review of the evaluation of FSIs, see case example 31.

Case Example 31. Documenting a Midpoint Evaluation Report

Scope of the Evaluation

Ongoing communication between the primary evaluators and the primary funders occurred weekly by telephone and e-mail and bimonthly through face-to-face meetings. A kickoff forum was held with the evaluation team and funders to clarify the scope and activities of the evaluation. The primary evaluator also attended two meetings with FSI directors to discuss the evaluation.

A formal report, "Results from Year One," was published and distributed to the state funders and directors of the thirty-eight FSIs. This report began with a three-page executive summary of the results from the site interviews and first round of telephone surveys. The main report contained the following sections:

1. Introduction
   a. Evaluation goals
   b. Evaluation design
   c. Use of this report
2. Site-visit findings
   a. Child and/or student measures and desired results
   b. Family environment measures and desired results
   c. Agency and/or school access measures and desired results
   d. Multiagency collaboration measures and desired results
   e. FSI evaluation activities
3. Telephone survey findings
   a. How to read this section
   b. FSI results
   c. FSI comparison group results
4. Discussion and recommendations
   a. Family support: measures of desired community change and agency change
   b. Family health and stability: measures of desired family change and child change
   c. Recommendations: continued telephone survey and implementation of common evaluation tool
5. Appendixes
   a. Goals and objectives
   b. Glossary of terms
   c. Telephone survey tables
   d. Budget

The report documented that the original goals, objectives, and timelines were met. The original evaluation questions remained relevant from the evaluators' standpoints.

Adherence to SCREAM Values

Strengths of client systems were captured through open-ended interviews with FSI stakeholders. The open-ended, qualitative focus-group format gave staff and clients an opportunity to tell their stories of the success of the FSIs even if there was not measurable evidence of those successes. There was some criticism from stakeholders that the instrument used to measure family functioning could actually be perceived as focusing on dysfunction rather than healthy functioning.

Culturally, FSIs located in urban areas had a higher African American population than did the rural FSIs, which had a predominantly white population. There were more female than male participants in the telephone survey. The modal age group represented in the survey was between twenty-five and forty-four. There was a wide range among participants on education and income.

Resources were adequate to complete the evaluation tasks.

Approval of the *ethical* guidelines needed to be resubmitted at the end of each year of the grant.

The one-year report became the basis on which to reexamine the original stakeholder *agreement*.

Multiple systems' desired results were reported in the focus groups.

Theory Building and Testing

Four different agency practice logic models emerged from the focus-group data:

1. *Community-change model*: The goal is to create change in the community-wide delivery system. Activities are intended to increase service coordination and community involvement. The short-term results are changes in the community that will eventually lead to improved functioning for families and children in the community.
2. *Agency-change model*: The goal is increased members of families with access to agency services. Activities are intended to increase parent involvement, increase child involvement, expand service capacity, establish positive rapport between staff and families, and provide families with supportive services such as transportation to the agency. The short-term results are changes in the agency's accessibility, which will eventually lead to improved functioning for families and children in the community.
3. *Family-change model*: The goal is to improve conditions for families. Activities are intended to decrease child abuse and neglect, help families meet their physical needs, increase parent knowledge and positive parenting behavior, reduce stress for parents, and improve health for children and parents. The short-term results are changes in the family that will lead to changes for children and the larger community.
4. *Child-change model*: The goal is to improve child physical, emotional, educational, and social behaviors. Activities are intended to increase school performance, increase positive social interactions with peers and

adults, and promote positive emotional development for children. The short-term results are changes in the child that will eventually lead to improved functioning for families and the larger community.

These four logic models did support the literature review findings about the range of family support programs. At the same time, not all the models identified family functioning as a short-term result. This became a data-collection issue because family functioning was being measured by consumers of all FSIs, not just the agencies following a family-change model.

Preliminary Results from Data Collection

Results from the two data-collection approaches were reported. The four different types of agency-change models emerged from the qualitative focus groups. There was no significant difference on the Family Assessment Device (FAD) between the FSI participants and the comparison group. Both groups were reporting healthy family functioning. The evaluation question addressed by the survey became more of a descriptive than an explanatory question because a true random sample of the FSI participants was not obtained.

The above format is a logic model for conceptualizing evaluations and demonstrating the sequential connection between each component of evaluation. The original background information and the original evaluation questions become the foundation for all other decisions. This format is similar to the working contract used by social service workers in clinical settings. It is flexible, allowing for changes based on feedback from key stakeholders.

Evaluations and the documents resulting from them can be part of a larger grant for program planning or implementation. Be clear about whether the agency report and evaluation report will be mailed to the funders together or separately. Agencies are sometimes requested to submit evaluation reports as part of the periodic program reports. In such cases, distinguish between the evaluation report and the program report, clarifying who authored each.

DOCUMENTING CHANGES TO THE EVALUATION

The evaluation process itself should be evaluated. This should occur continuously through communication between the primary evaluator and the primary stakeholders authorizing the evaluation. Formal, written feedback about the evaluation should be provided every three to six months, with a major review conducted no later than the midpoint of the evaluation.

All aspects of the evaluation should be reviewed. The following are some questions to consider about the performance of the evaluation team:

- Is the evaluation team following the stakeholder agreement plan and any other applicable formal contracts?
- Are the evaluators communicating with an agreed-on representative of the funding source or evaluation stakeholder group regarding the progress of the evaluation?
- Is the required documentation (e.g., six-month reports, literature reviews, evaluation training material) following the agreed-on format and content?
- Are the evaluators following ethical guidelines in conducting the evaluation?
- Is the evaluation team following the agreed-on timeline for conducting evaluation tasks and submitting results?

In addition to evaluating the performance of the evaluation team, some stakeholders may want to change the focus and scope of an evaluation after the original proposal is accepted. Evaluation contracts should allow at the latest a midpoint negotiation of the evaluation goals, questions, and tasks based on stakeholder input about the evaluation. Some of the reasons stakeholders may request a change in the evaluation focus are the following:

- Sometimes with the clarification of the evaluation process comes the realization that the actual evaluation activities are very different from expectations based on the evaluation proposal. Questions therefore arise that must be addressed.
- Ramifications of the evaluation decisions also become clear as the evaluation activities are implemented. Stakeholders and participants often become nervous about how the evaluation findings will affect future program decisions.
- Stakeholders may decide that certain evaluation questions need to be added or removed for reasons having nothing to do with the evaluation itself.
- Preliminary results may lead to a change in the scope of the evaluation.

- Stakeholders may want the evaluation team to play a more active role in training agency staff about the evaluation process. Stakeholders may want the evaluators to serve the role of facilitator or educator rather than the role of outside, objective evaluator. Or the opposite may be preferred. Maybe the stakeholders feel the evaluator has too much influence on agency practices and should be more objective and unobtrusive.

For an example of the process involved in evaluating changes to the two-year evaluation of FSIs, see case example 32.

Case Example 32. Evaluating an Evaluation

Evaluating the Original Scope of the Evaluation

The first-year report became the basis for evaluating whether changes should be made to the original scope, goals, and activities of the evaluation. The evaluators proposed that a common evaluation tool could be administered with ten FSIs during the second year of the grant. Other stakeholders emphasized the importance of FSIs measuring child outcomes, especially related to school performance. Some stakeholders wanted the evaluators to provide more technical assistance to help FSI staff conduct self-evaluations since very few FSIs had conducted credible evaluations of their programs.

Evaluating the Original Adherence to SCREAM Values

- *Strengths* of client systems were captured in all four types of FSI logic models. All FSIs had embraced the philosophy of the family support movement to encourage positive agency-client interaction. Stakeholders never questioned the evaluation's emphasis on strengths. Some stakeholders did question whether the agency and community change models resulted in short-term changes in families and children.
- *Culturally competent* evaluation practices were followed. The qualitative focus groups did capture the cultural diversity of the FSI client so stakeholders rightfully pointed out that the telephone survey missed lower-income families with no access to a telephone.
- *Resources* continued to be appropriate to complete the original evaluation activities. Some stakeholders felt, however, that the resources used for the telephone survey and proposed common evaluation tool could be better spent on helping agencies conduct self-evaluations.

- Any changes to the *ethical* guidelines continued to be submitted and approved by the institutional review board.
- The contractual *agreement* for the evaluation was up for negotiation based on feedback from the first-year report.
- *Multiple* systems were captured in the focus group data. Some stakeholders did not agree that the funding should support change models that do not target short-term child and family results.

Original Theory Guiding Evaluation Decisions

Even though all FSIs had the long-term desired result of improving family functioning, there were two separate, additional long-term results expected across FSIs: (1) improved school readiness and (2) the prevention of child abuse and neglect. There was disagreement among stakeholders about whether it was feasible for FSIs to achieve all three long-term results. The focus from stakeholders for literature reviews also moved toward evidence-based practices to improve school performance.

Original Data-Collection Approaches Guiding Evaluation Decisions

Much descriptive information was learned from the qualitative focus groups. At the same time, several stakeholders wanted to see the FSIs collect more measurable child and family outcomes. There was also discussion about whether to continue the second and third telephone surveys since the original hypothesis was not upheld by the findings to date. The evaluators emphasized that the longitudinal nature of the telephone survey design could still produce significant results in the second and third measures:

- Stakeholders did agree to continue the second and third telephone surveys, but with the addition of outcome measures related to school success.
- Stakeholders chose not to implement a comprehensive, multiple-level outcomes measure due to not having the resources to adequately implement the measures.
- Stakeholders chose to have the evaluators conduct a comprehensive review of the evidence-based literature related to child outcome measures. This evaluation product was published after the evaluation was completed.

Any changes to the original evaluation plan must be documented and agreed on. This can mean establishing an entirely new contract with the same evaluators or simply making additions to the original proposal. Evaluation is negotiation. All of chapter 5 was devoted to the many issues that influence evaluation stakeholders' decisions. Key stakeholders, including consumers, should be given the opportunity to offer feedback about the evaluation. The evaluators are stakeholders too and need to make their positions on the evaluation decisions clear. If agreement about proposed changes cannot be reached, the option that the evaluation contract can be discontinued should exist.

For an example of the changes agreed on in the evaluation of the FSIs on the basis of the midpoint review, see case example 33.

Case Example 33. Documenting Changes Made to an Evaluation

Changes to the Original Scope of the Evaluation

On the basis of the points discussed in case example 31, a new evaluation plan was written and approved by the evaluation advisory board. The following were changes to the original scope of the evaluation:

1. Add these descriptive evaluation questions:
   a. Do school-based FSIs report positive changes in school performance?
   b. What are the most valid and reliable instruments that FSIs can implement to measure desired child and family outcomes?
   c. Are parents becoming more involved in their children's school performance?
2. Add these data-collection tasks:
   a. All school-based FSIs must provide actual results of school performance that minimally include pass rates of proficiency scores, attendance, retention, and graduation.
   b. The evaluators will add to the telephone survey questions that ask participants how involved they are in their child's education and whether their child has improved in school.
   c. The evaluators will conduct literature reviews of standardized instruments that measure child health, family health, and parents' involvement in their child's school performance.
3. Omit the original evaluation goal to develop and administer a common evaluation tool across a selected number of FSIs.

Changes to Adherence to the SCREAM Values

- *Strengths* of client systems will be a focus of the instrument critiques listed in item 2 above. Administration of the FAD for times 2 and 3 will continue to measure healthy family functioning. No new qualitative data were collected from the FSI sites during the second year of the evaluation.
- *Culturally competent* instruments will be a focus of the instrument critiques in item 2. The telephone survey was repeated with the same participants as in time 1. Recidivism among participants did not vary across cultural groups.
- *Resources* continued to be appropriate to complete the revised evaluation activities.
- *Ethical* guidelines continued to be followed. Changes to the telephone survey were approved by the university's institutional review board.
- *Agreement* was reached by all stakeholders to the changes suggested.
- *Multiple* systems measurements were now focused primarily on family functioning as measured by the FAD and child and family outcomes through the instrument critiques. The agency and community-based results emphasized by stakeholders at some FSIs were not being measured in the second year.

Changes to the Theory Driving Evaluation Decisions

The child and family change logic models became the primary focus in the second year. Even more specifically, the logic model that focused on school-based FSIs mandated that the requirement to measure school performance become more important. The literature review shifted toward a critical review of rigorous, credible instruments that measured child health, family health, and parent involvement.

Changes to Data Collection

The administration of the quantitative telephone survey continued during times 2 and 3. The proposal to implement a common evaluation tool across ten selected FSIs was not approved. Rather, this data-collection task was replaced with the tasks involving completing the instrument critiques.

THE FINAL REPORT

There is usually one formal evaluation report that needs to be submitted to at least one source, usually the funder of the evaluation or of the program being evaluated. The report must follow the guidelines required by the funder for that final report. Common formats for the final report are described later in this section. Evaluators can adapt the final report to meet the needs of other key stakeholders described next.

Consumer Audience.

Consumers are the persons who utilize the intervention being evaluated. In many evaluations, all of the consumers or a sample of the consumers are recruited to be participants in the data-collection process. It is a requirement of the institutional review board (IRB) at most universities that the "consent to participate" form contain a sentence informing the potential participant on how she or he can obtain results of the evaluation.

In many situations an evaluation website is established so that consumers and other stakeholders can access information regarding the progress of the evaluation and findings from the evaluation. Be clear about what information will be made available on a public website. To protect confidentiality of the participants, raw data should not be made available to consumers or the general public. Raw data are the narrative and numerical responses to questions before the data are reduced to themes or statistical analysis. Evaluators are obligated only to report the aggregate or group data of the evaluation to consumers or the general public. Reporting group data is one way to ensure the confidentiality of individual responses. In terms of ethics, individual survey or instrument responses and individual or group narratives must be kept in a secure location not accessible to anyone besides the evaluators.

The aggregation and interpretation of data is time consuming. Some consumers may want to know the evaluation results shortly after completing a data-collection instrument. In many situations, the full analysis of the group data and the interpretation of that data may not occur for six to twelve months after the data were collected. By having an evaluation website, consumers can continually search for evaluation updates on their own.

Program staff, not evaluators, choose whether and how to announce to consumers that the final evaluation report is available. An important component of the plan-implement-evaluate-change cycle is that evaluation data are shared with key stakeholders and used to make programmatic changes. Thus, evaluation sections on an agency website can be one method to invite feedback from consumers on the findings from an evaluation. For example, the Council on Social Work Education (CSWE) requires social work education programs to have an assessment feedback loop. This assessment loop must demonstrate how students, faculty, and community advisory persons have access to annual assessment findings and how those findings are used to make program changes. Many social work education programs post their annual assessment reports to a program website. This annual assessment report should contain information about how program changes were made from the data. Social work education programs can also post the self-study that is required every eight years and the CSWE Commission of Accreditation response to the self-study and site visit report.

Decide which information will be shared with persons participating in qualitative, open-ended individual interviews. It was mentioned earlier that one method of achieving credibility of qualitative data is to complete a member check. A member check is providing the participant with the evaluator's interpretation of the interview. This interpretation can be in the form of a full verbatim transcript, a paraphrased transcript removing utterances and repeated content, a summary of the interview, or a theme analysis of the interview. Focus-group data are reported as aggregate themes or collective responses to the questions and not as individual responses to the questions.

The general community can also be considered potential consumers of the service. The general community can be taxpayers if the program is funded publicly, persons who are eligible for the services, residents where the agency is located, family members of consumers, or consumer advocates. For example, members of the National Alliance for the Mentally Ill were interested in the results of the evaluation of mental health competencies. Posting a public evaluation website allows all interested persons to have access to the data one chooses to post to that website.

Staff Audience.

Program staff can be planners and participants of the evaluation. Staff can also be from the agency delivering the intervention or agencies collaborating on the intervention.

Even though the final evaluation report will contain collective, aggregate data, stakeholders should decide ahead of time how site-specific data will be reported. For example, in an evaluation of the integration of school and mental health services, staff from thirty-seven schools participated in a survey. The survey contained questions about the respondents' knowledge of mental health issues for youth and the process for making a mental health referral. The survey was conducted two times. During the first time, there was a 25 percent response rate. The collective findings across the entire school district were reported to the general public, but the directors of the grant used school-specific results to target those schools that needed focused training on mental health issues.

Staff also included persons at different administrative levels: direct-line staff, supervisors, program managers, vice presidents, presidents, and board of directors. Stakeholders should identify ahead of time how site-specific or staff-specific data will be utilized. Potential participants need to be informed of how the data may be used also, especially if the data will be used to make decisions to keep or eliminate programs.

Academic Audience.

A theme of this book is that evaluations produce findings that help agencies make practice and planning decisions and contribute to evidence-based knowledge in the social sciences. Academic audiences may include honors, thesis, or dissertation committees or teachers of research courses for persons using part or all of the evaluation as part of their studies. Academic audiences may also be readers of peer-reviewed journals in which evaluation findings are published and presentations at professional organization's conferences or annual meetings.

Stakeholders of an evaluation must agree that the student or evaluator be able to submit academic products from the evaluation. Include such an agreement in writing as part of the evaluation contract. Respect confidentiality of participants in all academic reports. If desired by the agency, do not disclose the name of the agency in any publications or presentations. Include consumers and agency stakeholders as coauthors of submitted articles and presentations. Formats for academic submissions will be discussed later.

Funder Audience.

The funders have legal rights to all of the data as long as the data do not infringe on participants' right to confidentiality. Funders prefer a summary of the evaluation findings to be as brief as possible. I also provide the funders with comprehensive results to be accountable for how the summary was drawn from the original data. Thus, I provide funders with the SPSS codebook, descriptive data of the value responses to each variable on a data-collection tool, results of all co-relational and causal statistical tests run, and all graphs or diagrams completed. Similarly, I provide all transcriptions and theme analyses completed. Later, I discuss common formats for the final report that are often requested by funders.

Final Report Format.

The final evaluation report summarizes all the evaluation activities, results, and analyses of the results. Many stakeholders request that the final report include a recommendations section based on the findings of the evaluation. Clarify from the beginning whether recommendations are expected and, if so, how those recommendations will be utilized. Patton (2012) states that discussing utilization of the evaluation is necessary before the evaluation begins.

In general, the final report should contain the following components:

1. Evaluation background and context (material covered in parts 1 and 3)
2. Evaluation questions (material covered in part 1)
3. Literature review (material covered in part 4)
4. Logic model (material covered in part 4) (not present in all evaluations)
5. Methods (material covered in part 5)
6. Findings (material covered in part 5)
7. Discussion (connecting the findings to the original evaluation questions, purpose, and scope of the evaluation).
8. Appendixes (evaluation outputs listed in checklist 3 and repeated in the appendix to this book).

Evaluation is a teaching and learning opportunity. In some evaluations, stakeholders request structured training materials that they can use once the evaluation is completed. Examples of such training materials include the following:

- Annotated bibliographies and literature reviews related to the evaluation questions

- Critiques of standardized instruments that measure the desired outcomes
- A basic outline of evaluation tasks similar to the evaluation decision-making questions in the appendix

For an example of material contained in the final report of the FSI evaluation, see case example 34.

Case Example 34. Items Contained in the Final Report of the Evaluation of Family Support Interventions

A formal report, "A Combined Methods Evaluation of Family Support Interventions (FSIs): Final Report of Results," was published and distributed in hard copy and on CD to the state funders. The printed copy of the report was distributed to the directors of the thirty-eight FSIs. This report began with a twenty-page executive summary of the results from the entire survey that also contained a recommendations for future evaluations section.

The main report contained the following sections:

Section I. Evaluation background and context
Section II. Review of first-year site interview results
Section III. FSI consumer survey findings
Section IV. Discussion
Section V. Recommendations for future evaluations
Appendixes:

   A. Steps to conducting program evaluation
   B. Steps to conducting program evaluation applied to the FSI evaluation
   C. Site interview questions
   D. Phone survey questions
   E. Glossary of evaluation terms
   F. Evaluation resources
   G. Examples of evaluation questions related to school-based FSI logic models
   H. Examples of evaluation questions related to the theorized impacts of collaboration
   I. Promotional indicators for FSIs
   J. Resources for conducting culturally competent evaluation
   K. Demographic tables
   L. Statistical tables for telephone survey (CD-ROM only)

Three separate documents were submitted that contained instrument critiques of:

A. Child health
B. Family health
C. Parent involvement

Notice that the final report began with an executive summary, which is a brief (three- to twenty-page) synopsis of the evaluation activities. Some stakeholders, especially policy makers, take the time to read only the executive summary. Make sure, therefore, that it demonstrates the connection between the scope of the evaluation, the evaluation questions, the values driving the evaluation, the theories underlying the evaluation, the methods used to collect the data, and the findings reported. The executive summary should contain any limitations of the evaluation and how the evaluation results can be utilized.

The exploratory research with parents described in this book was not a formal evaluation of an agency intervention. Therefore, there was no contractual agreement related to submission of evaluation reports. The researcher did, however, have an ethical obligation to provide the results to the participants. He informed all participants how they could obtain a copy of the final report, which in this case was his dissertation. Expecting that the participants would not request that verbose academic document, the researcher did mail or hand deliver to each participant her narrative, which was about twenty pages long. And with permission from each participant, he also verbally reported the findings of the research to the agency workers who helped facilitate contact with the participants.

The published products from this study were the researcher's dissertation, a presentation to parents and agency workers of National Head Start, and an article in a journal published by Head Start (Brun, 1997). Head Start parents and staff were chosen as an audience for dissemination because one goal of Head Start is to support the strengths of families. Readers must determine for themselves whether the themes from the dissertation study and excerpts from the parent participants can be applied to similar families they help.

In the evaluation of the strengths-based case management (SBCM), progress reports were provided to the director of the program. All participants, consumers and social service workers, were informed that they could obtain the results of the evaluation. Only the director requested written results. Be clear about what information you will provide to those requesting the results. Provide a brief summary and information about how a more detailed report can be obtained, for example, by contacting the funder for a copy of the final report, tracking down publications related to the evaluation, or attending conferences at which the evaluation is to be discussed.

The evaluator provided a summary presentation to the staff of the SBCM. The director attended the presentation and discussed ways in which the staff could make program changes based on feedback from the consumer participants. The evaluator mailed or hand delivered the summaries of the interviews to each consumer participant. The director of the agency and the evaluator presented results of the evaluation at an NASW conference and had a cowritten article published in *Social Work* (Brun & Rapp, 2001). Readers of the article can determine how the authors' analysis of the SBCM program can be applied to their own social service setting.

Think of each evaluation as an opportunity to improve practice and contribute to the knowledge base. Consider presenting your results at local, state, national, and international conferences. Consider submitting the findings to professional journals. Work with other stakeholders to accomplish these activities. For more information on report writing and submitting evaluation findings for publication, consult the "Further Resources" section at the end of this chapter.

MAJOR POINTS

We have now come full circle. Documenting the decisions made at each step in the evaluation makes writing the final report much easier and shows the connection between all the decisions. Such documentation also shows the integration of planning, implementation, and evaluation of programs. Documentation of values, theories, and data-collection approaches guiding the evaluation keeps the practitioner accountable. Evaluation, like practice, goes through a cycle of planning, implementing, evaluating, and changing. Material to consider in preliminary and final evaluation reports was discussed. This book ends with the encouragement to share the findings of your evaluation with others at conferences and in professional journals.

CRITICAL-THINKING QUESTIONS

1. Now that you have come to the last chapter, have your views about evaluation changed since you first started this book?
2. Are you more optimistic or more pessimistic about the place of evaluation in the social service setting?
3. Are you more confident or less confident in your evaluation skills?
4. Do you see this book helping you with future evaluations?
5. How can you utilize the lists, case examples, and figures in this book for evaluations?
6. As a student, do you see yourself as a future practitioner-evaluator?
7. As a practitioner, do you see yourself as a practitioner-evaluator?

FURTHER RESOURCES

Drisko, J. (1997). Strengthening qualitative studies and reports: Standards to promote academic integrity. *Journal of Social Work Education, 33*(1), 185–197.

Padgett, D. (2004). Spreading the word: Writing up and disseminating qualitative research. In D. Padgett (Ed.), *The qualitative research experience* (pp. 285–296). Belmont, CA: Wadsworth/Thomson Learning.

Thyer, B. (2002). How to write up a social work outcome study for publication. *Journal of Social Work Research and Evaluation, 3*(2), 215–224.

Torres, R., Preskill, H., & Piontak, M. (2005). *Evaluation strategies for communicating and reporting: Enhancing learning in organizations.* Thousand Oaks, CA: Sage.

Westerfelt, A., & Dietz, T. (2010). *Planning and conducting agency-based research: A workbook for social work students in field placements* (4th ed.). Boston, MA: Allyn & Bacon.

DOCUMENTATION TASKS

Have you documented the following evaluation decisions?

___ Original evaluation plan
___ Adherence to the SCREAM values
___ Logic model that guided evaluation decisions
___ Review of evidence-based practice that guided evaluation decisions
___ Data-collection decisions
___ Evaluation progress reports
___ Changes to the evaluation

Preparing the final evaluation report

Who is the audience?

___ Consumers
___ Staff
___ Academic
___ Funders

Have you included all of the following components of the final report?

1. Evaluation background and context
2. Evaluation questions
3. Literature review
4. Logic model
5. Methods
6. Findings
7. Discussion
8. Appendixes

What are the evaluation documentation outputs?

___ Written evaluation proposal or plan
___ Written evaluation logic model
___ Written amendments to the evaluation plan (approved and signed by key stakeholders)
___ Written evaluation progress reports submitted every _____ months

___ Written final evaluation report containing the following
components:
   ___ Executive summary
   ___ Key stakeholders overseeing the evaluation
   ___ Purpose and scope of evaluation
   ___ Evaluation questions
   ___ Evaluation methodology
   ___ Copy of all data-collection tools used
   ___ Evaluation findings: Summary
   ___ Evaluation findings: All statistical tables
   ___ Evaluation findings: All narrative responses
   ___ Discussion of findings
   ___ Recommendations
   ___ Bibliography
   ___ Literature review
   ___ Written educational material on how to conduct
   evaluations
___ Presentations on _____ given to the following stake-
holders: ___
___ Manuscripts written by _____ to be submitted to _____
___ Call for papers written by ____ to be submitted to _____

APPENDIX

EVALUATION DECISION-MAKING QUESTIONS OUTLINE

When reviewing this outline, check the items that have been completed for the evaluation and fill in the blanks.

PART ONE: CLARIFY THE PURPOSE AND SCOPE OF THE EVALUATION

Chapter 1: Purpose of Evaluation

Why evaluate?
 ___ Evaluation is good practice.
 ___ Evaluation improves services.
 ___ Evaluation is accountability—summative evaluation.
 ___ The evaluation process is beneficial—formative evaluation.
 ___ Evaluation is applied research that builds knowledge.
 ___ Other: _____

Who wants the evaluation?
 ___ Recipients/consumers/clients of the services: _____
 ___ Funders: _____
 ___ Service providers: _____
 ___ Community members: _____
 ___ Evaluators: _____
 ___ Other: _____

What are the goals of the evaluation?
 ___ To improve existing programs by measuring program outcomes—summative evaluation.
 ___ To conduct a needs assessment and plan needed programs—formative evaluation.
 ___ To build knowledge
 ___ Other: _____

What are the expected outputs of the evaluation and due dates?
 ___ Written evaluation proposal or plan due ___
 ___ Written evaluation logic model due ___

___ Written amendments to an existing evaluation plan due ___
___ Written evaluation progress reports due _____
___ Written final evaluation report due ___
___ Executive summary due ___
___ Recommendations due ___
___ Bibliography due ___
___ Literature review due ___
___ Presentation on the evaluation findings due ___
___ Peer-reviewed manuscript on the evaluation due ___
___ Call for papers submission due ___
___ Response to request for proposals (RFP) submission due ___
___ Other: _____

Chapter 2: Scope of the Evaluation

Which current interventions will be evaluated?

What exploratory evaluation questions are being asked?

What explanatory evaluation questions are being asked?

What descriptive evaluation questions are being asked?

PART 2: VALUE-DRIVEN EVALUATION DECISIONS

Chapter Three: S C R E A M

What strengths will be measured in the evaluation?
    Participants' strengths: _____
    Agency strengths: _____

Community strengths: _____

Other strengths: _____

What culturally competent steps will be taken in the evaluation?

Appropriate language: _____

Respectful interactions: _____

Participant involvement in planning the evaluation: _____

Other: _____

What are the resources available for the evaluation?

Available funds: _____

In-kind resources _____

Hourly amount of time needed: _____

Other: _____

What multiple-systems-level results will be measured in the evaluation?

Individual results _____

Family or group results _____

Agency results _____

Community results _____

Chapter 4: Ethical Guidelines for Evaluations

Have the following ethical guidelines been followed?

_____ Evaluation approved by an institutional review board (IRB) or equivalent.

_____ Written stakeholder agreement plan is complete.

_____ There is no potential harm for participants.

_____ Informed consent form is prepared.

_____ Confidentiality of participants is protected.

_____ Voluntary participation is assured.

_____ Participants are openly aware of all aspects of participating in the evaluation.

_____ Evaluation procedures are respectful of the cultures of all participants.

_____ Procedures for evaluating the evaluation are agreed upon.

_____ Evaluators openly discussed potential conflicts of interests or values.

_____ Benefits of conducting the evaluation are stated.

_____ Other: _____

PART THREE: NEGOTIATING WITH STAKEHOLDERS

Chapter 5: The Politics of Evaluation

Has an evaluation agreement plan with the following information been completed?

   ___ List authorizing stakeholders, their constituency, their tasks, and timeline.

       _____ from _____ will do _____ by _____.
       _____ from _____ will do _____ by _____.
       _____ from _____ will do _____ by _____.

   ___ List evaluation advisory board members, their constituency, their tasks, and timeline.

       _____ from _____ will do _____ by _____.
       _____ from _____ will do _____ by _____.
       _____ from _____ will do _____ by _____.

   ___ List evaluation team members, their constituency, their tasks, and timeline.

       _____ from _____ will do _____ by _____.
       _____ from _____ will do _____ by _____.
       _____ from _____ will do _____ by _____.

PART FOUR: THEORY-DRIVEN EVALUATION DECISIONS

Chapter 6: Developing a Logic Model

What is the logic model for one to three interventions being evaluated?

Intervention 1   Goal   Strategies   Short-term results   Long-term results

Intervention 2   Goal   Strategies   Short-term results   Long-term results

Intervention 3   Goal   Strategies   Short-term results   Long-term results

___ Are the goals, strategies, and results logically and theoretically
linked?
___ Are the SCREAM values addressed in the logic model?
___ What are the valid, reliable, and credible measures of the results?

Chapter 7: Conducting Literature Reviews

What are the sources used for the literature review?

What are the keywords used for the literature search?

What are five to ten possible abstracts related to the evaluation?

For each of the five to ten full articles reviewed, address the following
items:
Proper APA citation

Research or evaluation questions posed by the authors

Research design: Qualitative, experimental, quasi-experimental, single
systems

Research protocol:
Sample: How selected? Sample size, sample demographics

Data collection: List the instruments used to answer questions, observe, or analyze secondary documents

Data analysis: Themes or statistical

Findings

Implications of this study to your evaluation

PART FIVE: DATA-DRIVEN EVALUATION DECISIONS

Chapters 8–11: Research Methods: Qualitative, Quantitative, and Mixed Methods

What information is being transformed into data?

What are the exploratory evaluation questions being asked?

How are participants purposively selected?

Which data-collection methods are being used? Attach data-collection tools.
___ Open-ended individual interviews
___ Open-ended focus groups
___ Open-ended written surveys
___ Open-ended observation
___ Open-ended analysis of secondary documents

How is a theme analysis of the data being conducted?

How is the credibility of the data-collection methods ensured?
___ Member checking
___ Peer debriefing
___ Evaluation audit
___ Triangulation
___ Other: _____

What are the descriptive evaluation questions being asked?

What is the overall research design?
___ Qualitative
___ Quasi-experimental
___ Single systems

How are participants selected?
___ Purposively
___ Randomly

Which data-collection method is being used? Attach data-collection tools.
___ Open-ended individual interviews
___ Open-ended focus groups
___ Open-ended written surveys
___ Open-ended observation
___ Open-ended analysis of secondary documents
___ Closed-ended individual interviews
___ Closed-ended focus groups
___ Closed-ended written surveys
___ Closed-ended observation
___ Closed-ended analysis of secondary documents

How are the data being analyzed?
___ Theme analysis
___ Statistical analysis

How is the credibility of the data-collection methods ensured?
___ Member checking
___ Peer debriefing
___ Evaluation audit
___ Triangulation
___ Reducing threats to validity
___ Increasing reliability
___ Other: _____

What are the explanatory evaluation questions being asked?

What is the overall quantitative research design?
___ Experimental
___ Single systems

How are the participants randomly selected?

Which data-collection method is being used? Attach data-collection tools.
   ___ Closed-ended individual interviews
   ___ Closed-ended focus groups
   ___ Closed-ended written surveys
   ___ Closed-ended observation
   ___ Closed-ended analysis of secondary documents

What statistical analyses are being conducted?

How is the credibility of the data-collection methods ensured?
   ___ Reducing threats to validity
   ___ Increasing reliability
   ___ Other: _____

PART SIX: DOCUMENTING EVALUATION DECISIONS

Chapter 12: Ongoing Evaluation Reports

Have you documented the following evaluation decisions?
   ___ Original evaluation plan
   ___ Adherence to the SCREAM values
   ___ Logic model that guided evaluation decisions
   ___ Review of evidence-based practice that guided evaluation decisions
   ___ Data-collection decisions
   ___ Evaluation progress reports
   ___ Changes to the evaluation

Preparing the final evaluation report
   Who is the audience?
      Consumers ___
      Staff ___
      Academic ___
      Funders ___

Have you included all of the following components of the final report?
1. Evaluation background and context
2. Evaluation questions
3. Literature review
4. Logic model
5. Methods
6. Findings
7. Discussion
8. Appendixes

What are the evaluation documentation outputs?
___ Written evaluation proposal or plan
___ Written evaluation logic model
___ Written amendments to the evaluation plan (approved and signed by key stakeholders)
___ Written evaluation progress reports submitted every _____ months
___ Written final evaluation report containing the following components:
    ___ Executive summary
    ___ Key stakeholders overseeing the evaluation
    ___ Purpose and scope of evaluation
    ___ Evaluation questions
    ___ Evaluation methodology
    ___ Copy of all data-collection tools used
    ___ Evaluation findings: Summary
    ___ Evaluation findings: All statistical tables
    ___ Evaluation findings: All narrative responses
    ___ Discussion of findings
    ___ Recommendations
    ___ Bibliography
    ___ Literature review
    ___ Written educational material on how to conduct evaluations
___ Presentations on _____ given to the following stakeholders: ___
___ Manuscripts written by _____ to be submitted to _____
___ Call for Papers written by ____ to be submitted to _____

GLOSSARY

ABA design. A single-system evaluation design in which a baseline (A) is measured, the intervention (B) is implemented, and then the intervention is discontinued (A).

analysis of variance. Statistical test of whether to reject the null hypothesis by comparing the means of more than two samples. The levels of measurement are the same as with *t*-tests.

baseline. A measure of performance of a client, student, worker, teacher, organization, or community prior to implementing an intervention or program. Baseline is the point with which to compare the results using the same measure of performance after the intervention.

biases. Influences on the results that cannot be attributed to the intervention or program being evaluated.

bivariate analysis. Statistics that analyze two or more variables at a time.

categories. During qualitative analysis, labels given to groupings of codes addressing similar topics.

chi-square. Statistic used to test the null hypothesis between variables measured at all levels, but other tests may be more appropriate for nonnominal data.

classic experimental design. A research design in which participants are randomly selected and assigned to intervention and control groups, and pre- and post-intervention ordinal-level and higher measures of results are given to both groups.

code of ethics. An organization's written statement of the values, principles, and behaviors expected of all members.

codes. During qualitative analysis, symbols or labels given to words or phrases that compose a single idea.

community. Persons who belong to a constituency (e.g., neighborhood, city, school district) affected by the intervention and evaluation.

comparison group. Persons who received a different intervention than the intervention predicted to create client change.

consent form. Form signed by the evaluation participants and evaluators that specifically states the parameters of participation, including that information will be kept confidential and that participation is voluntary.

consumers. Those persons who receive the intervention.

content analysis. Analysis, qualitatively or quantitatively, of secondary data.

context. Rich and thick description of evaluation participants and the evaluation setting in a qualitative research design to determine whether the results may apply to other populations.

control group. Persons who do not receive an intervention.

correlations. Statistics that analyze how values on one variable change in relation to values on a second variable.

credibility. The rigorous and systematic collection of qualitative and quantitative data according to the most widely accepted procedures cited in the research and evaluation literature.

cross-tabulations. Conducted with two or more variables and display the frequency and percentages of responses in each cell.

culture. The values, beliefs, customs, language, and behaviors passed on among individuals, families, communities, and societies.

data. Information systematically collected for specific evaluation and research purposes.

dependent variables. The changes or results related to or caused by the intervention or program.

descriptive evaluation questions. Open-ended or closed-ended questions posed about the demographics, attitudes, behaviors, or knowledge of clients, students, workers, teachers, or community members and aspects of an intervention that will lead to program improvement and knowledge building. Descriptive questions implement qualitative or quantitative research designs.

descriptive statistics. Numerical meaning attributed to the distribution of quantitatively collected data.

empirical. The published, peer-reviewed dissemination of the results of studies that applied credible data-collection methods. Empirical research includes credible qualitative and quantitative approaches.

evaluation. The systematic collection and analysis of information about one or more social service interventions and targeted clients to improve practice, planning, and accountability and to contribute to knowledge building.

evaluation advisory board. Those stakeholders overseeing the planning and implementation of an evaluation, whether or not it is required.

evaluation audit. A review of the evaluation decisions by a person not connected to the evaluation.

evaluation stakeholder plan. The written document that delineates the tasks for the people responsible for overseeing and completing an evaluation.

evaluation team. The people responsible for carrying out the evaluation tasks.

evaluators. Those persons who design and carry out the systematic collection and analysis of information to improve program practice, planning, and accountability.

evidenced-based practice. An intervention or program shown through empirical evaluation methods to have the desired impact on client or student outcomes.

evidence-informed practice. An intervention or program based on evidence from empirical research and evaluation of theory of change conducted by practitioners and planners.

explanatory evaluation questions. Closed-ended questions to test whether an intervention produced the desired results for clients, students, workers, teachers, or community members that will lead to program improvement and knowledge building. Explanatory evaluation questions implement quantitative research designs.

exploratory evaluation questions. Open-ended questions posed to clients, students, workers, teachers, or community members about their experiences or circumstances that will lead to program improvement and knowledge building. Exploratory evaluation questions implement qualitative research designs.

external validity. The ability to generalize evaluation results from the participants to the larger population.

externally driven evaluations. Evaluations initiated by stakeholders outside the local agency, such as state or federal funding sources.

extraneous variables. Characteristics other than the intervention or program that form alternative reasons for changes in clients or students.

focus groups. The collection of data by asking questions of more than one person at the same time.

formative evaluation. Planning evaluations in which data are collected to determine whether there is a need for a program or data are collected about current agency or school processes for the purpose of improving an intervention or program. Also called process evaluations.

frequency. The number of times the value for a variable occurred.

funders. Those individuals who represent the source that is financing the intervention and who have input into the evaluation activities.

generalized. Being able to assume that the results of the sample accurately apply to the larger population from where the sample was drawn.

goals. General, abstract statements about the desired processes, outcomes, or results of an intervention or program.

hypothesis. Predicts the causal relationship between a program or intervention and desired results in clients, students, workers, teachers, agencies, or communities.

independent variables. The intervention or program hypothesized to affect changes or results in clients, students, workers, teachers, agencies, schools, or communities.

inferential statistics. The numerical meaning attributed to the relationship between quantitatively collected data.

inputs. The sources determining the goals, objectives, and results of a logic model.

institutional review board. Formal structure within an organization to approve the evaluation, ensure that it will be conducted ethically, and ensure that steps are being taken so that people participating in evaluations are not harmed, physically or emotionally.

internally driven evaluations. Evaluations initiated by stakeholders within the agency or those connected locally to the agency, such as a board of directors or a community advisory group.

internal validity. The ability to attribute desired results to the evaluated intervention or program controlling for other factors that might be affecting changes.

interrater reliability. Consistent data collection by multiple persons.

interval. Level of measurement in which numbers are assigned by rank ordering different values along equal intervals.

interventions. Those services delivered to an identified client or client system with intended theoretical goals and desired results.

interview guide. A set of general, open-ended questions used in qualitative research designs to answer exploratory evaluation questions.

intrarater reliability. Consistent data collection by the same person.

keyword literature search. Locating abstracts of evidence-based research by using the search function of an abstract database, online library book catalog, or other computerized system in which published scholarship has been compiled and categorized.

levels of measurement. The variables used for statistical analysis grouped by the ability to make inferences from the data.

leveraging. The allocation of funds and other resources by organizations other than the primary funder.

literature review. A tool to compare relevant evaluations and research conducted by others as the research relates to a current evaluation.

logic model. An organization's clarification of the connection between intervention and program goals, strategies, and expected results.

mean. Measure of central tendency that is the average of all values of that variable.

measures of central tendency. Statistics that illustrate how values are distributed among respondents and include mean, mode, and median.

measures of variability. Statistics that measure how spread out values are, including range, variance, and standard deviation.

median. Measure of central tendency that is the midpoint of all values of that variable.

member checking. Seeking feedback from the participants about the evaluator's reporting, and in some cases, interpretation, of the information collected.

mixed methods. The gathering of information using open- and closed-ended questions to build and test theory and to answer descriptive evaluation questions.

mode. Measure of central tendency that is value of a variable that occurs most often.

multiple-baseline design. A single-system design that measures the impact of the intervention across different behaviors, persons, or settings.

multiple-level systems. The individuals, families, groups, organizations, and communities that are the targets for change and the sources for creating change.

natural setting. The environment most comfortable for evaluation participants, usually their home, work, agency, or school setting.

needs assessment. The collection of data to determine whether there is an issue or problem shared by large groups of people that requires intervention.

nominal. The level of measurement in which numbers are used to name a value.

non-directional hypothesis. A statement that there is a relationship between the intervention and desired results without being able to state whether that relationship is positive or negative.

null hypothesis. A statement that there is no relationship between the intervention and desired results.

objectives. Measurable expectations that are necessary for reaching an intervention or program goal. Objectives are usually a subset of goals and are written in measurable terms.

objectivity. The process of identifying and reducing evaluator biases and influences that distort the data-collection process.

operationalize. To define the effective components of an intervention, also called the independent variables, and to define the measurable results of the intervention, also called the dependent variables.

ordinal. The level of measurement in which numbers assign more value to some responses than to others.

outcomes. Desired results connected to an intervention or program.

outlier. A result that was not similar to any other participant.

paradigm. Worldview about how knowledge is gained.

participants. Called research subjects in studies, those persons from whom data are gathered through interviews, surveys, observations, and documents to answer evaluation questions.

peer debriefing. Consultation about the evaluation process from persons selected for their expertise.

percentages. The number of times a value was selected divided by the number of participants responding to the variable measured.

petition for approval of research involving human subjects. The formal application that must be submitted to an institutional review board before beginning evaluation and research. The application demonstrates the evaluator's adherence to meeting required ethical guidelines of evaluation and research.

population. The group to which results can be generalized.

positivist. A paradigm that views the world as measurable and predictable.

post-positivist. A paradigm that begins with the assumption that one can never be totally objective.

practice evaluation. Evaluating one's own practice or intervention.

primary investigator. The assigned coordinator of the evaluation. Also called principal investigator.

processes. Analysis of the way an intervention or program is implemented.

program evaluation. Evaluating one or more interventions targeted to multiple persons.

purposive selection. Participants chosen on the basis of specific criteria addressed in an evaluation question.

qualitative approach. The gathering of information using open-ended evaluation questions to build theory in order to answer exploratory and descriptive evaluation questions.

quantitative approach. The gathering of information using closed-ended questions to test theory in order to answer descriptive and explanatory evaluation questions and statements.

quasi-experimental designs. Quantitative research designs used to answer descriptive evaluation questions. These designs often lack random selection to a control group.

random controlled trials. Random selection of participants into intervention or control groups.

random selection. Also called random controlled trials. Participants in the larger population have an equal chance of being selected to participate in the evaluation.

range. Measure of variability that lists values from lowest to highest and indicates the distance between those values.

ratio. Level of measurement in which numbers are assigned by rank ordering different values along equal intervals and there is an absolute zero point.

regression analysis. Statistical test of the strength of change predicted to occur as a result of the intervention.

reliability. The consistent measurement of the same concept.

research. The implementation of reliable, valid, and credible methods to empirically explore, describe, or explain a theorized relationship between variables.

research design. The conditions for collecting data in the most rigorous manner appropriate to the research or evaluation question being asked. The research design is the procedural map for data collection.

research protocol. The following steps for implementing a research design: select participants, collect data, analyze data, and ensure credibility of the data.

resources. The time, materials, and training needed to complete evaluation tasks. Some agencies set aside no time or budget for evaluation.

response rate. The number of persons who complete the survey divided by the number of persons who received the survey.

results. The desired changes related to specific strategies. The term *results* is used to conceptualize change as being both processes and outcomes.

retention rate. The number of persons who continued to participate in multiple data collection activities divided by the number of persons originally in the evaluation.

sample. Participants selected from a larger population to participate in the evaluation.

SCREAM. Acronym used to remind evaluators to measure participants' strengths, to implement culturally competent evaluations, to implement the evaluation feasibly utilizing one's available resources, to conduct the evaluation ethically, to reach agreement on the evaluation process with all stakeholders, and to measure multiple-level systems.

service providers. Those persons responsible for implementing the intervention.

single-system design. An evaluation or research study in which the desired results are measured both before and after an intervention has been administered to a single system, which can be an individual, family, group, organization, or community.

social service program. One or more interventions delivered to achieve specified goals and desired results for identified needs of clients.

standard deviation. Measure of variance that is the square root of the variance.

stakeholders. Those persons affected by the intervention or program and the process, results, and reports of the evaluation. Stakeholders can include funders, service providers, consumers of services, community members, and those individuals involved in the planning, implementation, and utilization of the evaluation.

statistical analysis. Converting quantitative information into numerical values to reduce large amounts of information into a format that can be more easily understood and applied.

statistical power. The ability of a statistical test to correctly reject the null hypothesis.

statistical significance. Measurement of a relationship between the intervention and results outside an acceptable level for chance. The .05 level is most commonly used and implies that the evaluator will accept that five times out of one hundred the results were due to chance rather than the intervention.

strategies. Actual interventions employed to reach the stated goals.

stratified random sample. Persons from each of the identified demographic groups are randomly selected.

strengths. Behaviors and beliefs that help individuals, families, and communities reach their optimal level of social functioning.

summative evaluations. Program evaluations where data are collected to measure specific outcomes expected of the intervention. Also called outcome evaluations.

systematic review. An analysis of the most rigorous, evidence-based studies conducted about the effectiveness of the same intervention.

theme. Meaning attributed to the narrative data collected qualitatively.

theme analysis. Conversion of qualitative information into codes, categories, and themes to reduce large amounts of information into a format that can be more easily understood and applied.

theme redundancy. When conceptual patterns or themes will be repeated if persons possessing the same characteristics are selected; the assumption that no new themes will emerge if similar participants are selected for the evaluation.

theory. The connection between concepts to hypothesize a causal relationship or describe a noncausal relationship between concepts.

theory building. The process of exploring or describing what one learns while gathering information. Theory building occurs in formative evaluations.

theory of change. The description or explanation between an intervention or program and the desired results.

theory testing. The process of gathering information to describe or explain the relationship between interventions and client change. Theory testing occurs in summative evaluations.

triangulation. The process of implementing multiple data-collection methods in the same evaluation.

trustworthiness. The accurate description of the concepts and realities as intended by the participants in the evaluation.

***t*-test.** Statistical test of whether to reject the null hypothesis by comparing the means of two samples.

type I error. Occurs when the null hypothesis is rejected, and thus an erroneous claim is made that there was a relationship between intervention and change.

type II error. Occurs when the null hypothesis is not rejected and a true relationship between intervention and change is not identified.

unidirectional hypothesis. A statement that there is a relationship between the intervention and desired results and stating whether that relationship is positive or negative.

univariate analysis. Statistics that describe one variable at a time.

validity. Accurately describing or explaining the intended concepts when generalizing the results from the sample to the larger population.

values. Preferences, beliefs, cherished ideas, worldviews, assumptions, traditions, and morals that consciously and unconsciously shape and influence decisions of individuals and groups.

variance. Measure of variability that is the squared difference of all scores from the mean.

REFERENCES

American Evaluation Association. (2004). *American Evaluation Association guiding principles for evaluators.* Retrieved from http://www.eval.org/p/cm/ld/fid=51.

American Psychological Association. (2011). *Publication manual of the American Psychological Association* (6th ed.). Washington, DC: Author.

Babbie, E., Halley, F., & Zaino, J. (2012). *Adventures in social research: Data analysis using IBM SPSS Statistics* (8th ed.). Los Angeles, CA: Sage.

Bloom, M., Fischer, J., & Orme, J. (2009). *Evaluating practice: Guidelines for the accountable professional* (6th ed.). Boston, MA: Pearson/Allyn & Bacon.

Brun, C. (1997). A model to assess parental strengths of Head Start consumers: Results from a qualitative study of the lives of six women labeled "at-risk" for child neglect. *National Head Start Association Research Quarterly, 1*(2), 74–83.

Brun, C., & Giga, S. (1999). Organizing on behalf of families: Facilitating a community application to a state block grant to prevent teenage pregnancies. *Child and Adolescent Social Work Journal, 16*(1), 23–26.

Brun, C., & Rapp, R. (2001). Strengths-based case management: Individuals' perspectives on strengths and the case manager relationship. *Social Work, 46*(3), 278–288.

Campbell Collaboration. (n.d.). *What is a systematic review?* Retrieved from http://www.campbellcollaboration.org/what_is_a_systematic_review/.

Campbell, D., & Stanley, J. (1963). *Experimental and quasi-experimental designs for research.* Chicago, IL: Rand McNally.

Clasen, C., Meyer, C., Brun, C., Mase, W., & Cauley, K. (2003). Development of the Competency Assessment Tool—Mental Health, an instrument to assess core competencies for mental health care workers. *Psychiatric Rehabilitation Journal, 27*(1), 10–17.

Cook, T., & Campbell, D. (1979). *Quasi-experimentation: Design and analysis issues for field settings.* Chicago, IL: Rand McNally.

Corbin, J., & Strauss, A. (2008). *Basics of qualitative research* (3rd ed.). Los Angeles, CA: Sage.

Corcoran, K., & Fischer, J. (2007). *Measures for clinical practice and research: A sourcebook* (4th ed., Vols. 1–2). New York, NY: Oxford University Press.

Council on Social Work Education. (2012). *Education Policy and Accreditation Standards.* Alexandria, VA: Author. Retrieved from http://www.cswe.org/File.aspx?id=41861.

Dudley, J. (2013). *Social work evaluation: Enhancing what we do* (2nd ed.). Chicago, IL: Lyceum Books.

Epstein, N., Baldwin, L., & Bishop, D. (1982). Family Assessment Device. Providence, RI: Brown University and Butler Hospital Family Research Program.

Evans, C., & Fisher, M. (1999). Collaborative evaluation with service users: Moving towards user-controlled research. In I. Shaw & J. Lishman (Eds.), *Evaluation and social work practice* (pp. 101–117). Thousand Oaks, CA: Sage.

Fetterman, D., & Wandersman, A. (2005). *Empowerment evaluation principles in practice*. New York, NY: Guilford Press.

Fong, R., & Furuto, S. (Eds.). (2001). *Culturally competent practice: Skills, interventions, and evaluations*. Boston, MA: Allyn & Bacon.

Gambrill, E. (2013). *Social work practice: A critical thinkers' guide* (3rd ed.). New York, NY: Oxford University Press.

Gambrill, E., & Gibbs, L. (2009). *Critical thinking for helping professionals: A skills-based workbook*. New York, NY: Oxford University Press.

Gibbs, L. (2003). *Evidence-based practice for the helping professions: A practical guide with integrated multimedia*. Pacific Grove, CA: Thomson Brooks/Cole.

Ginsberg, L. (2001). *Social work evaluation: Principles and methods*. Boston, MA: Allyn & Bacon.

Government Performance Results Act. (1993). *Senate Committee on Government Affairs GPRA Report*. Retrieved from http://www.whitehouse.gov/omb/mgmt-gpra/gprptm.

Grinnell, R., Gabor, P., & Unrau, Y. (2012). *Program evaluation for social workers: Foundations of evidence-based programs* (6th ed.). New York, NY: Oxford University Press.

Holloway, S. (2012). *Some suggestions on educational program assessment and continuous improvement for the 2008 EPAS*. Alexandria, VA: Council on Social Work Education. Retrieved from http://www.cswe.org/File.aspx?id=31582.

International Association of Schools of Social Work. (2004). *Ethics in social work, statement of principles*. Retrieved from http://www.iassw-aiets.org/ethics-in-social-work-statement-of-principles.

International Federation of Social Workers. (2012). *Statement of ethical principles*. Retrieved from http://ifsw.org/policies/statement-of-ethical-principles/.

King, J., Stevahn, L., Ghere, G., & Minnema, J. (2001). Toward a taxonomy of essential evaluator competencies. *American Journal of Evaluation, 22*(2), 229–247.

Kretzmann, J., & McKnight, J. (1993). *Building communities from the inside out: A path toward finding and mobilizing a community's assets*. Evanston, IL: Asset Based Community Development Institute for Policy Research, Northwestern University.

Krueger, R., & Casey, M. (2009). *Focus groups: A practical guide for applied research* (4th ed.). Los Angeles, CA: Sage.

Leviton, L. (2003). Commentary: Engaging the community in evaluation: Bumpy, time consuming, and important. *American Journal of Evaluation*, 24(1), 85–90.

Marsh, J. (2003). Chewing on cardboard and other pleasures of knowledge utilization. *Social Work*, 48(3), 293–294.

McClintock, C. (2003). Commentary: The evaluator as scholar/practitioner/ change agent. *American Journal of Evaluation*, 24(1), 91–96.

Mertens, D. (2003). The inclusive view of evaluation: Visions for the new millennium. In S. Donaldson & M. Scriven (Eds.), *Evaluating social programs and problems: Visions for the new millennium* (pp. 91–108). Mahwah, NJ: Erlbaum.

Meyer, C., Brun, C., Yung, B., Clasen, C., Cauley, K., & Mase, W. (2004). Evaluation of social marketing efforts designed to increase enrollment in the Children's Health Insurance Program (CHIP). *Journal of Nonprofit and Public Sector Marketing*, 12(2), 87–104.

Meyer, C., Yung, B., Ranbom, L., Cauley, K., Brun, C., & Fuller, B. (2001). *Medicaid outreach expansion evaluation* (Final evaluation report submitted to the Ohio Department of Jobs and Family Services). Dayton, OH: Wright State University.

Morris, M. (2003). Ethical challenges: You want to ask them what?!?!?! *American Journal of Evaluation*, 24(1), 81–84.

National Association of Social Workers. (2008). *Code of ethics of the National Association of Social Workers*. Retrieved from http://www.socialworkers.org/ pubs/code/code.asp.

Nevo, I., & Slonim-Nevo, V. (2011). The myth of evidence-based practice: Towards evidence-informed practice. *British Journal of Social Work*, 41, 1176–1197.

Patton, M. (2012). *Essentials of utilization-focused evaluation* (5th ed.). Los Angeles, CA: Sage.

Paul, R., & Elder, L. (2006). *The miniature guide to critical thinking: Concepts and tools*. Dillon Beach, CA: Foundation for Critical Thinking.

Posavac, E. J. (2011). *Program evaluation: Methods and case studies* (8th ed.). Boston, MA: Prentice Hall.

Potocky-Tripodi, M., & Tripodi, T. (2003). Twelve steps for quantitative analysts anonymous: On recovery from dependence on statistical significance testing, or (effect) size matters. *Journal of Social Work Research and Evaluation*, 4(2), 139–144.

Rapp, R. (2011). *Effectiveness of strengths-based case management with substance abusers throughout the treatment continuum* (Doctoral thesis, University of Ghent, Belgium). Retrieved from http://hdl.handle.net/1854/LU-1842861.

Royse, D., Thyer, B., & Padgett, D. (2010). *Program evaluation: An introduction* (5th ed.). Belmont, CA: Wadsworth Cengage Learning.

Sawin, K., Harrigan, M., & Woog, P. (Eds.). (1995). *Measures of family functioning for research and practice.* New York, NY: Springer.

Smith, M., & Brun, C. (2006). An analysis of selected measures of child well-being for use at school- and community-based family resource centers. *Child Welfare, 84*(6), 985–1010.

Thyer, B. (2001). What is the role of theory in research on social work practice? *Journal of Social Work Education, 37*(1), 9–25.

Thyer, B. (2002). How to write up a social work outcome study for publication. *Journal of Social Work Research and Evaluation, 3*(2), 215–224.

Twill, S., & Buckheister, N. (2009). A descriptive study of economic human rights violations. *Journal of Poverty, 13*(4), 365–383.

Twill, S., Purvis, T., & Norris, M. (2011). Weeds and seeds: Reflections from a gardening project for juvenile offenders. *Journal of Therapeutic Horticulture, 21*(1), 13–20. Retrieved from http://ahta.org/ahta-journal-therapeutic-horticulture.

United Way of America. (1998). *Community impact. A new paradigm emerging: A white paper on change in the United Way movement.* Alexandria, VA: Author.

U.S. Department of Health and Human Services. (1979). *The Belmont report.* Retrieved from http://www.hhs.gov/ohrp/humansubjects/guidance/belmont.html.

U.S. Department of Health and Human Services. (2013). *Health information privacy.* Retrieved from http://www.hhs.gov/ocr/privacy/.

U.S. Department of Health and Human Services, Centers for Disease Control and Prevention. (2011). *U.S. public health service syphilis study at Tuskegee.* Retrieved from http://www.cdc.gov/tuskegee/index.html.

Wilson, S., Lipsey, M., Tanner-Smith, E., Huang, C., & Steinka-Fry, K. (2011). *Dropout prevention and intervention programs: Effects on school completion and dropout among school-aged children and youth* (A systematic review published on the Campbell Collaboration Library of Systematic Reviews). Retrieved from http://campbellcollaboration.org/lib/project/158/.

Wright State University Institutional Review Board. (2013). *Required elements of informed consent.* Retrieved from http://www.wright.edu/rsp/subjects.html.

Yarbrough, D., Shulha, L., Hopson, R., & Caruthers, F. (Eds.). (2011). *The program evaluation standards: A guide for evaluators and evaluation users* (3rd ed.). Los Angeles, CA: Sage.

INDEX

CPSIA information can be obtained
at www.ICGtesting.com
Printed in the USA
BVHW090410191220
595002BV00004B/9

9 780190 615468